On D-Day—June 6, 1944—soldiers of the 9th Canadian Infantry Brigade swarm ashore at Bernières-sur-Mer, France. The Normandy invasion, the greatest amphibious operation in history, was the opening phase of Operation Overlord, the Allies' master plan for the liberation of German-occupied Europe.

THE SECOND FRONT

This volume is one of a series that chronicles
in full the events of the Second World War.
Previous books in the series include:

Prelude to War
Blitzkrieg
The Battle of Britain
The Rising Sun
The Battle of the Atlantic
Russia Besieged
The War in the Desert
The Home Front: U.S.A.
China-Burma-India
Island Fighting
The Italian Campaign
Partisans and Guerrillas

WORLD WAR II · TIME-LIFE BOOKS · ALEXANDRIA, VIRGINIA

BY DOUGLAS BOTTING
AND THE EDITORS OF TIME-LIFE BOOKS

THE SECOND FRONT

Time-Life Books Inc.
is a wholly owned subsidiary of
TIME INCORPORATED

Founder: Henry R. Luce 1898-1967

Editor-in-Chief: Henry Anatole Grunwald
President: J. Richard Munro
Chairman of the Board: Ralph P. Davidson
Executive Vice President: Clifford J. Grum
Chairman, Executive Committee: James R. Shepley
Editorial Director: Ralph Graves
Group Vice President, Books: Joan D. Manley
Vice Chairman: Arthur Temple

TIME-LIFE BOOKS INC.

Managing Editor: Jerry Korn
Executive Editor: David Maness
Assistant Managing Editors: Dale M. Brown
(planning), George Constable, Martin Mann,
John Paul Porter, Gerry Schremp (acting)
Art Director: Tom Suzuki
Chief of Research: David L. Harrison
Director of Photography: Robert G. Mason
Assistant Art Director: Arnold C. Holeywell
Assistant Chief of Research: Carolyn L. Sackett
Assistant Director of Photography: Dolores A. Littles

Chairman: John D. McSweeney
President: Carl G. Jaeger
Executive Vice Presidents: John Steven Maxwell,
David J. Walsh
Vice Presidents: George Artandi (comptroller);
Stephen L. Bair (legal counsel); Peter G. Barnes;
Nicholas Benton (public relations);
John L. Canova; Beatrice T. Dobie (personnel);
Carol Flaumenhaft (consumer affairs);
James L. Mercer (Europe/South Pacific);
Herbert Sorkin (production); Paul R. Stewart
(marketing)

WORLD WAR II

Editorial Staff for *The Second Front*
Editor: William K. Goolrick
Picture Editor/Designer: Raymond Ripper
Picture Editor: Robin Richman
Text Editors: Gerald Simons, Henry Woodhead
Staff Writers: Malachy J. Duffy, Brian McGinn,
Tyler Mathisen, Teresa M. C. R. Pruden
Chief Researcher: Frances G. Youssef
Researchers: Marion F. Briggs, Loretta Y. Britten,
Christine Bowie Dove, Oobie Gleysteen,
Pat Good, Chadwick Gregson
Art Assistant: Mary Louise Mooney
Editorial Assistant: Connie Strawbridge

Editorial Production
Production Editor: Douglas B. Graham
Operations Manager: Gennaro C. Esposito,
Gordon E. Buck (assistant)
Assistant Production Editor: Feliciano Madrid
Quality Control: Robert L. Young (director),
James J. Cox (assistant), Daniel J. McSweeney,
Michael G. Wight (associates)
Art Coordinator: Anne B. Landry
Copy Staff: Susan B. Galloway (chief),
Patricia Graber, Victoria Lee, Celia Beattie
Picture Department: Alvin L. Ferrell
Traffic: Kimberly K. Lewis

Correspondents: Elisabeth Kraemer (Bonn);
Margot Hapgood, Dorothy Bacon, Lesley Coleman
(London); Susan Jonas, Lucy T. Voulgaris (New
York); Maria Vincenza Aloisi, Josephine du Brusle
(Paris); Ann Natanson (Rome). Valuable assistance
was also provided by: Judy Aspinall (London);
Carolyn T. Chubet, Miriam Hsia, Christina
Lieberman (New York); M. T. Hirschkoff (Paris);
Mimi Murphy (Rome); Traudl Lessing (Vienna)

The Author: DOUGLAS BOTTING was born in
London in 1934 and was educated at Oxford University. His interest in military affairs began with
service in the British Army; he enlisted as an infantry subaltern and served in the King's African Rifles
in East Africa. Subsequently he traveled widely as
writer and film maker on scientific and explora-
tory expeditions to Arabia, Africa, Amazonia and
Arctic Siberia. He has written several books on
history and travel, including three volumes for
Time-Life Books: *Wilderness Europe* in The
World's Wild Places series, *Rio de Janeiro* in The
Great Cities series, and *The Pirates* in The Seafarers
series.

The Consultant: COLONEL JOHN R. ELTING, USA
(Ret.), is a military historian and author of *The
Battle of Bunker's Hill, The Battles of Saratoga* and
Military History and Atlas of the Napoleonic Wars.
He edited *Military Uniforms in America: The Era
of the American Revolution, 1755-1795* and *Mili-
tary Uniforms in America: Years of Growth, 1796-
1851,* and was associate editor of *The West Point
Atlas of American Wars.*

Library of Congress Cataloguing in Publication Data

Botting, Douglas.
    The second front.

    (World War II; v. 13)
    Bibliography: p.
    Includes index.
    1. Operation Overlord. 2. World War, 1939-1945—
Campaigns—France—Normandy. 3. Dieppe Raid, 1942.
4. France—History—German occupation, 1940-1945.
I. Time-Life Books. II. Title. III. Series.
D756.5.N6B6   940.54'21   78-3405
ISBN 0-8094-2500-9
ISBN 0-8094-2499-1 (lib. bdg.)
ISBN 0-8094-2498-3 (retail ed.)

For information about any Time-Life book, please write:

Reader Information
Time-Life Books
541 North Fairbanks Court
Chicago, Illinois 60611

CONTENTS

HITLER'S ATLANTIC WALL

The Atlantic Wall—beach obstacles, hidden gun batteries and, behind the bomb-damaged sea wall, barbed-wire entanglements—guards a French coastal village.

"IMPREGNABLE FRONT" FOR FORTRESS EUROPE

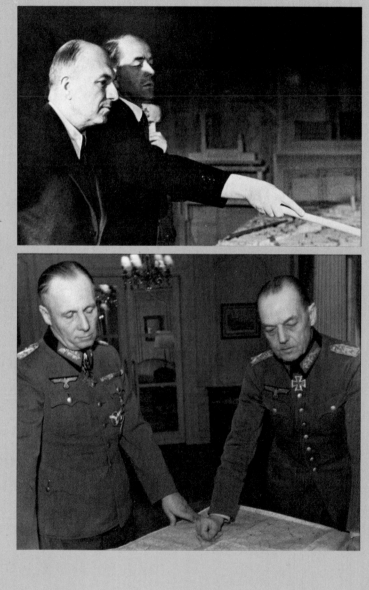

Todt and Speer (below, with pointer) supervised construction of the Wall. Rommel (bottom, left) and Rundstedt were charged with its defense.

In December 1941, Adolf Hitler boasted to the world that his Third Reich controlled the entire west coast of Europe from the Arctic Ocean to the Bay of Biscay. "It is my unshakable decision," the Führer added, "to make this front impregnable against every enemy." To keep his vow, Hitler conceived of an awesome defense line—a broad band of concrete, steel, guns and troops that would follow the shoreline for 2,400 miles. He called it the Atlantic Wall. In the next two and a half years, it became an obsessive project for him. For the Allied invasion planners it became the most formidable defensive barrier of the War.

Hitler ordered the building of 15,000 permanent strong points, which were to be manned by 300,000 troops. The defense posts, many of which he designed himself, were built by the German agency for military public works, Organization Todt, under its namesake, Dr. Fritz Todt, and his successor, Reich Minister Albert Speer. Construction officially started early in 1942, with the heaviest concentration of defenses rising along the narrowest part of the English Channel, between the Netherlands and Le Havre in Normandy. For two years, a quarter of a million men worked night and day. They used more than a million tons of steel and poured more than 20 million cubic yards of concrete.

The Wall inspired confidence in practically every German. There were a few skeptics, of course. The top commander in the West, Field Marshal Gerd von Rundstedt, doubted that the Wall alone could stop an Allied attack. At first, Field Marshal Erwin Rommel, the former commander of the famous Afrika Korps, called the Wall a "figment of Hitler's 'cloud cuckoo land.'" But after he was appointed inspector of coastal defenses in the West, Rommel set out to strengthen and deepen the defense line. He implanted mine-tipped obstacles along open beaches and flooded great inland areas to impede airborne invaders. His many improvements gave added weight to the German Propaganda Ministry's confident claims for the Wall: "This is why an enemy attack, even the most powerful and furious possible to imagine, is bound to fail."

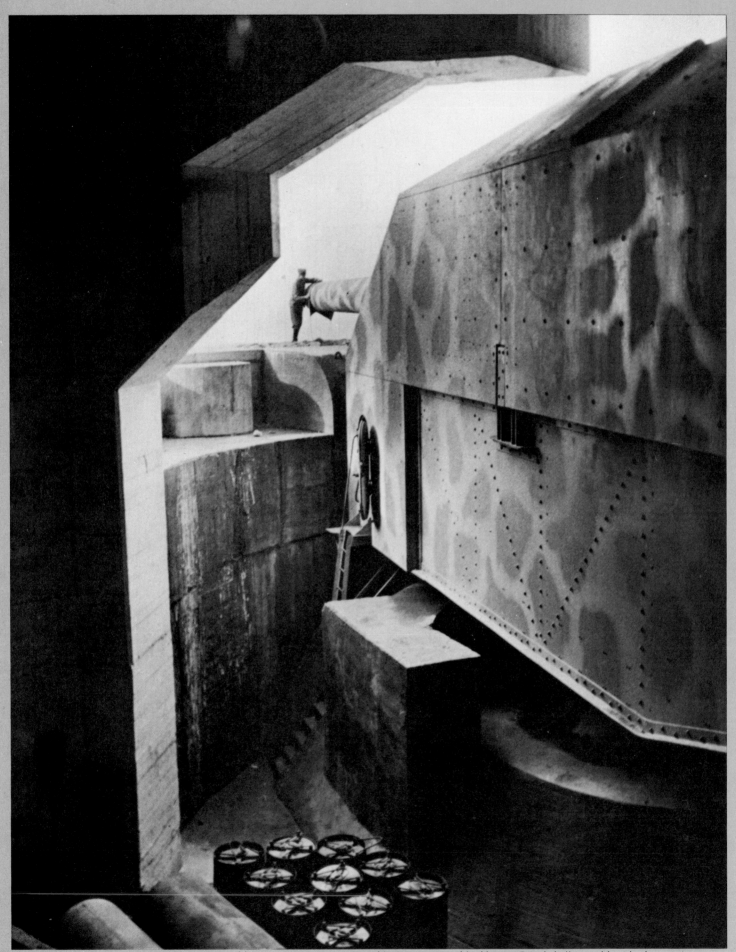

A powerful coastal gun, its muzzle being serviced by a German, points seaward from a concrete blockhouse. Cased shells stand beside the rotating turret.

French laborers prepare to pour concrete into wooden forms to make steel-reinforced bunker walls.

Weary Frenchmen hired by the Germans are marched off to excavate for a sea-front fortification.

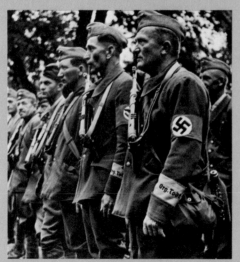

Overage Germans worked on the Atlantic Wall.

French colonial workmen enjoy a rice break.

Walls of a giant U-boat pen, being built by thousands of conscripted laborers, rise at the port of Bordeaux in 1942. Each open bay had docks on both sides.

MIGHTY INSTALLATIONS BUILT BY SLAVE LABOR

The Atlantic Wall was constructed largely by slave labor. To make up for German manpower that had been drained off by the armed forces and war industries, prisoners of war and civilians who had been rounded up in occupied countries were brought to Organization Todt to work on the mighty coastal defenses. At the peak of construction in 1943, fully 90 per cent of the workers in Organization Todt were conscripted foreigners. The rest included paid French volunteers, and German technicians and supervisors.

Under close guard and a great deal of pressure, the conscripts did backbreaking labor around the clock. On the heavily fortified Channel Islands, they toiled seven days a week, at least 12 hours a day, with a 10- to 30-minute break for lunch. Their rations were insufficient for such strenuous labor, and they were issued no work clothes. One Sunday a month they were given a half day off.

Most of the conscripts were put to work on the largest and most elaborate of the Atlantic Wall installations. These were the ports containing U-boat bases, whose artillery and machine-gun nests were designed to defend the harbor as well as the submarines. Each of the biggest bases—in France at Brest, Lorient, Saint-Nazaire and La Pallice—was built by a work gang composed of up to 15,000 men. The gang was supposed to build a base—construction that would take three years under normal conditions—in six months. Some crews came close, and the men who faltered were simply replaced.

OBSERVATION TOWER WITH RADAR

SUPPLY BUNKER UNDER CONSTRUCTION

FOOD STORAGE BUNKER WITH REFRIGERATION

PERSONNEL BUNKERS

CREATING DEFENSES FOR SPECIAL FUNCTIONS

The German planners designed almost 700 standard units for the tens of thousands of individual defense works of the Atlantic Wall. Then, using selected units, they put together an emplacement tailor-made for each specific function. There were heavy coastal-gun sites and antiaircraft positions, artillery and machine-gun pillboxes, ammunition bunkers, multistory observation towers, communications posts and medical facilities. Huge supply bunkers with facilities for storing water and refrigerating food were built in compliance with Hitler's directive that the troops "must never be

A sampling of concrete defense structures, differing in functions (labels), displays the monolithic massiveness common to most Atlantic Wall strong points.

forced to surrender because of a shortage of ammunition, rations or water."

The centerpiece of most defense complexes was the gun emplacement. Weapons were housed beneath stepped overhangs that gave them maximum arcs of fire while preventing enemy shells from falling into the blockhouse. Many sites had air-conditioned magazines and conveyors to move shells to the guns.

The larger batteries had heavy concrete bunkers for gun crews. These accommodations generally housed from 10 to 150 men, who slept in double or triple tiers on steel-framed bunks that folded against the walls when not in use. Though space was at a premium, some complexes had recreation areas, libraries, well-equipped kitchens and mess halls. One bunker even had an officers' bar, complete with wood paneling and upholstered chairs.

A gun emplacement masquerades as a house with curtained windows and a balustrade along the roof.

An observation post (center) is painted to resembl

A German antitank gun pokes out of a bunker disguised as a modest villa in southwest France.

Disguised as the Strand Café, this seaside lookou

EXPERTS IN THE ART OF CAMOUFLAGE

In 1942 Lieut. General Rudolf Schmetzer, German Inspector of Land Defense West, laid down the principle that camouflage was as important as thick concrete. Heeding his dictum, local commanders spared no effort to hide or disguise their posithe dark-beamed, Norman-style residence at right.

post displays false windows and painted curtains.

The figure of a matron, painted in a bunker's false window, draws mock salutes from passing Germans.

tions. The Fifteenth Army, which was deployed along the Channel coast from Ostend, Belgium, to Caen in Normandy, even formed a special study group—consisting of a botanist, zoologist, geologist, engineer, tank expert, artilleryman and infantryman—to come up with new and better ways to make the army's bastions look like something else.

In towns all along the Atlantic Wall, defense works were carefully disguised as local buildings by means of false roofs, painted windows and dummy doors. Many observation posts were made to look like churches, complete with steeples. And the concrete façades of gun batteries carved into seaside cliffs were painted to match the rock formations.

The most common type of camouflage was more effective but much less esoteric: plain dirt. Since many of the defense positions were built underground for protection, the Germans simply covered them over with protective layers of earth, leaving openings only for guns and for observation purposes. And the defenders were much too shrewd to let raw earth betray an underground bunker or command post. Atop the positions they placed a cover of natural vegetation.

A German soldier on guard duty patrols a beach lined with tetrahedral antitank obstacles, a number of them supporting the rifles of his off-duty comrades.

A row of curved obstructions composed of metal rails protects a village on the French coast. These objects were designed by the Germans to snag tanks.

A pair of horses tow a formidable antitank barrier, known as a "Belgian Gate," into position. The gates were approximately nine feet high and nine feet wide.

THE CHANNEL COAST: "ZONE OF DEATH"

To defend the open beaches along the crucial Channel coast, Field Marshal Rommel spun out a steel spider web to entrap and destroy any foolhardy attackers. By June 1944 the Germans had barricaded the shoreline from Cherbourg to Calais with half a million assorted anti-invasion obstacles and more than four million mines planted in depth.

Great logs and steel beams were driven into the sand and tipped with mines or metal cutters to gut landing craft. Hedgehogs—twisted steel girders welded together—studded tidal flats. Concrete antitank obstacles lined the beaches.

Rommel, who designed many of the obstacles himself, warned the Allies against challenging this "zone of death." He also said, "The war will be won or lost on the beaches," and by the eve of D-Day, he had done his best to win it there.

The low tide exposes rows of mines and wooden stakes guarding a possible Allied landing site.

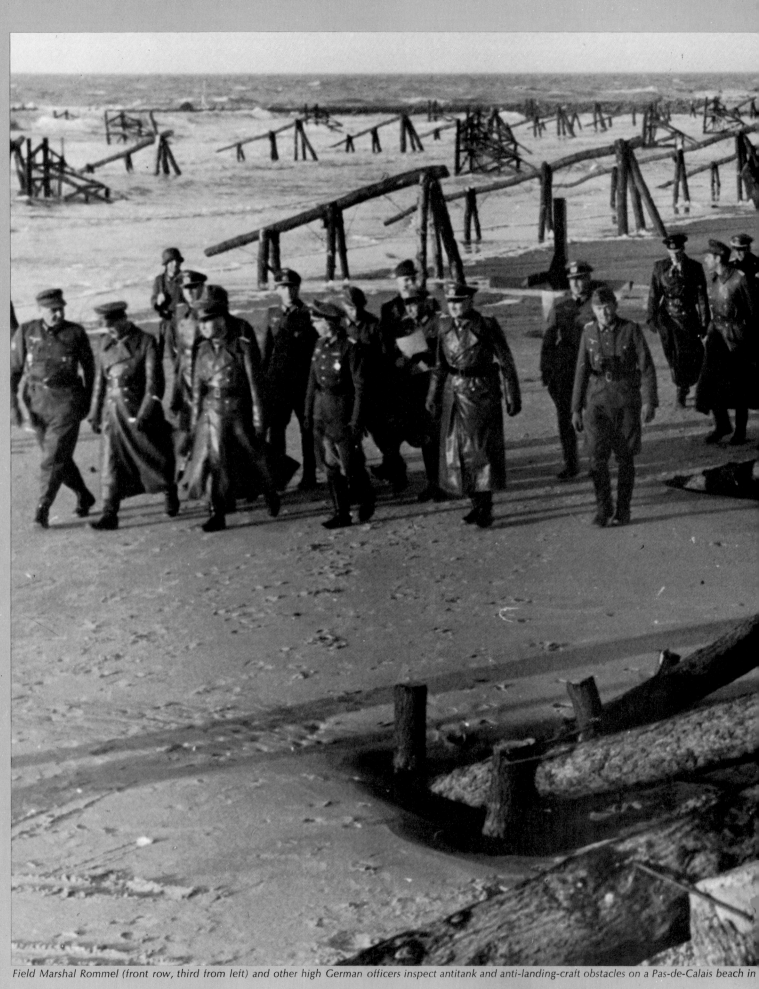

Field Marshal Rommel (front row, third from left) and other high German officers inspect antitank and anti-landing-craft obstacles on a Pas-de-Calais beach in

April 1944. Rommel expressed satisfaction with the defenses in this sector of the Atlantic Wall, but he was disappointed with those along the Normandy coast.

1

On the afternoon of June 4, 1940, as 338,000 soldiers were being evacuated from Dunkirk in the desperate effort to save the British Army from annihilation by the German blitzkrieg then steam-rolling across France, Prime Minister Winston Churchill made a stirring, but seemingly unlikely, promise to the House of Commons. "Britain will fight on," he thundered, "if necessary for years . . . if necessary alone. . . . We shall go back."

On that dark day for British fortunes, and in the darker ones to come, the prospect of Britain's Army recrossing the Channel and defeating Germany on the soil of Europe was remote indeed. At a time when Britain was gearing up its meager resources for a last-ditch defense to stave off an expected German invasion, an offensive of its own seemed out of the question. But on the day Churchill made his vow, a British planner in the War Office conceived the idea of a force of specially trained commandos to carry out guerrilla raids against the German Occupation forces across the English Channel. It was the modest beginning of an effort to strike back, an effort that would culminate four years later in the launching of a vast Allied armada and the opening, on the beaches of France, of a western front against Germany.

Less than three weeks after Dunkirk, the commandos struck. On June 23, the day after France signed her humiliating armistice with Germany and Hitler crowed that Britain had been "driven from the Continent forever," a party of 120 British Commandos raided Boulogne on the French coast and inflicted such damage as they could with 20 Tommy guns—half the number that Britain possessed at the time. The raid was not particularly successful. No prisoners were captured, little information was gained, and part of the Commando force, which on its return to England landed at another port than the one intended, suffered the humiliation of being arrested by military police and held for a short while as a party of deserters.

The Commandos had no illusions about the importance of the Boulogne raid. As one of their officers put it: "We went there merely to show the Hun we can go back any time we bloody well feel like it."

The Commado strikes continued, against far-ranging targets in France, Norway, Italy and Libya. Their objectives were always limited: to destroy enemy defenses or industrial plants or utilities, to capture prisoners and garner infor-

REHEARSALS FOR INVASION

mation—and generally to boost Allied morale. While they served to harass the Axis and to keep them constantly on the alert, the attacks did little to change the course of the War. The Commando raids were mere pinpricks in the hide of the Axis behemoth. It was the best that Britain could do.

Even though Churchill dreamed of an invasion of the Continent and British strategists had been studying that possibility since October 1940, there was no hope that Britain could launch an effective offensive so long as it was fighting a defensive war alone in the West. It needed friends—allies to fight on its side. Eventually it got them. In June 1941, Hitler turned his armies eastward and invaded Russia. As enormous battles raged, with the Germans penetrating deeper and deeper into the vast country across a broad front, Stalin begain exhorting Churchill to open a second front at the earliest possible moment and thereby relieve his hard-pressed armies. Six months later, after the Japanese attack on Pearl Harbor in December 1941, the United States joined the war against the Axis, and Britain, Russia and America were now united in what came to be called the Grand Alliance. The opening of a second front no longer seemed so remote.

As interest in an invasion mounted late in 1941, the British organization that conducted the Commando raids, the Combined Operations Command, was given a new chief and a new direction. Captain the Lord Louis Mountbatten, a cousin of the King and a brilliant and forceful organizer who had been a destroyer commander at the start of the War, was put in charge. Under his dynamic leadership, Combined Operations became less an organization for pinprick raiding parties and more an embryo invasion headquarters.

Accordingly, the Commando raids became less important for the damage they inflicted and more and more valuable for gathering the experience and information necessary for planning a full-fledged invasion of Europe. No one knew exactly what was required, what snags might arise, what defenses would be encountered. It was essential to find out.

There was no lack of ideas. The planners at Combined Operations were wildly unorthodox young men, and in the first months of 1942 they dreamed up many fanciful schemes. The boldest and most far-fetched was to land and drive an armored column to Paris, shoot up the German Army headquarters at the Hotel Crillon, rekindle the flame on the Tomb of the Unknown Warrior, then drive back to the Channel for reembarkation to England.

Fortunately, a cooler but no less imaginative head prevailed. As his senior staff officer, Mountbatten had chosen a highly creative Royal Navy officer, 40-year-old Captain John Hughes-Hallett, who later became one of the outstanding planners of D-Day. It was Hughes-Hallett who devised perhaps the most brazenly impudent and successful Commando operation of the War—the Saint-Nazaire raid *(pages 24-25)*, which took the Germans by surprise and knocked out the only dry dock on the Atlantic coast that was capable of servicing their newest and mightiest battleship, the *Tirpitz*. The destruction of the dry dock prevented the *Tirpitz* from venturing into the Atlantic and wreaking havoc on the Allied convoy routes.

The success of the Saint-Nazaire raid was misleading, however. It gave Hughes-Hallet and his Combined Operations planners the mistaken impression that it was feasible to attack other heavily fortified ports by direct assault, provided only that the defenders were taken by surprise.

In the meantime, the pressure on Britain and America to launch a second front had been mounting. The German armies had plunged even deeper into the Soviet Union, and Russian losses were appalling. Millions of soldiers, and as many civilians, had been killed in battle or had perished of starvation, cold and disease. Stalin demanded a major military diversion from the Western Allies. "A second front is essential," he said, "and therefore must be possible." A great public clamor for supporting the Russians arose in Britain, Canada and the United States. In British cities billboards and walls blossomed with the hand-painted injunction SECOND FRONT NOW.

In the judgment of American military chiefs, the Soviet Union was in such desperate straits that it might soon be knocked out of the War, freeing a mass of German soldiers and equipment for an invasion of Great Britain. To counteract an anticipated Russian collapse, and possibly to prevent it, General George C. Marshall, American Chief of Staff, ordered plans prepared for an emergency invasion of France. Two connected plans were drawn up by his protégé, Major General Dwight D. Eisenhower, and in April Marshall presented them to Churchill. The first plan, bearing the code name Operation *Sledgehammer*, called for landing some 12 divisions (10 of them British) in the autumn of 1942. The *Sledgehammer* force would establish a bridgehead and wait to be joined by a larger army—Operation *Roundup*—in the spring of 1943, when many more American troops would be available.

These plans drew strong but opposite reactions from British strategists. They were enthusiastic about *Roundup*, but they emphatically rejected *Sledgehammer*. The Germans were too strong, they argued, and the Allies too weak. There were not enough men and not yet enough materials for such a vast operation; there were not sufficient craft to carry them in or aircraft to cover them. Though America's capacity for war production was immense, the British argued, the U.S. was not yet geared for total war and its arsenals as yet were empty. The British were adamant that

there could be no second front in 1942, and they got the Americans to agree to a smaller invasion of North Africa in the autumn under General Eisenhower.

The idea of opening a second front had not been abandoned entirely. But instead of the real thing, there would be a dress rehearsal at a French port. At this stage of the War, both British and American strategists alike thought that any full-scale invasion of Europe, when it came, would have to aim at a port, and seize it intact, as the only way of getting supplies and reinforcements ashore quickly. With this in mind, a few weeks after the Saint-Nazaire raid the Anglo-American invasion planning group known as the Combined Commanders, headed by Eisenhower and General Sir Bernard Paget, sent Combined Operations a list of French ports and a polite request: "Please raid one of these ports in sufficient strength to persuade the enemy to react as if he were faced with actual invasion."

From the list of ports Mountbatten and his planners chose Dieppe, on the English Channel. Dieppe had several advantages over other possible targets. It was near enough to be reached by ship under cover of darkness, it was well within the operating range of RAF fighter planes, and its defenses were strong enough to ensure a major German reaction, from which the invasion planners hoped to learn much.

Specifically, the Dieppe raid would afford practice in handling an assault fleet off an enemy coast, in trying out new kinds of assault craft and equipment, in capturing and holding an enemy port. It would have the additional practical benefit of destroying German defenses, dock and rail installations, gasoline dumps and radar stations. And there would be the bonus of captured secret documents and prisoners. The raid had two strategic purposes as well—to force the Luftwaffe into a decisive air battle and to relieve German pressure on Russia by drawing troops and warplanes away from the Eastern Front.

For the main assault force, Combined Operations called upon the services of the 2nd Canadian Division, under the command of Major-General John Hamilton "Ham" Roberts, a respected artillery officer whose military career dated back to World War I. The Canadians had been based in England since 1939 and now, 150,000 men strong, they formed the backbone of the island's anti-invasion defenses while the British Army fought in the Middle East and South-

In this 1942 London Daily Mail cartoon, Prime Minister Winston Churchill is reminded of his long-standing promise to invade Europe by three "children," representing Britain's Army, Navy and Air Force. The cartoon reflected the growing clamor in England for the opening of a second front on the Continent to help relieve the Soviet Union in its desperate struggle against the Germans. The Soviet Ambassador to England demanded immediate action, saying, "There is no time to wait until the last button is sewn to the last uniform of the last soldier."

east Asia. During their two and a half years in England they had not seen any combat and they had gained a reputation as the most overexercised and underemployed army in the War. The Canadian government knew its men were frustrated and demoralized by inactivity and was pressuring the British government to send them into action at the earliest opportunity. Dieppe provided that opportunity.

The plan for the Dieppe raid, which bore the code name Operation *Jubilee,* evolved painfully, with many alterations, as spring gave way to summer. The attack was to be carried out on an 11-mile front, with Dieppe roughly in the center. The terrain was formidable. Two high headlands flanked the beach at the town, and beyond the headlands to either side rose unscalable chalk cliffs. Moreover, these natural defenses had been skillfully strengthened with artillery pillboxes, antiaircraft batteries and machine-gun nests. Combined Operations disregarded British intelligence estimates of the strength of the Dieppe defenses and judged that the German garrison in the area was no cause for concern. It consisted predominantly of raw recruits, older soldiers judged unfit for combat duty and Polish conscripts who had failed to qualify for their Army in 1939. But the terrain and the strength of its defenses more than made up for the garrison's shortcomings.

The final plan of attack called for landing six infantry battalions, one tank regiment, two Commando formations and various support units in five separate operations. On the outer flanks, several miles to either side of Dieppe, British Commando units would destroy two big coastal batteries, at the hamlets of Berneval and Varengeville, to prevent them from firing on the invasion fleet. Just to the east and west of the town, two Canadian regiments would knock out the German gun emplacements on the pair of headlands overlooking Dieppe.

Thus protected, the main assault force would land on the mile-long beach in front of the town. This force, consisting of two Canadian infantry regiments, would capture Dieppe and throw up a defensive perimeter around the Allied beachhead. Then tanks and foot soldiers would pass through the perimeter and attack a German airfield and the headquarters of the German 302nd Infantry Division, both within four miles of Dieppe. As soon as the port had been secured, another Commando unit would come in to seize the invasion barges that the Germans had stockpiled.

All in all, the plan was overambitious and hopelessly inflexible. In typescript it ran to 199 pages. It made no allowances for enemy interference in the attack, nor did it allow for individual initiative by the Canadian unit commanders—their every move was spelled out. Only the Commandos demanded—and got—the right to attack their assigned objective in any manner they saw fit.

The most grievous deficiencies in the plan were the most elementary ones. No overall commander was appointed; the naval forces and the landing parties would have coequal chiefs. There was to be no preliminary aerial bombardment and only brief naval shelling. Heavier bombardment had been ruled out partly because of the planners' concern for the safety of the townspeople, partly because of their fears that the resulting rubble would make the streets impassable to tanks, and partly because the Royal Navy could not spare any battleships and the RAF declined to contribute any bombers. Nor would any paratroopers be landed behind Dieppe to draw off some of the shore-front defenders; airborne attacks were considered too susceptible to cancellation due to adverse weather. Just as at Saint-Nazaire, surprise was supposed to win the day.

As final preparations for the Dieppe raid were made in August, the Allies' fortunes in Europe were at their lowest ebb, the Germans' at their fullest. Between the English Channel and the Black Sea, and between Norway and the islands of Greece, more than 400 million people had fallen under Hitler's rule. The German Afrika Korps under Field Marshal Erwin Rommel had defeated the British at Tobruk in Libya and was driving them eastward into Egypt. In the Atlantic, German U-boats were sinking merchant ships at a faster rate than replacements could be built. In the Far East, the all-conquering Japanese were threatening India, raising Allied fears that Japan might link up in the Middle East with its German and Italian allies and establish an Axis dominion over half the world.

The Dieppe raid, if all went as planned, would be one bright and inspiring light in the darkness.

Through the late hours of August 18, 1942, and the early hours of August 19, the Allied strike force steamed across the English Channel toward Dieppe. It was a beautiful,

A DARING STRIKE STAGED BY COMMANDOS AND AN ELDERLY DESTROYER

The Campbeltown, embedded in the gate of the great dry dock, is examined by Germans on the morning after the Saint-Nazaire raid. Even though the ship later blew up and destroyed the gate, German propagandists used this picture in stories calling the raid "new proof of England's military impotence."

Months after the raid, the remnants of the Campbeltown (circle) lie in the drained dry dock. The pump house (cross) and the old harbor entrance (rectangle) were wrecked by the British. Later, the Germans built a sand embankment to protect the dock's smashed gate (arrow), where the ship blew up.

Just after midnight on March 28, 1942, 630 British Commandos and sailors raced up the Loire estuary toward Saint-Nazaire aboard 18 small armed boats and one obsolete American Lend-Lease destroyer, the Campbeltown. Their mission was to wreck the only dry dock on the Atlantic coast big enough to handle Germany's huge battleship, the Tirpitz, thereby reducing her ability to stage devastating attacks on transatlantic convoys bound for the British Isles.

The raiders' main weapon of destruction was the Campbeltown herself; concealed above her fuel compartment were five tons of high explosives connected to delayed-action fuses. To confuse the German defenders, the British had disguised the destroyer as a German torpedo boat, cutting her funnels aslant and topping her masts with captured German battle flags.

The ship's disguise fooled the Germans just long enough. Although they spotted the floating time bomb more than a mile from her target, they waited until the old destroyer was approximately half a mile from the dry dock before firing. With machine-gun bullets and artillery shells battering her armored hull, the Campbeltown burst through an antitorpedo net, smashed into the huge dry-dock gate and stuck there at dead center (arrow, above right), her bow crumpled by the impact. The men aboard set their time fuses and abandoned ship.

Meanwhile, combat units and demolition teams from the small boats were busily wrecking other port facilities, including the water pumps and operating equipment for the dry dock. The boats provided cover fire, and one of them released delayed-action torpedoes into a metal gate blocking the old entrance to the harbor. Caught in a deadly cross fire, 10 of the small boats were hit and began sinking. At 2:50 a.m., Naval Commander R. E. D. Ryder (right) gave the order to withdraw. The eight vessels that were still afloat managed to rescue only 271 men.

In spite of the heavy losses, the raid turned out to be a smashing success—though how smashing was not apparent at first. The following morning, while curious Germans (above left) poked around the Campbeltown, time fuses detonated her charges. A tremendous explosion ripped the destroyer in half and blew aside the dry-dock gate, and a great surge of water carried the vessel's aft section through the gap into the dock itself. The blast killed more than 200 Germans.

Two days later, as the German work details were cleaning up the wreckage, the delayed-action torpedoes exploded and destroyed the old harbor entrance.

Though the Germans spent 18 months and huge sums of money trying to repair the dry dock for the Tirpitz, the battleship remained in northern waters, unable to impede the shipment of Britain-bound American manpower and supplies.

balmy summer night. The sea was calm, the wind quiet. For much of the voyage the moon shone down, illuminating the low silhouettes of 237 blacked-out Royal Navy ships—destroyers, troop carriers, tank landing craft, assault boats and antiaircraft barges traveling in parallel columns. For the members of the invasion force—nearly 5,000 Canadian infantrymen and tank crews, 1,100-odd British Commandos, 15 Free French soldiers, five expatriate German interpreters and a complement of 50 U.S. Rangers, the new American counterpart of the British Commandos—these were the last moments of peace and reflection.

The fleet passed easily through the German coastal minefield, which had been cleared hours earlier by 15 British minesweepers. Just before 3 a.m. the ships drew up about 12 miles from the coast, and their crews began to prepare the landing craft for the run to the shore. Everything was going exactly according to plan. Radio silence had been maintained; no enemy ships or planes had appeared. There seemed every chance that Operation *Jubilee* would hold on to its most crucial asset—surprise.

The troop ships lowered their landing craft into the water, and the men of the four preliminary assault forces clambered down into them. These forces—one each assigned to destroy the two outlying coastal batteries and to overrun the two coastal headland positions—were scheduled to land at 4:50 a.m., just before dawn. If the Berneval and Varengeville coastal batteries were not silenced, their big guns would be turned on the *Jubilee* fleet with full fury. If the headlands were not neutralized, the main assault force, scheduled to land on the Dieppe beach at 5:20 a.m., would fall prey to raking fire from both sides. To keep the element of surprise, the four assault teams would have to land at the same time. Any deviation in their schedule and they would pay the consequences of landing against enemy forces that would by then be fully alerted by the sounds of combat up or down the coast.

Soon after 3 a.m. the four flotillas of landing craft began to follow behind the gunboats guiding them to their respective beaches. For 37 minutes all went well. Then disaster struck. At 3:47 on the far left of the strung-out assault forces, men aboard the 23 landing craft of No. 3 Commando were suddenly startled to see the silhouette of a darkened ship dead ahead. Before the crews could take evasive action, a star shell shot into the sky, illuminating the black sea in its brilliant glow and revealing the unmistakable outline of a German convoy of five small cargo ships and three armed escorts steaming southwestward along the coast in the direction of Dieppe.

It was the cruelest luck imaginable—a few minutes earlier or later and the two flotillas would have passed each other unobserved in the darkness. But it need never have happened. Since 10:40 the previous evening the convoy had been observed on radar, first at Dover, and later at the Royal Navy headquarters in Portsmouth by a young Wren with a brother in No. 3 Commando. Two warnings had been radioed to the *Jubilee* fleet, but because of some technical breakdown on the headquarters ship, the destroyer H.M.S. *Calpe*, neither message had been received. For the lack of warning, the 460 men of No. 3 Commando were virtually helpless as the Germans opened fire. Most of the landing craft were unarmed and unarmored wooden boats, whose only defense was to speed off in all directions.

But the British gunboats accompanying this part of the invasion fleet put up a stiff fight. Jagged flickers of orange,

marking the muzzle blast of their guns, erupted across the dark sea. A German ship exploded and burned on the water. The flames revealed another German ship sinking fast and three more retreating into the darkness. The British gunboat leading the Commando landing craft was stopped by a shell in its boilers. Some of the landing craft went down. Some turned back. Five on the left and a solitary one on the right held their course. As a coherent force No. 3 Commando had all but ceased to exist.

The roar and flash of gunfire caused confusion for miles around. The British destroyer escort, five miles away to the east, thought the battle was taking place on the land. The headquarters ship had no idea where the gunfire was coming from. German sentries in their lookouts on the cliffs raised the alarm, but some of their superiors thought the sea battle was a routine convoy interception and gave no order to stand to. At 4:15 a.m. the gunfire died down, then ceased. For the next half hour all was quiet on the water.

To the men on board the solitary landing craft now spearheading the Commando 3 attack, the quiet seemed ominous and unreal. To Lieutenant Henry Thomas Buckee,

The biggest raid of the War, launched at daybreak on August 19, 1942, by some 6,000 British and Canadian troops, was a complex operation involving five assaults on the German-held French port of Dieppe and its outlying defenses. To permit the British fleet to approach Dieppe safely, Commandos attacked the long-range gun batteries at Berneval and Varengeville. Both of these two-pronged assaults prevented the enemy guns from firing on the fleet. To knock out guns that threatened the main assault on Dieppe itself, other units attacked batteries on top of the flanking headlands at Puys and Pourville. These attacks were bloody failures. When the main assault force hit the beach at Dieppe, the troops were mowed down by heavy fire from both headlands—as well as from shore-front machine-gun nests. Following a desperate morning-long battle, the raiders withdrew. Their casualties totaled 4,394 dead, wounded, missing and taken prisoner—more than two thirds of the whole force.

the landing craft commander, Major Peter Young, the officer in charge, and the five sailors and 19 soldiers with them, it seemed as if they were about to attack the armed might of German-occupied Europe completely on their own. They could see no sign of any other Allied soldiers or ships, not even the other stragglers from their own force. The men were on schedule, but they felt very vulnerable and alone as their boat drew close to the French cliffs and their objective, the Berneval gun battery that controlled the easterly sea approaches to Dieppe.

As the solitary landing craft came in below the cliffs to the east of Dieppe, Lieutenant Buckee said to Major Young:

"There you are, there's your beach."

"What do we do now?" the major asked.

"My orders are to land even if there's only one boat."

"Those are my orders too," Young agreed. "We are to land whatever happens, even if we have to swim."

At 4:45 a.m., five minutes early, the landing craft touched down at the edge of the secluded beach of Belleville, and the 20 Commandos raced up the rocky beach and into the mouth of a deep gully. It was the only exit from the beach, and the Germans had strung barbed wire up and down its flanks. The Commandos used the wire as climbing ropes and pulled themselves up the gully to the top of the cliff. Then they spread out around the gun battery and, using scrub brush for cover, opened fire. Outnumbered by more than 10 to 1, they could only hope to distract the 200-man German garrison from the main assault on Dieppe farther down the coast.

For about an hour and a half the Commandos pestered the battery. At one point the exasperated Germans swiveled a big 6-inch gun around and attempted to blast the Commandos out with artillery shells at a range of 150 yards. But the gun could not be depressed low enough to hit such a close target, and the shells roared harmlessly out over the French countryside. Eventually the Commandos' ammunition ran low, and Major Young's handful of men were forced to withdraw to the beach and reembark at 8:10 a.m. They did not lose a man.

The other landing craft of No. 3 Commando managed to reach their beach 20 minutes late. All the advantage of surprise was gone. They landed in broad daylight in the face of the determined fire of a fully alerted enemy. None reached the Berneval battery. Many were gunned down in the boats, on the beach and in the gully beyond. Some hid in the nearby hamlet of Petit Berneval but were later betrayed by the villagers and rounded up. At the end of the morning 38 of those who had landed lay dead and 82 were prisoners. Among the dead was 19-year-old Ranger Lieutenant Edwin Loustalot. He was the first American soldier of the War to be killed on European soil.

At the opposite end of the landing area, 11 miles west of the Berneval battery, No. 4 Commando was right on time to make its assault against the other coastal battery, at Varengeville. This force was led imperturbably by Lieut. Colonel the Lord Lovat, chief of Clan Fraser, who went into battle dressed as if for a Highlands sporting expedition—in corduroy slacks and a gray sweater and packing a Winchester hunting rifle. His 252 Commandos landed in two groups on adjacent beaches and quickly mounted their pincers attack on the six-gun battery. The 112 defenders were overwhelmed by a bayonet and knife attack of such fury and efficiency that it left only four of the Germans alive. The Commandos blew up the six big guns and set fire to the battery installations. Then, at precisely 7:30, just as planned, they reembarked and went home, taking with them their wounded, the four German survivors and some new-laid eggs presented by an elderly Frenchwoman.

The British Commando attacks on the outer flanks had accomplished their objectives, preventing the big coastal batteries from bombarding the naval force assembled off Dieppe during the most crucial part of the raid. But the two other preliminary assaults, intended to secure the headlands flanking the beach at Dieppe, soon collapsed, dooming the main attack on the town itself.

To the east of Dieppe, the landing craft carrying the Royal Regiment of Canada became badly scattered as they began their run into the little resort beach at Puys. The Royals lost 17 precious minutes while their boats regrouped. During the delay a German soldier at Puys, awakened by the gunfire at Berneval to the east, had rushed to his gun and began firing into the night, rousing his comrades. By the time the Royals landed at Puys the Germans were waiting for them.

German fire raked the landing craft, clanging against the metal-sided wooden boats or piercing them entirely. The men sprawled, clung to the deck and watched blue and white tracer bullets rushing by overhead with a sharp sound like dry twigs snapping. Then the landing craft touched down, and their ramps were lowered and the men stood up. The butchery began.

Fewer than 100 Germans defended Puys against more than 650 Canadian invaders. But their guns, mounted in concrete pillboxes and fortified houses on the rugged headland, commanded the entire 200 yards of pebbly beach. First, German snipers singled out officers and signalmen and put bullets through their heads or their radio sets, thus depriving the Royals of both leadership and communications. Heavy machine guns, antitank and antiaircraft guns, mortars and rifle fire smashed the Royals at almost point-blank range. The beach was scourged with orange flame, roaring shell bursts, flying shrapnel and showers of pebbles.

As the soldiers began jumping into the shallow water, they were cut to pieces, blown to bits, disemboweled, blinded, mangled and killed. Fewer than 20 men in the first wave reached the relative safety of the sea wall, some 50 yards from the boats. In minutes the beach was littered with the dead and dying. A blast of machine-gun fire cut off the legs of a sergeant, and as he fell the same burst severed his hand at the wrist. Along the water's edge the spume of the waves flopped blood-pink on the shore.

As the newly arrived landing craft lowered their ramps, their crouching human cargo was exposed to the direct aim of machine-gun fire from concrete pillboxes in the sea wall, and the men in the first rows were slaughtered. The men behind them were so shocked by the bloody spectacle that

Towering over the French coast three and a half miles to the west of Dieppe, the 80-foot-high lighthouse at Pointe d'Ailly guided the gunboats and landing craft of No. 4 Commando—one of four units that preceded the main invasion force—as the troops on board prepared their predawn attack on enemy gun emplacements. Even though the beacon was a help to the Commandos, one officer remarked that under its light," we felt like thieves in an alley when the policeman's torch shines."

they froze in the landing craft and had to be forced out at pistol point by Naval officers, who threatened to shoot them if they did not disembark. They ran into the withering fire, and within three minutes the Royal Regiment, the crack battalion of the Canadian Army Overseas, had virtually ceased to exist.

Some men did succeed in crossing the beach to the sea wall, moving miraculously through small gaps between the machine guns' field of fire. But the sea wall was 10 to 12 feet high, and the esplanade above it was wreathed with dense coils of barbed wire and swept with still more machine-gun bursts. It was suicidal to try to scale the wall but almost as dangerous to remain huddled below it, caught in constant enfilading fire. Before long the living and the dead formed a compact mass at the base of the wall.

Some men lay there, pretending to be dead, knowing that the slightest movement would bring gunfire down on them. Others were driven by rage and despair to acts of spectacular foolhardiness. One soldier went berserk and stood up in full view of the Germans, firing his Bren gun at them and screaming as he did so; he was still screaming when a hail of lead lifted him off his feet. A lone lieutenant charged a pillbox on the sea wall, heedlessly wading forward in a stream of bullets, and as he died he flung a grenade through the gun slit. Another officer attacked the headland all by himself, clawing his way up the high chalk cliff. As he climbed, Germans and Canadians alike stopped firing and watched in awe. He was about 80 feet up when his strength gave out and he clung to the cliff unable to move up or down. At that moment a single shot rang out across the almost silent beach, and the officer shuddered and fell backward into space.

A few men led charmed lives. Under constant heavy fire they went about their duties like sleepwalkers. One man, Corporal L. G. Ellis, managed to climb up a flight of stairs in the sea wall. He made his way inland, wandered about aimlessly, killed a sniper, dodged a shell, shot up Puys village, returned to the sea wall, ran down the beach, took off his clothes, waded through the sticky, blood-filmed water and the bobbing bodies, then swam safely out to sea.

Landing in the Royals' second wave, Lieut. Colonel Douglas Catto attempted to organize his ravaged battalion on the beach. Cutting through the coils of barbed wire on top of the sea wall, Catto and 20 men rushed up onto high ground beyond. The Germans at once unleashed a drenching fire that isolated Catto from his regiment.

On the beach, panic had broken out. When a landing craft tried to withdraw, it was stormed by hysterical soldiers who rose from the heaps of dead along the sea wall. In their efforts to climb aboard they overwhelmed the craft by the sheer weight of their numbers, as the sailors tried in vain to beat them off with the boat hooks. The craft, ramp down and doors jammed open, began to fill with water while German fire riddled most of the men on board. About 50 yards from the shore the sinking craft was hit by a shell and capsized. Some men clung to the upturned hull and were ultimately saved, but those who floundered in the water nearby were machine-gunned to death.

By 7 a.m. the end was near. The Germans emerged from their fortified gun emplacements on the cliffs and dropped stick grenades down on the Royals wriggling and ducking among the rocks below. Shortly after 8 a.m. the Germans saw a white handkerchief knotted to a rifle barrel being waved above the sea wall at the western end of the beach and ceased their fire. At 8:35 a.m. the men of the German garrison reported to their commander, General Conrad Haase: "Puys firmly in our hands; the enemy has lost about 500 men prisoners and dead."

Exactly 278 Canadians were taken captive, more than a third of them wounded. Lieut. Colonel Catto and his party were the last to surrender, at about 4:30 that afternoon. Of the 650 men who had actually landed at Puys, 67 returned to England that day. One of them was Corporal Ellis, who had spent two and a half hours swimming about before he was fished from the sea. The Royals had suffered 94.5 per cent casualties.

While the Royals were dying in droves, another Canadian regiment, the South Saskatchewan, was struggling to take the west headland overlooking the Dieppe beach. Unlike the Royals, the South Saskatchewans had landed at the little resort of Pourville, two miles to the west of Dieppe, nearly on time—and achieved almost total surprise. They rapidly overran Pourville and began their attack on the German installations in and around the fortified farm called Les Quatre Vents, or The Four Winds, on the headland.

Half an hour after the Sasks hit the beach, the follow-up battalion, the Queen's Own Cameron Highlanders of Canada, landed at Pourville with a bagpiper playing Scottish battle tunes—the sounds of his instrument were mistaken by some Canadians on shore for the squeaking wheels of German horse-drawn artillery. Some of the Camerons reinforced the South Sasks; others advanced inland toward the airfield at Saint Aubin, and after penetrating about a mile they laid low in a wood and waited for the Canadian tanks that were supposed to join them from the main landing at Dieppe. But no tanks came and eventually the outgunned Camerons fell back to the beach.

In and around Pourville, the Saskatchewans had bogged down in fruitless actions against stiffening German resistance. The farm, a radar station and an antiaircraft battery on the headland remained in German hands. Having failed to take their objectives in time, both the Sasks and the Camerons began a fighting retreat from Pourville to the beach. There, under increasing German fire, they watched for boats to come to evacuate them. They waited—and died—for one hour.

At 5:20 a.m., when the main attack on Dieppe got under way, the commanders aboard the headquarters ship *Calpe* had no inkling of the failure at Pourville or the calamity at Puys. General Roberts, commanding the ground forces, might have had time to cancel at least part of the assault had word reached him that the two headland landings had gone wrong. But he and Captain Hughes-Hallett, commanding the naval forces, were forced to operate in a vacuum until it was much too late to save the main force from pointless sacrifice in a campaign already lost.

The naval smoke screens, set up to conceal the ships from enemy gunners, also hid the joint commanders' view of the fighting on the beaches. Communications between the *Calpe* and the shore had broken down as radio operators were killed on the beaches and their radios destroyed. To confuse matters even more, the Germans transmitted deceptive messages, such as "Royal Regiment of Canada not landed." In sum, the commanders could not form any clear picture of the preliminary assaults. Not until nearly three hours after the first landings at Puys did the commanders receive trustworthy information that the Royals were in trouble. The pathetic message, much delayed in retransmission, read: "Is there any chance of getting us off?" By then there was little the commanders could do to change the course of events at Puys or anywhere else.

The plan for the main assault at Dieppe called for landing two regiments of Canadian infantry—the Royal Hamilton Light Infantry on the western half of the beach, the Essex Scottish on the eastern half. Their first mission was to knock out the German defenses so that the tanks of the Calgary Regiment could move on into the town.

As the landing craft carrying the 1,552 infantrymen and tank crews sped in toward Dieppe, the 4-inch guns of four British destroyers opened up with a 10-minute bombardment of the fortified beach-front buildings along the Boulevard de Verdun. At the same time, 50 cannon-firing Hurricanes swooped down in a brief low-level attack against the German defenses. To the men in the landing craft, the sea and air bombardment seemed outrageously inadequate, as indeed it was. When the boats had about 200 yards to go, three red flares burst in the air, signaling the end of the abbreviated bombardment. The ships' guns ceased firing. The Hurricanes flew away. Pinned down no longer, the Germans retaliated with a fearsome mortar barrage.

The Canadians bore up under German fire all the way to the beach. There they were pinned down, wounded and

Surrounded by battle-weary men, Lieut. Colonel the Lord Lovat, leader of No. 4 Commando, checks his casualty list after returning to Newhaven, England, from the disastrous Dieppe raid. Lord Lovat executed his attack with such precision and dash that only 12 of his 252 men were lost.

killed. The naval shelling had done little but set houses on fire. The cannon of the RAF Hurricanes had barely chipped the thick concrete of the German pillboxes.

The sea front was held by only a single company of enemy infantry, but the positions of the Germans were virtually unassailable. Soldiers were firing from the roofs and windows of the houses along the boulevard and from the casino on the beach. Other Germans poured down enfilading fire from the headlands and from machine-gun nests in the eastern cliffs.

These machine guns, unreported by British intelligence, cut broad swaths through the Essex Scottish, which landed almost below the eastern cliffs. Within 25 minutes of its landing, the regiment had lost 30 to 40 per cent of its men. In the next 45 minutes its casualties mounted to nearly 80 per cent. One group of about 15 Scots managed to cross the sea wall, blasting through the barbed wire on top. They raced across bullet-torn lawns, reached the houses beyond and fought their way to the docks. There they ran into impenetrable fire and were forced to fall back to the beach.

At the western end of the beach the Hamiltons fared a little better. Those nearest fought their way into the casino, whose front abutted the sea wall, and battled the defenders from room to room. In an hour the Canadians captured the lower floors of the casino, but the top floor remained in German hands throughout the morning. From the cover of this building, several small parties of Canadians dashed into the town. Two groups fought their way to a movie theater and then on to the Church of Saint-Rémy, but they were forced to withdraw.

The tanks of the Calgary Regiment, which had landed behind the assault forces, had even less luck in penetrating the Dieppe defenses. No matter what the crewmen tried, their tanks—27 of the new Churchill type that had never before been in action—could not break into the town. Several of these were put out of action shortly after landing. Fifteen climbed over the sea wall, but strong, concrete antitank barriers denied them entrance to the streets leading into Dieppe. As they rumbled about the esplanade, the tanks were easily picked off by German antitank guns. A few survivors returned to the beach, where they took up a hull-down position for a final fight.

All this time the commanders on board the *Calpe* had received no sure indication of how the main assault was faring. General Roberts did get a message saying that the Essex Scottish had fought their way into town. Thinking that meant the whole regiment and not just the few survivors who had done so, Roberts ordered part of his reserves, the French Canadians of the Fusiliers Mont-Royal, to land in support. He assumed he was exploiting success; in fact he was reinforcing failure.

At 7 a.m. the Mont-Royals went in. Nearly 200 men in bullet-riddled wooden boats were landed in the wrong place, on an isolated little beach below the west cliff, from where they could neither move nor take any part in the fighting. The rest of the Mont-Royals landed in the right place but met the fate of the regiments that had preceded them there. Most stayed pinned down in hollows on the rocky beach or behind the hulks of wrecked tanks. Only one group of Mont-Royals was able to scramble off the beach and penetrate the town. Led by Sergeant Pierre Dubuc, they fought their way as far as the docks. There their ammunition ran out and they were forced to surrender. They obeyed the Germans' orders to strip to their underclothes and line up against a wall. Then the nearly naked Mont-Royals overpowered their guard and fled through the streets back to the beach. Since they were without uniforms they were fired on by neither side.

At 8:30 a.m., General Roberts was informed that the casino had fallen into Canadian hands and that the western part of the beach was under Canadian control. Believing that the tanks were entering the town, he ordered in the last of his reserves, the Royal Marine Commandos. They moved forward under the cover of a smoke screen and supporting naval fire. But when they emerged from the smoke they saw before them a nightmarish panorama of burning landing craft, disabled tanks and dead and wounded soldiers amid erupting shells fired at point-blank range.

The Commando leader, Colonel J. P. Phillips, put on a pair of white gloves and, turning his back to the enemy, motioned to the following boats to turn back from the slaughter. Phillips continued to signal after everyone else on his craft was killed. Then he too fell. But most of the craft did turn back, escaping annihilation.

No objectives had been taken, and German resistance

was intensifying as reinforcements arrived. The 10th Panzer Division from Amiens was moving on Pourville, and German reinforcements were getting ready to rush the beaches. Time after time, British destroyers ran a gauntlet of shellfire to blast away at the German positions, one ship coming in so close that her stern touched the bottom as she turned. At one point in the action German officers wearing white dress uniforms could be seen through binoculars by the men on the beach. The officers had drinks in their hands and cigars in their mouths and were enjoying the victorious scene from a terrace on the west headland.

At 9 a.m. Captain Hughes-Hallett advised General Roberts that if the men on the beaches were to be evacuated, the decision would have to be made at once; it would take time to organize the rescue ships. The withdrawal was fixed for the earliest time possible, 11 a.m. That meant two more hours of hell for the men on the beaches.

Overhead the RAF got the battle it wanted. Its 74 Allied squadrons met the Luftwaffe, which flew in like hornets from bases as far away as Germany, Belgium and Holland. Over the beaches and the fleet the two air forces fought a massive battle. The RAF lost 106 planes to the Germans' 48.

The evacuation was a horror from the start. As the rescue ships' sirens screamed out their urgent summons, the soldiers on the Dieppe beaches struggled down to the water's edge in dazed little groups, many falling along the way. As their fire diminished, the Germans' intensified, and the survivors clustered helpless in the midst of an appalling barrage. The men in the tanks, sacrificing all hope of escape for themselves, kept up such covering fire as they could and prevented the Germans from storming the beach. An RAF Hurricane formation saved many soldiers by laying a smoke screen between them and German machine guns that were only 200 yards away.

But there was no withstanding the massed artillery bombardment, which by now had been reinforced by additional guns. Canadians died en masse at the water's edge. Many others died in the sea when their landing craft, overloaded with desperate men, capsized or were blown apart. In one overcrowded boat the Canadians shot their German prisoners and heaved the bodies overboard to lighten the sinking craft. All told, only 370 Canadians managed to escape the beach at Dieppe; 1,600 stayed there, 500 of them dead, the rest prisoners.

At the same time, the shattered troops who had tried unsuccessfully to take the west headland dominating the Dieppe beach were being evacuated from the beach at Pourville—with much the same harrowing results. Approximately 690 soldiers were killed or wounded. The living were forced to construct a parapet out of the bodies of the dead to cover their retreat. All together, 601 men were eventually extricated from Pourville.

At 12:20 the last attempts at evacuation were abandoned. Half an hour later, the *Calpe* sailed close to the shore at high speed to give short-range covering fire for any men who might still be alive on the beach. For the first time General Roberts was able to see the battlefield for himself. He could not make out any signs of life. At 1:08 p.m. he received his last message from the senior officer alive on shore: "Our people have surrendered." On that battered beach, the walking wounded began to drag their crippled comrades out of the water, saving them from drowning as the tide came in. Then they sat on the stones and wept.

Aboard the *Calpe*, a message from General Roberts was attached to the leg of a carrier pigeon and dispatched to the headquarters of the Canadian Army in England. "Very heavy losses in men and ships," read the message. "Did everything possible to get men off, but in order to get any home had to come to sad decision to abandon remainder. This was joint decision by Force Commanders. Obviously operation completely lacked surprise."

At 1:30 the remnants of the fleet and the remnants of the 2nd Canadian Division set course for England. "The journey back," a British Marine recorded afterward, "was one of utter misery. The mess deck was crowded with survivors, wounded lay around everywhere, a stench of mutilated humanity prevailed. I was in a state of utter shock. I lay on the deck and tried to gather my shattered wits together. I had no knowledge of what our role had been, I knew even less of what, if anything, we had achieved. I suppose someone, somewhere, was able to make a pattern of the day's events. I couldn't."

At 5:40 p.m. Field Marshal Gerd von Rundstedt, Commander in Chief of the German Army West, recorded in his diary: "No armed Englishman remains on the Continent."

In the ships taking them back across the Channel the shocked survivors fell into a deathlike sleep. Some were found still asleep in dark corners of their vessels 24 hours after their return to England. Five hospitals worked without a break for two days and two nights. In one operating room eight doctors at four tables did surgery for 40 hours nonstop. One doctor alone did 167 operations in a single night. "When some of the lads awakened from the ether," one survivor recalled, "they lived the battle all over again. The language was so cruel it was no wonder the nurses wore earplugs."

The Dieppe raid—a gallant, ill-planned rehearsal for the Second Front—was in almost every respect a disaster for the Allies. Of the 5,100 troops who actually landed, 3,648 failed to return. The Commandos, fighting on their own initiative, had fared well, suffering only 247 dead, wounded and prisoners. Not so the Canadians, who had been obliged to fight by the book; 907 were killed, and 1,946 taken prisoner, 568 of them wounded—virtually wiping out the 2nd Canadian Division. The Royal Navy lost a destroyer, 33 landing craft and 550 men. The RAF lost another 153 men. The German losses were light: 316 in the Army, 113 in the Navy, 162 in the Luftwaffe—a total of 591, of whom 297 had been killed.

The Dieppe raid was a great German victory. Marshal Henri Philippe Pétain and Pierre Laval, heads of the French Vichy government, were the first to congratulate the German High Command for the "rapid clearing of French soil."

Strategically, from the British point of view the assault was a total loss: it not only failed to cripple the Luftwaffe, it also failed to relieve German pressure on the Russian front. But it served some purposes. The action convinced Hitler that it was possible to repel an invasion at the water's edge. It deluded him into believing that the Allies' next invasion would be directed against a port and thus led him to neglect the defense of the open beaches. For the British, as Churchill later wrote of the raid, "it was a mine of experience." It taught the Second Front planners that no invasion could succeed if it was directed against a fortified port rather than open beaches. It proved that surprise was not so important or reliable as a massive and prolonged preliminary bombardment from sea and air, together with overwhelming close-fire support during the initial stages of the attack. It also showed that, once control of the air was established, a large fleet could be maintained off an enemy coast indefinitely; that tanks and signal parties should not be landed before beaches had been secured; and that attacks against heavily defended areas should be developed around the flanks rather than head on.

Many of these lessons were not new, but their importance was doubly underlined after Dieppe. So, too, was the need for a properly trained permanent naval force to operate landing craft, for properly organized headquarters ships, for special armored vehicles to protect the beach demolition squads, and for many other technical innovations in equipment and their use. Medical analysis of wounds pointed up the need for better designed landing craft to cut down on the number of casualties. "For every soldier who died at Dieppe," said Mountbatten later, "10 were saved on D-Day."

The Second Front planners took all of these lessons to heart, as several shrewd Germans expected they would.

"It would be an error," advised Field Marshal von Rundstedt in his summary of the Dieppe raid, "to believe that the enemy will mount his next operation in the same manner. . . . Next time he will do things differently."

AFTERMATH OF A TRAGIC RAID

In the aftermath of the disastrous Dieppe raid, wounded Canadian soldiers lie on the beach beside an abandoned tank, while a landing craft burns on the water.

STARTLING EVENTS IN DIEPPE

At 2 p.m. on August 19, 1942, the bewildered citizens of the port city of Dieppe, France, slowly emerged from their homes and stared about them. Their city was a shambles. Buildings had been gutted by shells, and streets were littered with roof tiles, shattered glass and fallen telephone lines. Hundreds of prisoners, bloodstained and pale, were being marched to collection points by German guards. On the beach lay battered tanks and wrecked landing craft. Bodies were everywhere—some hanging on barbed wire, many huddled under the sea wall.

What the stunned people of Dieppe were seeing was the aftermath of one of the biggest and boldest commando raids of the War, in which some 6,000 British and Canadian troops had stormed ashore at dawn along a broad front, and, after eight hours of fierce fighting, had withdrawn in bloody defeat. The population, warned by a BBC broadcast "to refrain from all action which might compromise its safety," had remained under cover throughout the raid.

More than 400 dead raiders were found right after the attackers withdrew, and within the next four days the sea washed up 475 more. The Germans buried the dead in a mass grave and permitted the townspeople to cover the mound with hundreds of wreaths and flowers. A few days after the burial, the Germans made an unexpected show of respect for their fallen enemies. The Wehrmacht Graves Commission sent coffins to Dieppe, and 500 soldiers reburied the dead in individual graves with full military honors.

Then the Germans made another surprising gesture: they rewarded the townspeople for taking no part in the raid. Hitler sent Dieppe a gift of 10 million francs and, more important, he announced that he was releasing French prisoners of war from Dieppe.

It happened that the Dieppe officials had only a sketchy list of local prisoners of war, so they asked the townspeople to supply them with the proper names and addresses—all that the Germans required for releasing a POW. The officials were not too fussy about verifying the names and addresses given them; they simply handed the long list over to the German authorities. Thus, in a happy epilogue to the tragic raid, hundreds of Frenchmen were allowed to go home—including many who had never set foot in Dieppe.

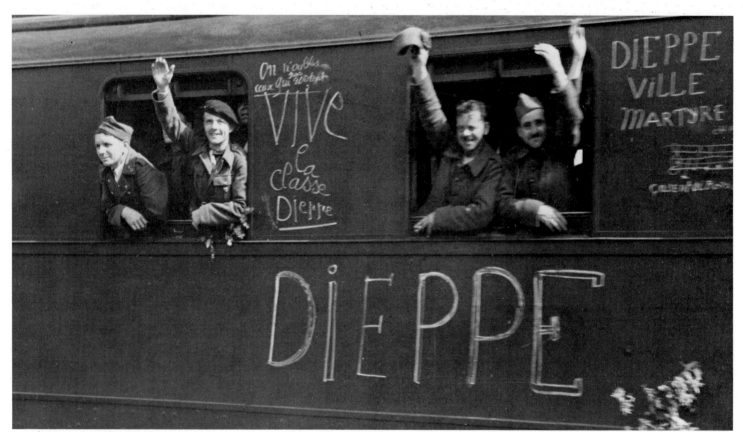

French POWs, freed by Hitler to reward Dieppe citizens for taking no part in the raid, wave joyously from a homeward-bound train covered with graffiti.

After the morning-long battle, townspeople of Dieppe sweep up the debris in front of a barbershop. By 4 p.m. nearly all of the stores were open again.

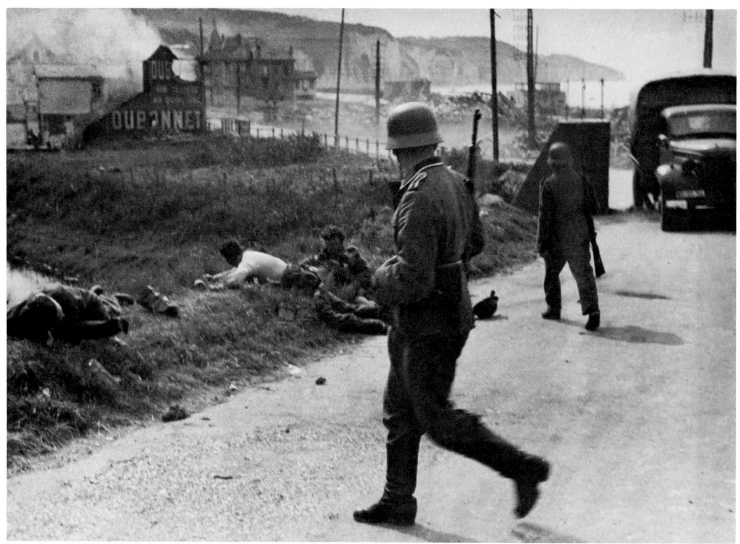

Wounded Canadians, rounded up by German soldiers, lie waiting on the roadside for transportation at Pourville, scene of bloody fighting west of Dieppe.

Under guard at a waterfront assembly point, Canadian prisoners await orders from the Germans. A few captives served as stretcher-bearers for the wounded.

Canadian prisoners march in a grim parade through Dieppe. Captives were searched, questioned and registered before being sent to POW camps in Germany.

HARSH TREATMENT FOR CAPTURED RAIDERS

In the hours after the raid, more than 2,000 captured Canadian and British troops were herded together in Dieppe. Some of the prisoners were dressed only in their underclothes and makeshift shoes made of rubber strips torn from their Mae West life jackets; these soldiers had been left behind during the raiders' desperate withdrawal, and had stripped off their uniforms and boots and swum out to sea, trying in vain to catch an outbound landing craft.

More than 500 prisoners were badly injured. One man with a huge abdominal wound struggled along holding back his intestines with his hands. However, despite their wounds and their defeat, many POWs marched in step with their heads high. They received treatment at a Dieppe hospital and, in a week, were sent to prison camps in Germany.

Unfortunately, a relic of the raid added to the sufferings of the imprisoned raiders. On the battle-torn beach, inside a waterproof package, a German officer found a copy of the British plan for the Dieppe operation. The plan contained orders that "wherever possible, prisoners' hands will be tied to prevent destruction of their documents." The Germans were infuriated by what they called these "Wild West measures." Then came a further provocation: the British raided one of the Channel Islands on October 4 and tied up several defenders. In retaliation, the Germans kept the Dieppe prisoners bound with ropes and handcuffs from 8 a.m. to 9 p.m. They pursued the practice for more than a year before relenting.

A Luftwaffe officer studies Allied equipment left on a landing craft. The square marker on the craft identified it to others heading shoreward during the raid.

Laden with captured gear, a German leaves a beach to the dead.

LESSONS LEARNED FROM THE SPOILS OF BATTLE

The Dieppe raid left behind an enormous and valuable booty. The Germans collected several landing craft, 28 Churchill tanks, one command car, 80 mortars, six self-propelled guns, 60 antitank rifles and some 1,500 small arms. They carefully studied all the captured matériel, but they were most interested in the 43-ton Churchills. These were the Allies' latest tanks, specially waterproofed to operate in six feet of water.

German technicians ran thorough tests on the Churchills and wrote detailed reports on the tanks' strengths and weaknesses. Months later, a British spy stole copies of the reports and forwarded them to London. The British welcomed the Germans' shrewd analysis of the tanks' defects and used it in designing later tanks.

The Germans' final assessment of the Dieppe raid was equally astute, if less palatable to the British. The German High Command called it an "amateur undertaking" that was "carried out in opposition to all good military sense."

A tank landing craft, one of several stranded on the beach at Dieppe, gives the Germans a rare opportunity to analyze the recent progress of British designers.

At a German base near Paris, General Sepp Dietrich, the noted tank corps leader, examines a captured Churchill, brought from Dieppe for study and display.

On the day after the raid, the camouflaged Dieppe casino, where room-to-room fighting raged for hours, stands as a battered reminder of the Germans' victory.

On the 12th of March, 1943, British Lieut. General Sir Frederick E. Morgan stepped into a crowded elevator at New Scotland Yard, London, on his way to a meeting at Combined Operations Headquarters, the amphibious command run by Admiral Mountbatten. The admiral himself jumped into the elevator at the last minute and greeted Morgan warmly. In spite of the crowd of people around them, Mountbatten congratulated Morgan on his appointment as Chief of Staff to the Supreme Allied Commander (Designate), or COSSAC for short—a title used to describe Morgan's whole operation. COSSAC was the planning embryo for the Supreme Headquarters of the Allied Expeditionary Force, or SHAEF, which in 1944 would command the long-awaited invasion of occupied Europe.

Thus Morgan learned for the first time of the daunting assignment that was to engage all his energies for the next year. He was an excellent choice for the post, having had solid experience in both invasion planning and invasion operation. In 1942 he had been a task-force commander in the invasion of North Africa, and he had just completed preliminary planning for the invasion of Sicily, which was to take place in July. Morgan was also a self-starter with extraordinary executive ability.

Morgan immediately established headquarters in Norfolk House, St. James' Square, in London. He gathered together a small but rapidly growing staff of British and American officers; COSSAC had to be a joint effort since neither Britain nor the United States had the resources to mount the invasion alone. The staff was already hard at work when, in April, General Sir Alan Brooke, Chief of the Imperial General Staff, handed Morgan his orders from the Combined Chiefs of Staff.

"There it is," Brooke said. "It won't work but you must bloody well make it."

Morgan's orders called for the planning of a large-scale invasion of the Continent, to be launched as early as possible in 1944. This immediately forced him and his staff to make a giant leap in military logic. Since it was impossible to plan an invasion without deciding first its ultimate goal, COSSAC set as the objective the defeat of Germany on German soil and drew up a master plan—later code-named *Overlord*—that estimated the enormous numbers of troops

2

A British general lays the groundwork for "Overlord"
"We must take a port with us"
Crisis over a shortage in landing craft
SHAEF and Eisenhower take command
The magnificent deceptions of Operation "Fortitude"
Paving the way with saturation bombing
The countdown for invasion
Alarming last-minute German troop movements
History's most important weather forecast
Ike says go

OVERTURES TO OVERLORD

and the immense quantities of matériel that would be needed at various stages in the campaign to reach that goal. In effect, COSSAC worked backward through *Overlord* to its initial assault phase, Operation *Neptune.*

The planning of the invasion, which preoccupied Morgan and COSSAC throughout 1943, was a mind-boggling enterprise. No useful precedent existed. Unlike the massive invasion of Sicily, which would begin with most of the troops and supplies within striking distance in North Africa, the assault on Western Europe had to be started virtually from scratch, and it depended on the speculative dates when manpower and matériel would become available in the huge quantities needed. Somehow the COSSAC planners would have to produce soldiers by the millions, along with the millions of tons of paraphernalia needed to keep them living, moving and fighting. All this and more the COSSAC staff would have to do under great pressure, for the Combined Chiefs soon fixed May 1, 1944, as D-Day.

Fortunately, the planners had a wealth of data with which to begin detailed work. The sea approaches, winds, tides, nature of the beaches, their exits and hinterlands, the pros and cons of every port and beach that might be captured, airfields or ground suitable for building airfields, enemy coastal defenses, strength of enemy troops, location of enemy naval forces, the capacity of the assault area for the build-up of invasion forces—information about all these aspects of the possible invasion areas had been assiduously gathered by previous planners, using secret agents, aerial photos, Commando landing parties, even seaside picture postcards collected from prewar British tourists. All that COSSAC now had to do was dig through the files.

Morgan and COSSAC discarded old preconceptions in their search for the best area for the invasion. They considered regions as unlikely as Portugal and Norway, Denmark's Jutland and the Netherlands' Frisia—even Dunkirk. It was not just beaches they were looking for. "The landing beaches were just one x in an algebraic expression that contained half the alphabet. What was wanted was a lodgement area into which we could blast ourselves and from which our main bodies, having suitably concentrated themselves within it, could erupt to develop the campaign eastwards," Morgan wrote later.

Various factors determined the choice. One of the most important considerations was the range of friendly fighter aircraft. The Allies could not count on getting a firm foothold on the beaches without total supremacy in the air above them. Air supremacy could be gained only with an overwhelming cover of fighter planes. Since these fighters were based in England, it followed that the farther from England the invasion forces landed, the less time the planes could spend in the air over the beaches before having to turn back to refuel. In practice this meant that the invasion area had to be somewhere between Cherbourg and Flushing in the Netherlands.

The need for harbors further narrowed down the choice. Once they had landed, the invaders could not count on extending their beachhead into a staging area unless the rate of build-up of troops and matériel was greater than the Germans' rate of reinforcement with reserves. The build-up therefore depended on securing an area with wide beaches and large ports nearby, through which men and supplies could be rapidly unloaded.

Only two places were really suitable for the invasion—the Pas-de-Calais coast and the Caen sector of the Normandy coast to the west (*map, page 46*). The Pas-de-Calais was the more obvious choice. It was nearer England, so the seaborne journey of the invasion army would be shorter and simpler and air cover more easily provided. Once landed there, moreover, the Allied armies could be on the most direct route to Germany.

But because the Pas-de-Calais coast was the most obvious choice, it was also the most heavily defended section of Hitler's Atlantic Wall. Topographically it was also unsuitable. The high cliffs, narrow beaches and restricted exits would make it difficult to maintain a build-up on the beaches, so the Allies would be forced to capture a port immediately. In that respect as well the Pas-de-Calais was less than perfect. The capacity of the local ports of Calais and Boulogne was so small that the Allies would have to extend their staging area eastward or westward toward the big ports of Antwerp in Belgium or Le Havre in France, a difficult task against the expected opposition from the Germans. Finally, the English south-coast ports opposite the Pas-de-Calais were themselves too small to accommodate the invasion armada.

The Normandy coast had none of these drawbacks. "The

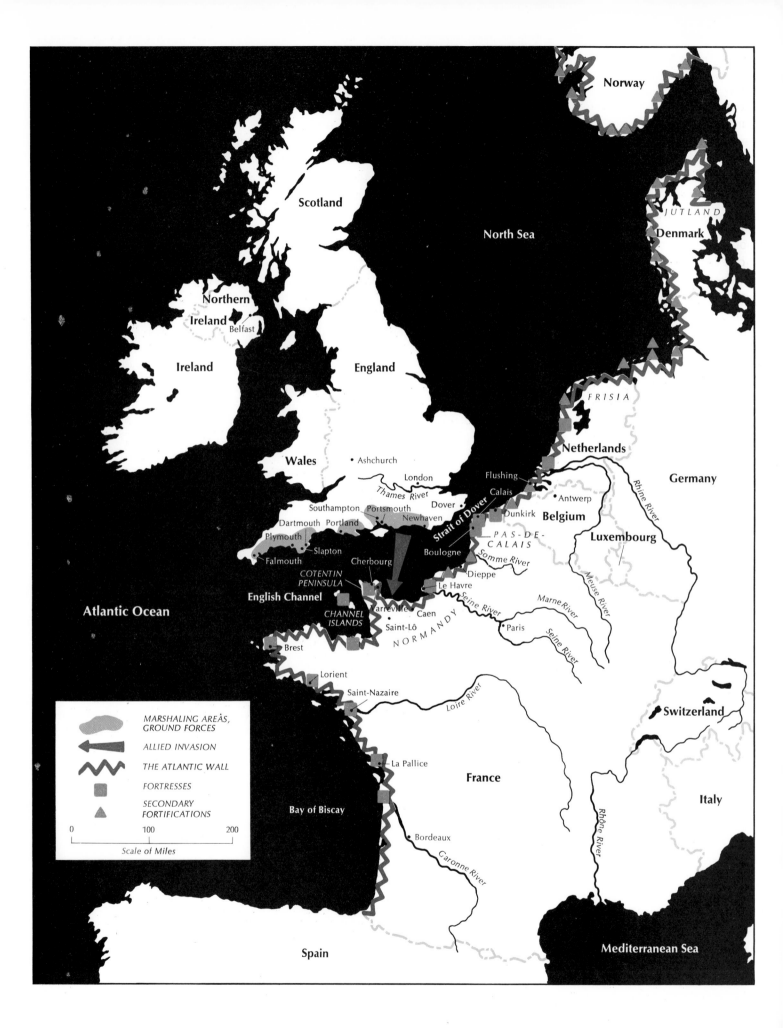

Norway

North Sea

JUTLAND

Denmark

Scotland

Northern
Ireland
• Belfast

Ireland

England

Netherlands

FRISIA

Germany

Wales   • Ashchurch

London

Flushing

Calais

Thames River

Dover

Antwerp

Belgium

Rhine River

Southampton Portsmouth

Newhaven

Dunkirk

Luxembourg

Dartmouth Portland

Strait of Dover

*P A S - D E -
C A L A I S*

Plymouth

Boulogne

Somme River

Falmouth   Slapton

Cherbourg

Dieppe

Meuse River

*COTENTIN
PENINSULA*

Le Havre

Marne River

English Channel

Varreville

Caen

Seine River

• Paris

*CHANNEL
ISLANDS*

Saint-Lô

Seine River

N O R M A N D Y

Atlantic Ocean

• Brest

Switzerland

Lorient

Saint-Nazaire

Loire River

MARSHALING AREAS,
GROUND FORCES

ALLIED INVASION

THE ATLANTIC WALL

La Pallice

Italy

FORTRESSES

SECONDARY
FORTIFICATIONS

France

0   100   200

Scale of Miles

Bay of Biscay

Rhône River

• Bordeaux

Caronne River

Spain

Mediterranean Sea

Caen sector is weakly held," COSSAC reported, "and the beaches are of high capacity and sheltered from the prevailing winds. Inland the terrain is suitable for airfield development and for the consolidation of the initial bridgeheads." Furthermore, the nearest major port, Cherbourg, was big enough to handle large amounts of matériel quickly. Normandy became the strike point.

The next problem was to determine the size of the assault. Since there were no existing guidelines for such an undertaking, the only thing to do was to make an arbitrary allocation of the forces that might be available at the time. However, the size of the invasion force was limited by the number of landing craft set aside for the assault. Morgan did not believe that enough craft would be available to transport more than three divisions on D-Day. He therefore proposed that the initial assault should be carried out along a 25-mile front by three seaborne divisions and two airborne divisions, with two additional seaborne divisions following up—a dangerously small force.

The English Channel and its weather were also factors to take into account. The Channel's big tides and extraordinary capacity for conjuring up storms often and on short notice had posed a serious problem in Britain's plans for small-scale, overnight Commando raids. Now the planners had to face the problems of using the Channel for a massive and prolonged amphibious operation.

COSSAC applied a lesson learned from the Dieppe raid: no major fortified port could be captured quickly by a frontal assault. Morgan set D-plus-14—14 days after D-Day—as the date for the capture of Cherbourg and calculated that it would take two or three months more to clear the mines and repair the damage left behind by the Germans. In the meantime, the invading troops would have to be supplied and reinforced on open beaches. But weather statistics showed that there were storms in the Channel every month of the year and that fair weather rarely lasted for more than four days at a stretch. It seemed that the only way to guarantee an uninterrupted flow of men and matériel to the Normandy front even in adverse weather was to provide sheltered water off the beaches. But how? The solution, worked out by British naval experts and construction engineers in 1943, proved to be one of the boldest and most original conceptions in military history: artificial harbors.

The basic idea of the artificial harbor had been dreamed up by Winston Churchill for a proposed invasion of Flanders in World War I. In 1917 he suggested building "a number of flat bottomed barges or caissons, made not of steel but of concrete, which would float when empty of water and thus could be towed across. On arrival the sea cocks would be opened and the caissons would settle on the bottom. By this means a torpedo- and weather-proof harbour would be created in the open sea."

Churchill's concept was brought to fruition by Hughes-Hallett, the driving force behind the raids on Saint-Nazaire and Dieppe, now a commodore and the senior Naval officer at COSSAC headquarters. In the summer of 1943, when the question of ports was raised at COSSAC, Hughes-Hallett remarked: "Well, all I can say is, if we can't capture a port we must take one with us." He believed that a large area of sheltered water could be created by sinking a line of ships in shoal waters off the invasion beaches. His scheme gave hope to the COSSAC planners. It was, they felt, the key to the whole operation.

The Combined Chiefs agreed to build two artificial harbors, later code-named Mulberry A (for the Americans) and Mulberry B (for the British)—together capable of handling 12,000 tons of stores and 2,500 vehicles a day. Since the harbors would have to be ready by May 1, 1944, only eight months were left for their design and construction.

A team consisting of the leading consultant engineers and naval contractors in Britain worked around the clock to solve the complex design problems of the Mulberries. The principal difficulty was the breakwater. Hughes-Hallett's sunken blockships alone would be inadequate. One bright idea was to create an artificial breakwater with an underwater wall of air bubbles, a method that was eventually rejected as being impractical on the scale demanded. The final plan incorporated the proposals of both Churchill and Hughes-Hallett: floating piers, caissons and blockships were all integral to the design.

More than 200 steel-and-concrete caissons were constructed; the largest, each as big as a five-story building, were 200 feet long, 55 feet wide and 60 feet high and weighed 6,000 tons. There were 23 floating pierheads, 10

On June 1, 1944, five days before D-Day, most of the million-odd German troops stationed in France and the Netherlands were dispersed along the Atlantic Wall, a 2,400-mile coastal barrier (saw-toothed line) of powerful fortresses (gray squares), lesser fortifications (gray triangles), innumerable machine-gun nests and long stretchers of formidable terrain. Most of the 3.5 million Allied troops in Britain were concentrated in southern England, in marshaling areas (shading) around the major embarkation ports. Across the English Channel, in the strongest sector of the Atlantic Wall, some 20 German divisions manned the French coast between two fortresses—the ports of Cherbourg, on the Cotentin Peninsula in Normandy, and Calais, well to the northeast. The Pas-de-Calais area, the closest to England and the likeliest invasion target, bristled with the mightiest defenses of all. But the Allies had their invasion site picked: a 59-mile stretch of the Normandy coastline west of Caen.

miles of steel roadway, 93 steel-and-concrete floats, each 200 feet long, 25 feet high and 2,000 tons in weight, and 74 cargo boats and obsolete warships to be used as block-ships. To tow these vast and unwieldly parts from their moorings in creeks and inlets around the British coast to their final, exact position off an enemy shore on the far side of a treacherous sea would require every heavy-duty tug in Britain and America.

The staff of COSSAC applied another lesson from the Dieppe raid in its planning: the need for armored support as soon as the infantry had landed. General Brooke reckoned that without armor the Atlantic Wall could not be breached except at an unacceptable cost in soldiers' lives. So in March 1943 he turned the 79th British Armored Division into an experimental formation with the task of developing special armor for the invasion. The division commander was Major-General Sir Percy C. S. Hobart, a veteran of World War I and one of the great pioneer tank theoreticians, whose early ideas had been adapted by the Germans in the creation of their panzer formations.

Hobart realized that the tanks used at Dieppe had never reached their objective because most of the demolition engineers who were to have cleared the way through obstructions had been killed almost as soon as they landed. His solution was to construct tanks that could do their own demolition work. Hobart and his staff eventually produced an amazing variety of specialized armored vehicles (pages 172-181), the most important of which were devices that enabled a 33-ton Sherman tank to take to the water and swim ashore under its own power.

Yet another lesson COSSAC learned from Dieppe was the need for stronger and closer fire support for the first wave of assault troops. Clearly, neither bombing nor naval shelling could totally silence the German defenders, many of whom would be back in action soon after the bombardment ceased. To prevent assault troops from being dangerously exposed to point-blank enemy fire as they closed in on the beaches, it was essential to fill what General Paget, Commander in Chief, Home Forces, aptly called "the gap between the barrage and the bayonet." COSSAC proposed that assault infantry should be accompanied by floating artillery—guns, mortars and rocket batteries mounted in landing craft and gunboats. Later General Sir Bernard L.

Montgomery, ground commander for the invasion, proposed that some tanks on landing craft following close behind the leading infantry should provide support while they waited to land. By using both these measures, the Overlord planners hoped to saturate the German defenses with close-range fire up to the moment of landing.

Of all the technological devices thought up for Overlord, none gave COSSAC greater anxiety than the specialized landing craft. At first sight, the problem seemed to be one of production. General Morgan pointed out to the Combined Chiefs in August 1943 that the allocation of landing craft for Overlord was inadequate. But the shortage continued and actually became more acute, driving Churchill to exclaim in exasperation, "the destinies of two great empires seemed to be tied up in some goddammed things called LSTs." American production was stepped up until it could be stepped up no more, and in Britain one quarter of all the steel for new ships went into landing-craft production. But it was not sufficient.

In the end the Allies had to resort to the drastic action of postponing D-Day for a month in order to allow shipyards more time to increase stocks of landing craft. In fact, however, the postponement of the greatest amphibious assault in history need never have happened. The shortage of landing craft was not so much a failure of production as of allocation. On May 1, 1944, the original D-Day, Admiral Ernest J. King had at his disposal as chief of U.S. Naval Operations some 31,123 landing craft, while a mere 2,493 were assigned to Overlord. King was stockpiling landing craft for island fighting in the Pacific, and eventually General Marshall had to order him to share the wealth.

The landing-craft problem brought to a head the tensions underlying the Allies' differing approaches to the strategy and politics of Overlord. Though the British had good cause for complaining about the shortage of landing craft, the Americans, for their part, viewed the British protestations as a reflection of a deep-down lack of commitment to any invasion of France in 1944. The British had never been in favor of the Americans' strategy of a straight stab into the heart of Germany. Their preference was for encirclement and slow strangulation—an approach that had involved the Allies in Mediterranean fighting that a large number of

Americans thought was peripheral to the main objectives of the War. After the invasion of Italy in September of 1943, Churchill proposed extending the Mediterranean campaign into the Balkans. While President Roosevelt was insisting that *Overlord* should have overriding priority in the assignment of forces in Europe, Churchill proposed allocating only six tenths to *Overlord,* three tenths to Italy and one tenth to the Balkans.

Many Americans, slowly growing aware of the labyrinthine complexity of European politics, began to feel that there was more to the British obsession with the Mediterranean and the Balkans then met the eye. They felt that the British were tailoring their wartime conduct to suit their postwar interests in the Mediterranean. They read into the British attitude toward *Overlord* a profoundly sinister intention: to delay the defeat of Germany so as to exhaust the U.S.S.R. and leave Britain the dominant power in Europe.

In fact, as General Morgan remarked about *Overlord,* "there were undoubtedly those who would not be heart-

British Lieut. General Sir Frederick E. Morgan, wearing a SHAEF shoulder patch on his uniform as one of the Supreme Headquarters' three deputy chiefs of staff, laid the initial groundwork for Operation Overlord in his earlier position as the Chief of Staff to the Supreme Allied Commander (COSSAC) between April and December of 1943. Morgan's successor, General Eisenhower, later wrote of him, "He had in the months preceding my arrival accomplished a mass of detailed planning, accumulation of data, and gathering of supply that made D-Day possible."

broken if the whole business were called off. There were other ways of winning the war." Russian victories on the Eastern Front meant that a second front to help the Russians was no longer the military or moral necessity it had formerly seemed to be. A powerful element, led by Air Chief Marshal Sir Arthur Harris, the head of the British Bomber Command, believed that Germany could be bombed into submission at less cost in money and manpower. It would just take longer. But Roosevelt wanted to win the War in 1944.

The British also entertained suspicions of the Americans. They doubted the Americans' tactical ability to carry out an invasion of the Continent and, later, their strategic capacity to do so. In 1943 General Morgan at COSSAC felt obliged to wonder why the Americans were so slow in delivering the landing craft, troops and matériel to solidify his plans for the invasion. "Were we really only taking part in a gigantic cover plan or hoax," he later recalled asking himself, "with the object of hoaxing, among others, ourselves?" With the United States so deeply committed to the war in the Pacific, and with Admiral King and other commanders arguing that the Pacific theater was of primary importance, the fate of *Overlord* always hung in the balance of global strategic priorities. Were the Americans procrastinating about *Overlord?* General Morgan had grounds to think so. Why, as late as November 1943, had various top U.S. commanders received no directives regarding their part in the invasion? Why, as November turned into December, was there not even a Supreme Commander to take charge? Were not the Americans furthering their interests in the Pacific at the expense of the liberation of Europe?

The biggest issue separating the British and the Americans was the matter of the ultimate goal of *Overlord.* "We tried in vain," Morgan later wrote, "to obtain some statement of a long term political object. The objective admittedly was Berlin, but an object and an objective are two different things." Was the object the destruction of Germany or the creation of a new Germany? Was it occupation or was it withdrawal?

The disagreement was political: essentially, the British argued that the Americans were abandoning Central Europe and the Balkans to the Soviet Union, while the Americans insisted that *Overlord's* only concern should be military victory. The U.S., by virtue of its superior resources in men and matériel, had become the dominant partner of the alliance, so the American view prevailed. But Churchill and other British leaders were never reconciled to it.

Until May of 1943 it seemed highly unlikely that the actual build-up for *Overlord* would meet COSSAC's projected schedule. Only small numbers of U.S. troops and small quantities of American supplies had been reaching Britain under a year-old Second Front logistics program called Operation *Bolero (pages 64-77)*. It took time for the United States to gear up industrially for total war and to recruit an army, and the U-boat toll on the Atlantic convoy crossings put a brake on the rate of build-up. But by May 1943 there had been a dramatic turnaround in the Battle of the Atlantic. U-boat losses rose and Allied shipping losses fell; meanwhile American shipyard output broke all records. The Allied leaders gave the go-ahead for a cross-Channel invasion in the spring of 1944.

By late autumn of 1943, the build-up in Britain was accelerating at an almost unmanageable rate. The target—1.5 million American servicemen in Britain by May 1944 and another million by February 1945—came within reach. At the same time, the British were fast building their own army to a total of 1.75 million; they also expected to have 175,000 Commonwealth forces and 40,000 troops from France, Norway, Belgium, Holland, Poland and Czechoslovakia. Thus, an army of about 3.5 million men would eventually be gathered in Britain, together with all the planes, ships, guns, tanks, trucks, ammunition, fuel, rations, clothing, medicines and other supplies required to sustain a force of that size. By early 1944 Britain was top-heavy with troops and matériel. "It was claimed facetiously at the time," General Eisenhower wrote later, "that only the great number of barrage balloons floating constantly in British skies kept the islands from sinking under the seas."

To the U.S. Army officers charged with organizing the supply build-up, Britain posed some surprising problems. An Army transportation chief declared that the country was "so cramped and small, the railroad equipment so tiny, the roads so small and crooked, and methods so entirely different" that American operating methods would have to be totally transformed. Most of the ports were antiquated and inadequate. The dock workers were few and elderly (at

Liverpool the average age of the dockers was 52), and restricted by archaic labor practices (union rules in Belfast, for example, made it advantageous to both employer and employee to discharge vessels as slowly as possible). Many of the winding roads of the English countryside and the narrow high streets of the towns were impassable for bulky military convoys. The railways were short of rolling stock and tunnels were too narrow for tanks on flatcars.

Complicating matters was the fact that the capacity of the ports was already strained. American imports for *Overlord*

A British war worker manufactures strips of aluminum foil for deceptive operations executed during the predaylight hours of D-Day morning. Since 1943, when the British began dropping the foil simply to jam enemy radar reception, they had learned the exact frequency of German radar from equipment captured in a Commando raid on Bruneval, France. Using this information, they cut the aluminum strips at precise lengths that would produce the same effect on German radar screens as an airplane. The foil, dropped in controlled patterns in a line toward the Pas-de-Calais area, helped to convince the Germans that a huge force of Allied aircraft was heading there, protecting an enormous invasion fleet.

represented only one tenth of the 25 million tons of freight that flowed through British ports each year to meet the country's civil and military needs. As the build-up reached a crescendo in the spring of 1944, Britain's limited port facilities and storage space reached the crisis point. An enormous backlog of cargo piled up in New York, and the danger grew that the invasion forces would not be properly supplied even in the midst of plenty. Churchill finally solved the problem by cutting Britain's own imports to allow room for the *Overlord* build-up.

Supplying the invasion forces was not entirely an American responsibility. Britain, despite its impoverishment and the overwhelming demands of its civilian population and armed forces, contributed greatly to the U.S. forces in a form of reverse Lend-Lease. The Quartermaster Corps of the U.S. Army in Britain acquired 63 per cent of its supplies from the British, the Corps of Engineers 58 per cent, the medical service 49 per cent and the Air Force 21 per cent, including 1,100 aircraft, mostly small transport and courier planes. As a whole, what the Americans called ETOUSA (European Theater of Operations, United States) received 31 per cent of all its supplies from Britain.

British and American authorities had at first believed that the huge influx of American servicemen into Britain would lead to disastrous cultural conflicts. There were strains, but the officials' worse fears proved to be unfounded. Considering the circumstances, the American invasion of Britain was in the main a friendly and harmonious affair *(pages 106-119)*. The British and the Americans saw in each other a new culture and a new way of life, though neither side was entirely convinced that it liked what it saw. To many of the British, the Americans were brash, bad mannered, tiresomely energetic and unpleasantly addicted to chewing gum and talking boisterously about the Brooklyn Dodgers baseball team. But for British girls at least, American boys were second only to German bombs as the most memorable experience of World War II.

By the autumn of 1943, a quiet crisis had gripped COSSAC and indeed the entire Allied military establishment in England: *Overlord* planning could not be jelled until someone was appointed to the post of Supreme Commander of the invasion forces. For a long time it had been assumed that the Supreme Commander would be a British general, and Churchill had already promised the job to General Brooke, the Chief of the Imperial General Staff. But it had gradually become clear that the majority of the force for *Overlord* would not be British but American and that the Supreme Commander should, therefore, be an American.

At first the consensus was that the American Chief of Staff, General Marshall, would be given the job. But Marshall was too valuable to President Roosevelt in Washington. For a time Roosevelt could not decide. At one point he proposed that Marshall should hold both jobs, but the British objected, on the reasonable grounds that Marshall would then be too powerful. Asked in October who the Supreme Commander was to be, Roosevelt said he had not made up his mind.

But if it was not to be Marshall, there was only one logical choice: General Dwight D. Eisenhower. Eisenhower had worked out the original invasion plan for the 1943 Operation *Roundup*; he had commanded three previous invasions in the European theater (North Africa, Sicily, Italy); he was a leader equally popular in both the American and British camps.

In December Roosevelt finally announced that Eisenhower was the man. COSSAC gave way to SHAEF (Supreme Headquarters of the Allied Expeditionary Force), and the embryo invasion headquarters became a full-fledged operational headquarters assigned to carry the war to the Germans without further delay.

General Eisenhower arrived in London to take up his duties in mid-January, 1944. In March the rapidly expanding SHAEF organization was moved from the old COSSAC headquarters in Norfolk House to a large encampment in Bushey Park near Henry VIII's old palace at Hampton Court by the Thames River in Middlesex. Here all the diverse departments of this huge and complex organization could be unified into a tented township that eventually held some 750 officers and 6,000 men. Eisenhower himself moved to a secluded home nearby, called Telegraph House, in an exclusive and leafy suburb on Kingston Hill. He did not care overmuch for big-city surroundings, and he eschewed the distracting social life of the capital. He had to. Few military men had ever assumed a burden as awesome as his.

To ease the burden, Eisenhower gathered around him a

galaxy of proven and talented military leaders. In selecting his top subordinates, he picked an extraordinary group of men who had already played decisive war roles. The man chosen as Deputy Supreme Commander was Air Chief Marshal Sir Arthur Tedder, who had been head of the RAF in the Middle East and the Allied air forces in the Mediterranean. The commander in chief of the Allied Naval Expeditionary Force was Admiral Sir Bertram H. Ramsay, who had planned the North Africa invasion and organized the brilliant rescue of the British Expeditionary Force from Dunkirk in 1940.

The commander of the Allied Expeditionary Air Force (comprising the RAF Second Tactical Air Force and the U.S. Ninth Air Force) was Air Chief Marshal Sir Trafford Leigh-Mallory, a tough and uncompromising airman who had commanded the famous 12 Group in the Battle of Britain, the air operations in the Dieppe raid and the RAF Fighter Command. Lieut. General Walter Bedell Smith, who had been Eisenhower's chief of staff throughout the North Africa and Mediterranean campaigns, was retained as his chief of staff for *Overlord,* while General Morgan, whose intimate knowledge of *Overlord* planning was irreplaceable, became deputy chief of staff.

For the all-important position of ground commander of the Allied armies during the initial assault and the establishment of the beachhead, Eisenhower wanted General Sir Harold R. L. G. Alexander, whom he regarded as an outstanding strategist. But Alexander could not be spared from his command of the Allied armies in Italy, and the job went to General Montgomery, whose Eighth Army the year before had decisively defeated Rommel's Afrika Korps. Montgomery's appointment pleased the British public and the British soldiers, who looked on him as a national hero, but it dismayed a number of senior American commanders, who found the man abrasive and egocentric.

Soon after Eisenhower's arrival in England, the Supreme Commander and his senior commanders reached agreement on a number of fundamental modifications of the original COSSAC plan. The three divisions provided by the old plan for the initial assault were simply not enough. There would be five divisions, and they would attack on a 50-mile front instead of the original 25-mile one. The new front reached from the mouth of the Orne River, near the important city of Caen, westward to Varreville on the east

coast of the Cotentin Peninsula, with its vitally needed port of Cherbourg. However, the beaches near Varreville were cut off from the interior by high cliffs, river valleys and lagoons flooded by the Germans; these would surely become a death trap to seaborne forces landing there without additional support. It would therefore be necessary to take the American airborne division earmarked originally for the capture of Caen and drop it on the Cotentin Peninsula instead, along with an extra airborne division not called for in the COSSAC plan.

Leigh-Mallory protested passionately against these airborne operations; he believed strongly (but, as it turned out, wrongly) that the powerful German antiaircraft defenses and the widespread marshes and waterways of the peninsula would inflict losses of more than 70 per cent among the aircraft and paratroopers involved. But Eisenhower, however, convinced that the support of airborne troops was essential, overruled him.

To allow the production of landing craft, D-Day had been put back from May to the first week of June. The postponement was a mixed blessing: it gave time for more strategic bombing of Germany and for more training of the assault forces, but it also gave Field Marshal Rommel, commander of Army Group B and the northwestern French coast, more time for strengthening Hitler's Atlantic Wall.

Thanks to the various Allied intelligence-gathering agencies, SHAEF knew almost as much as Rommel about the Atlantic Wall and the deployment of German units that would have some effect on the mission. In January 1944, the same month that saw Eisenhower taking up his duties, Rommel had been given command of the two armies, the Seventh and the Fifteenth, whose infantry and artillery held the invasion coast between Antwerp and the Loire River. But Hitler had imposed an elaborate chain of command designed to maintain his control over the troops by limiting his commanders' power. As far as the invasion front was concerned, it was unclear—both to Rommel and to SHAEF—who would control what forces. To be sure, the coastal artillery and defense of naval ports were definitely the responsibility of the Navy, while antiaircraft guns were the Luftwaffe's. But Rommel, even though he was Hitler's favorite general and a master of tank warfare, had only nominal control over most of the panzer forces; their deployment was entrusted to a headquarters known as Panzer Group West, under General Leo Geyr von Schweppenburg.

Geyr's views on the proper use of armor to repel the invasion differed sharply from those of Rommel. A row had broken out between the two commanders. It was not resolved until March, when Rommel appealed to the Führer and asked that all armored and motorized units be placed directly under his command.

Hitler's answer was a compromise. Of the seven available armored divisions in Western Europe, three (the 2nd, 21st and 116th) were assigned to Rommel as Army Group B tactical reserves. The remaining four (the 1st SS, 12th SS, 17th SS Panzer Grenadier and Panzer Lehr) were assigned to Supreme Headquarters, OKW; they would comprise a central strategic reserve that could not be moved without OKW's authority—that is, without Hitler's approval. This compromise achieved nothing and was to have a calamitous result for the Germans on D-Day. OB West, headquarters for all German forces in Western Europe, lacked the authority to deploy or assign to Rommel the Strategic Reserves. Of the three armored divisions actually under Rommel's command, only one, the 21st Panzer, was anywhere near the invasion area on D-Day.

Rommel realized that he could not rely on panzer support, and he knew that the Allies could establish mastery of the air over any invasion beach they chose. Under the circumstances he had no choice but to rely on the Atlantic Wall and its static defenses to repel any Allied invasion. So he launched an all-out campaign to strengthen the Wall by whatever means came to hand. His orders to his commanders said: "In the short time left before the great offensive starts, we must succeed in bringing all defenses to such a standard that they will hold up against the strongest attacks. The enemy must be annihilated before he reaches our main battlefield. We must stop him in the water, not only delaying him but destroying all his equipment while it is still afloat." Every soldier and every weapon was packed into the Atlantic Wall or held in very close reserve behind it. "The high water line," Rommel insisted, "must be the main fighting line."

Rommel's aim was to create a defensive belt around the entire coast, but mainly on the Fifteenth Army sector be-

tween Antwerp and the Orne River in Normandy and on the Seventh Army sector of Normandy west of the Orne. All through the spring of 1944 Rommel traveled up and down the Atlantic coast checking the construction work, encouraging the men. Lack of time, labor and materials prevented the completion of the Wall according to Rommel's final plan. Even so, by the end of May he had transformed the Wall into a formidable obstacle.

The staff officers at SHAEF were informed of Rommel's progress almost daily by Allied intelligence and reconnaissance flights, and they were profoundly disturbed when they learned that the invasion coast of Normandy between high water and low water was beginning to bristle with long parallel lines of special devices designed to impale or capsize assault landing craft—hedgehogs, tetrahedrons, dragons' teeth, curved rails and sharpened stakes tipped with mines. These obstacles threatened to wreak havoc among the initial assault waves, and they forced a number of

Off-duty soldiers play their accordions atop a camouflaged bunker of the Atlantic Wall. About 100 accordions were distributed by Field Marshal Rommel to boost the troops' morale and to reward them for passing a rigorous inspection of the Wall's gun emplacements and beach obstacles.

very important changes in SHAEF's plans for the assault.

It was now clear that in order to see their way through the obstacles, the invaders must land in daylight—not, as some planners had suggested, under cover of darkness. It was also clear that squads of special demolition engineers would now have to land very shortly after the first wave. Montgomery had intended the landings to be made at high tide, but this was now impossible because many of the landing craft would be wrecked on obstacles invisible just below the surface. On the other hand, if the landings were made at low tide to give the demolition squads maximum time to clear the obstacles before the tide covered them, the assault troops would have to cross a broad stretch of beach under heavy fire before they could reach the shelter of the dunes or the sea wall. Either way would mean heavy casualties.

Montgomery's solution was a hedge. He permitted the Americans to take their chances with a landing just after low tide, but he ordered his British and Canadian assault troops to land on a rising tide, when the main belt of obstacles was still above the water. For the British, at least, this would reduce the hazards to the landing craft and still give the engineers enough time to accomplish their job. But it would still leave the infantrymen exposed to enemy fire before their own support fire could be brought to bear. Montgomery therefore decided to revolutionize the technique of amphibious invasion by sending in armor in the vanguard of the assault. The floating Sherman tanks would now land in the first wave, other specialized tanks developed by Hobart would land in the second wave and the infantry in the third. Other tactical innovations were developed, but none were nearly as important as SHAEF's strategic efforts to take the enemy by surprise.

"Fortifications of concrete and steel, armed with modern fire power and fully manned by trained, resolute men, could only be overcome by surprise," Churchill later wrote. Only if Hitler was kept guessing as to the place, time, weight and aims of the invasion could the assault hope to achieve success. To coordinate various secret deceptive operations, Churchill established a central agency, the London Controlling Section (LCS), headed by two Englishmen, Colonel John Bevan and Lieut. Colonel Sir Ronald Wingate (a cousin of Lawrence of Arabia and of Orde Wingate of the

SOME PUZZLING COINCIDENCES

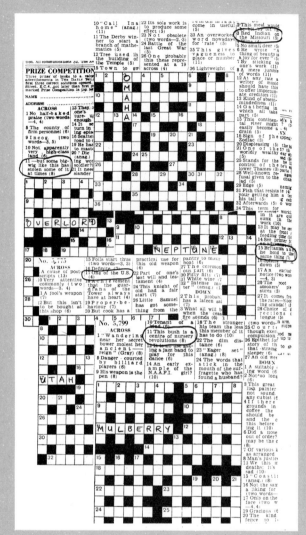

During the five weeks prior to D-Day, five crossword puzzles in London's *Daily Telegraph* horrified the SHAEF generals. Each contained a secret code word directly related to the impending invasion of Normandy: "Utah," "Omaha," "Mulberry," "Neptune" and "Overlord." The appearance of "Overlord" convinced the invasion planners that security had been breached.

Scotland Yard detectives questioned the puzzle compiler, Leonard Dawe. They discovered that he was an unassuming physics teacher who composed crosswords as a hobby. Dawe was convincingly bewildered by the interrogation, and the investigators finally drew the conclusion that it was all an amazing coincidence.

Burma campaign). In the words of an American member of the LCS, Colonel William H. Baumer: "Their object was to make Hitler run about like a blue arsed fly." Strategically, the deception campaign waged by the LCS and its associated intelligence agencies was either the first or the second most important factor in the outcome of D-Day, the other being Allied air supremacy.

The LCS leaked thousands of pieces of false information to the Germans through every intelligence outlet available—double agents, fake wireless transmissions, fictitious armies, the Resistance, calculated indiscretions. The aim of the campaign was twofold: first, to convince the Germans that the invasion would be at a different place and on a different date from the real one so they would not reinforce their defenses in the real invasion area with troops drawn from other fronts; and second, to delay their reaction to the Normandy landings by disrupting their communications, intelligence, supply and administrative systems.

Of all the multifarious activities surrounding D-Day, none was more extraordinary than the final deception program that was worked out by the LCS with the approval of the Joint Chiefs of Staff. It was in essence a credible war plan, drawn up at the highest political and strategic level. There were six principal deception plans, 36 subordinate ones and many more related stratagems. All around the perimeter of Europe thousands of guerrilla operations and Allied actions, rumors, feints, threats, raids and acts of sabotage were put into effect to bewilder the Germans and to keep their troops dispersed.

The deception plan most directly affecting the Normandy invasion was code-named *Fortitude*. The overall purpose of *Fortitude* was to tie down 90 German divisions, with all their air and naval support, in areas a safe distance from Normandy. One part of the plan was intended to bottle up 27 divisions in Scandinavia by making OKW believe that the Allies were about to make a diversionary landing in Norway. A deception organization, with a handful of men and women, was assigned to create a fictitious British Fourth Army of more than a quarter of a million men with headquarters under Edinburgh Castle. By April 1944 this ghost army was swamping German intelligence monitors with an endless stream of fake messages from fake divisions and corps, such as "80 Division requests 1,800 pairs of Kandahar ski bindings" and "VII Corps requires the promised demonstrators in the Bilgeri method of climbing rock faces." British agents in Norway, with help from the Russians, compounded the deception so successfully that the 27 German divisions stationed in Scandinavia were held there instead of being sent southward.

The key plan of *Fortitude* was calculated first to make the Germans believe that the invasion would take place in the Pas-de-Calais and then to make them believe, on D-Day itself, that the Normandy landings were merely a feint. Every possible trick was employed to make it seem that the invasion forces gathering in Britain were weighted toward southeastern England and pointed at Calais: British agents in neutral capitals even went around buying up all existing stocks of Michelin maps of the Pas-de-Calais. A fake army group of 50 divisions and a million men under the command of Lieut. General George S. Patton was established in southeastern England.

In fact Montgomery's 21st Army Group *was* assembling in the south of England—together with American troops that would form Bradley's 12th Army Group after the beachhead was secure. To Montgomery's group the Allies added a fictitious second, the First U.S. Army Group (FUSAG), consisting of the Canadian First Army, the American Third Army and 50 divisions that would come in directly from the United States. Though some of the 50 divisions in America were imaginary, the American Third Army and the Canadian First Army actually did exist and would eventually land in France. The trick was to persuade the Germans that they belonged to Patton's FUSAG and would form the main invasion force in the Pas-de-Calais on D-Day.

So while Montgomery's real army group was secretly assembling in southwestern England, Patton's nonexistent one appeared to be openly assembling in southeastern England. Fake landing craft, fabricated at Shepperton Film Studios near London, were moored in the Thames and other rivers in southeast England with laundry hanging realistically from their rigging. Fake ammunition dumps, hospitals, field kitchens, troop camps, guns and planes made of canvas and scaffolding crowded the fields, along with more than a brigade of inflated rubber tanks. Britain's leading architect, Sir Basil Spence, professor of architecture at the

Royal Academy, designed and constructed an enormous fake oil dock occupying three square miles of the foreshore at Dover, complete with jetties, storage tanks, pipelines, powerhouses and antiaircraft guns.

FUSAG was accepted as a real army by OKW and appeared in the official German listing of Allied forces. By May 1944 the Germans believed that there were 92 to 97 divisions assembling in Britain instead of the 35 that really were there; and though they were still uncertain when and where this huge force was going to land, they firmly favored the Pas-de-Calais. Captured documents showed that OKW had disposed its forces in accordance with the Allies' subversive intentions. An intercepted report revealed that Hitler's advisers continued to swallow the *Fortitude* deceptions and continued to believe that the invasion would hit the Pas-de-Calais, probably in July.

Of the Allies' real intentions the Germans learned precious little. The British and American counterintelligence agencies prevented the Germans from learning the secrets of *Neptune*. In Britain more than 100 German spies had been bribed or intimidated into transmitting erroneous information to Germany, forming an important element of the Allied deception campaign. The Germans' conventional sources of information had also failed them. Few Luftwaffe aircraft were able to penetrate the invasion assembly areas in southern England and return home safely, and Rommel complained in his weekly intelligence report for May 21 that "there are *no* results of air reconnaissance of the island for the entire period."

By contrast, Eisenhower on the eve of D-Day was the best informed military commander in history. He knew the enemy's order of battle, strength, defenses, supply, communications, morale, plans. The Germans could hardly conceal the movement of a tank from the reconnaissance aircraft or the prying eyes of the Resistance. Intelligence-gathering operations dealing with the Normandy invasion beaches started by COSSAC were intensified to an around-the-clock vigil under SHAEF. Swimmers, frogmen, Commandos and sea-level photo planes *(opposite)* constantly monitored the state of the beaches and the German defenses for the Inter-Services Topographical Unit at Oxford. In May 1944 alone, French agents sent to London 700 radio reports and 3,000 written dispatches on German military positions. By 1944 Admiral Ramsay had a continuous sea-level panoramic photostrip of the coastal invasion area made up of uncounted individual photos spliced together.

In mid-April the Allied intelligence-gathering network received shocking news. Aerial photos of the Orne valley revealed that the Germans were putting up antiglider obstacles in precisely the fields where the British were planning to land gliders on D-Day. Then air reconnaissance and agents' reports revealed intensive enemy ground activity in Normandy. The 21st Panzer Division was moved from Brittany to Caen, almost opposite the Second British Army invasion beaches, and the Panzer Lehr Division was moved to the area of Chartres–Le Mans, only a day from Caen.

The Allies' fears that their intentions were known to the Germans after all were increased when an infantry division and a parachute regiment were moved to the drop zones of the American airborne divisions at the base of the Cotentin Peninsula, and reports from agents indicated that the 17th SS Panzer Grenadier Division was getting ready to move north to Normandy from Poitiers.

In fact, these moves were not the result of the Germans' intelligence but of Hitler's intuition. On May 2, after a string of less successful guesses, Hitler had decided that there would be a strong Allied thrust in Normandy despite the fact that his staff continued to advise him that invasion would come in the Pas-de-Calais. He ordered reinforcements moved up to counter the attack. The SHAEF planners had to make rapid readjustments, among them altering the landing zones and objectives of the American 82nd Airborne Division. Facing the Allies in or near the invasion area, the Germans now had six infantry divisions and two panzer divisions, with two more panzer divisions 24 hours' march away. Normandy at the end of May was thus much more strongly held than it was only a few weeks before.

In the meantime, intense Allied aerial activity was cutting down the defense capability of the Germans. By the spring of 1944, Allied strategic bombing had so reduced German aircraft production that the Luftwaffe was reluctant to contest Allied sweeps over Germany. In April the Strategic Air Forces turned their attention to Germany's dwindling oil supply, and within a month they had cut oil production by 20 per cent. Marshaling yards, bridges and rail centers were

A CLOSE-UP PORTRAIT OF THE INVASION COAST

To prepare for the invasion, Allied reconnaissance planes flew hundreds of low-level sorties over the coast of Normandy, photographing the shoreline in minute detail. The photos were rushed to Oxford University, where the Inter-Services Topographical Unit had assembled a corps of draftsmen, geologists, photographic technicians and geographers. The corps carefully pieced together thousands of individual photos, forming a continuous sea-level panorama of the coast. The portrait was so accurate and detailed that the invasion warships could lay their guns according to grids superimposed on it.

The results so impressed General Eisenhower that he ordered 40,000 sets printed for tactical study by all of the assault units. To fill the enormous order, an air shuttle flew 730 miles of paper and 10 tons of chemicals from the U.S. every two days until the printing was finished.

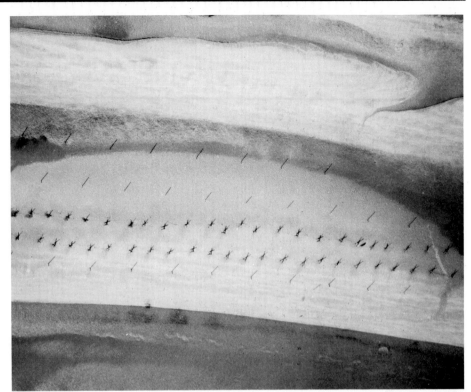

Every obstacle in this aerial photograph was transferred onto giant maps for tactical planning.

BERNIERES — SUR — MER

HOUSE 987848

Guided by low-level reconnaissance photographs of the Bernières-sur-Mer coast, landing-craft crews accurately put British troops ashore here on D-Day.

Based on aerial photos, a scale model of the Queen and Roger Beaches at Sword gave officers due to land there an in-depth sense of the problems ahead.

pounded by heavy bombers and attacked with rockets by fighter planes. Throughout the entire aerial campaign the Allies' deception strategy was maintained, and for every bomb that was dropped over the Normandy invasion area, two were dropped elsewhere in the northern part of France. By the eve of D-Day, the Germans' ability to react to the invasion had been crippled by tactical destruction of German communication systems, bridges, rail centers and rail lines leading to Normandy.

By May the great army that was to breach the Atlantic Wall was one of the most thoroughly trained assault forces ever to go into battle. Throughout the early part of 1944 all units had studied and practiced the highly specialized skills of their trade. Tank crews had learned how to handle amphibious tanks in the open sea; glider pilots had learned how to crash-land their craft behind German lines in the dark; demolition teams had learned how to dismantle mined contraptions of concrete and steel in a rising tide; infantrymen had been trained for amphibious operations; landing-craft crews had learned how to set down troops in the right place and at the right time on an open beach held by a powerful enemy. Most important, various branches of the service had to learn how to cooperate with one another—spotter planes with battleships, bomber planes with infantry, Army and Navy engineers with each other.

The SHAEF commanders stipulated that on D-Day every individual soldier should know exactly what specific task he had to accomplish against a specific objective. Exhaustive maneuvers were held, and great pains were taken to make the assault exercises resemble the real thing as closely as possible. An exact replica of the worrisome German battery near Merville was constructed in a secret field in Berkshire so that British paratroops and glider troops could rehearse their precision nighttime attack on the D-Day target. American Rangers practiced cliff assaults with London fire-brigade ladders mounted on amphibious trucks, or DUK-Ws.

After the last maneuvers in May, the soldiers returned to their marshaling areas. Final supplies were issued for the voyage, and the units were broken down into boatloads to await the final move to the ships. Then there was nothing to do but wait. Some units had to wait for a month. The soldiers were briefed for D-Day in the last week in May.

Each man was carefully instructed in his unit's task with the help of aerial photos, models, maps and sketches. RAF glider pilots and aircrews were briefed by means of a special film that tracked across a scale model of the exact terrain over which they would fly on their route to the drop zones. Projected through a blue filter, the film gave a good representation of moonlight conditions.

It was a dangerous time for security. Though the troops had not been told the place names of their assault areas, they knew a great deal, and if only a few men were indiscreet, German intelligence could piece together a correct overall picture. General Morgan had warned: "If the enemy obtains as much as forty-eight hours warning of the location of the assault area, the chances of success are small and any longer warning spells certain defeat."

SHAEF was thus forced to impose strict security arrangements on both troops and civilians. On April 1 all unauthorized visitors were banned from coastal zones 10 miles wide in the areas where the assault forces were being concentrated. On April 17 the British government took the unprecedented step of restricting the diplomatic privileges of all nations, forbidding diplomats and diplomatic couriers to enter or leave England and censoring hitherto immune diplomatic correspondence. All mail by British forces involved in *Overlord* was strictly censored, and on May 25 transatlantic telephone, radio and cable facilities were denied to American personnel and a 10-day delay was imposed on their mail to the States.

In the last week of May the troops were sealed in their camps behind barbed wire and armed guards. They were not allowed to mail letters or even to say goodbye to their families or girl friends. One Royal Engineer who broke out of his camp returned to his unit the night before embarkation and—much to the amusement of his comrades—was sent to invade France under close arrest. For the handful of officers who knew the complete *Overlord* plan, a new system of security classification known as Bigot was introduced; documents stamped Bigot were even more confidential than those stamped Top Secret. Even this was not foolproof. In a U.S. Army mail-sorting office in Chicago a half-opened packet from England was found to contain Bigot papers, and a complete Bigot list of radio transmission frequencies and ciphers for use in the invasion was found in a briefcase left in a taxicab at Waterloo Station in London.

The complete plan for *Overlord* was set forth in one last briefing three weeks before D-Day. The Supreme Commander and his deputy commanders and other chiefs gathered in the circular model room of the old St. Paul's School, in Hammersmith, London, to outline the plan for the King of England, the Prime Minister and the commanders of the units that would be involved, with the aid of a map as broad as a city street. King George VI sat on a hard narrow school bench in the front row, with Churchill on his right and Eisenhower on his left. "As we took those uncompromisingly hard and narrow seats," wrote American Rear Admiral Morton L. Deyo, "the room was hushed and the tension palpable. The first to rise and break the silence was the Supreme Commander himself. It had been said that his smile was worth twenty divisions. That day it was worth more. He spoke for ten minutes. Before the warmth of his quiet confidence the mists of doubt dissolved. When he had finished the tension had gone. Not often has one man been called upon to accept so great a burden of responsibility. But here was one at peace with his soul."

Montgomery got up to explain the plan of battle for the initial assault phase of *Overlord,* Operation *Neptune.* The ships and landing craft of the Allied Naval Expeditionary Force under the command of Admiral Ramsay would begin transporting the armies across the Channel to France on D-minus-1. Ramsay's immense naval armada was divided in two: an Eastern Task Force for the three British beaches code-named Gold, Juno and Sword, and a Western Task Force for the two American beaches code-named Omaha and Utah. Shortly after midnight, while the armada was approaching the 59-mile invasion front, two aerial fleets, one British and one American, would begin dropping parachutists and glider troops behind the German coastal defenses, and by daybreak on D-Day, the British 6th Airborne Division would have secured the eastern flank of the bridgehead, the American 82nd and 101st Airborne Divisions the western flank.

Montgomery now went on to the next phase. Shortly after dawn, following a massive preliminary aerial and naval bombardment of the German shore defenses, five seaborne assault divisions would begin landing on five beaches lying between the flanks held by the airborne divisions—three divisions of the British Second Army under General Sir Miles Dempsey on the British invasion sector between the Orne River and Port-en-Bessin, and two divisions of the American First Army under General Bradley on Omaha and Utah Beaches in the American sector between Port-en-Bessin and Varreville on the Cotentin Peninsula.

The British and American ground forces were to secure their separate beachheads on D-Day, then on D-plus-1 to link up the beachheads, and on D-plus-2 to D-plus-9 to expand northwest, west and south to form a staging area in which to build up strength for a breakout toward Paris and the Rhine. In order to achieve this initial aim it would be necessary, first, for the British to hold the left flank around Caen against German panzer counterattacks; second, for the British and Americans in the center to secure the plateau far enough inland to protect the artificial Mulberry harbors from direct German artillery fire; and third, for the Americans on the right to seal off the base of the Cotentin Peninsula and move on the port of Cherbourg, so vital for the long-term unloading of troops and matériel.

The build-up of men and supplies on the beaches and inland would be accomplished with complete air supremacy. The Allied Expeditionary Air Force of Air Chief Marshal Leigh-Mallory had at its disposal 3,467 heavy bombers and 1,645 medium, light and torpedo bombers, plus 5,409 fighters. All these would provide a continuous air umbrella over the invasion area and would range far and wide to interdict German movement both on land and in the air.

The plan had been worked out in meticulous detail. Nothing had been left to chance. Speaking of the importance of the troops' frame of mind, Montgomery said in conclusion: "We shall have to send the soldiers into this party 'seeing red.' They must see red. We must get them completely on their toes, having absolute faith in the plan; and imbued with infectious optimism and offensive eagerness. Nothing must stop them. Nothing. If we send them into battle in this way—then we shall succeed."

But there could not be any control over one sovereign factor—the weather. There were only three days in each two-week period of June when the right conditions of both light and tide prevailed—when low tide and first light more or less coincided. If the additional requirement of a late-

rising full moon for the airborne night drop was taken into account, the number of days when the invasion could take place was reduced to three a month.

On those three days, yet another set of requirements had to be met: to ensure the safe handling of the landing craft, onshore winds should not exceed 8 to 12 mph and offshore winds 13 to 18 mph; to increase the firing accuracy of the bombarding ships, visibility should not be less than three miles; to enable the bomber squadrons and the transports carrying airborne forces to find their targets accurately, there should be no more than six tenths cloud cover and the cloud base should not be below 3,000 feet; to prevent paratroopers from being widely scattered in the drop, the land wind should be less than 20 mph; there should be no ground fog or heavy mist and no prolonged high winds in the Channel in the days before D-Day.

Meteorological records showed that the odds against the occurrence of such ideal weather in early summer were 50 or 60 to 1. But the forward momentum of the D-Day machinery was such that the operation could not be postponed for more than a day or two once it had been set in motion. For this reason, perhaps, no one at SHAEF had seriously contemplated the possibility that weather conditions might put a stop to the whole tremendous venture. When, at the beginning of June, that possibility stared everyone in the face, the countdown to *Overlord* entered its most nerve-racking phase.

On May 8, Eisenhower set D-Day for June 5, with the 6th and 7th as suitable alternatives. For the rest of the month of May southern England and the Channel basked in beautiful summer sunshine and barely a breeze ruffled the surface of the Channel. It was perfect invasion weather. On May 29 the SHAEF Meteorologic Committee, a team of British and American weathermen headed by a dour Scot, RAF Group-Captain J. M. Stagg, made a guardedly optimistic long-range forecast of the weather for the first days of June. On the basis of that forecast, the D-Day machine was set in motion.

All over England men and vehicles were put on the move from the sealed camps to the waiting ships. Tanks and trucks, bearing the white star that was the symbol of liberation, rumbled toward the south-coast ports in convoys up to 100 miles long. Marching regiments of men in full com-

bat kit filed down the narrow streets to the quays at harbors all over southern England. They tramped past the air-raid shelters, the sandbagged doorways and the boarded-up seafront shops, down the drab warworn streets of the tired English towns. As they marched a vast communal excitement began to fill the air, and people came out to line the streets and cheer them on and wave and cry. No one, including the soldiers, knew exactly where the soldiers were going. But everyone in England realized that this was the start of a great event in history. Everyone knew that this was the opening of the Second Front, the vindication of the bitter years of defeat and deprivation, the final expression of a single collective international will.

By June 3 all the assault troops—some 170,000 of them—were aboard. On the ships they were briefed again with maps and aerial photos of the beach sections they were destined for, although security was still so strict that they remained in ignorance of the place names. They practiced embarkation drill, sorted out weapons and stores, and waited in a state of mounting tension for the word to go. Already some of the warships and Mulberry blockships that had the farthest to sail had set off from distant ports in Scotland and Northern Ireland. Eisenhower cabled General Marshall: "We have almost an even chance of having pretty fair conditions . . . only marked deterioration would discourage our plans." By that very evening the "marked deterioration" was already heading *Overlord's* way.

At 9:30 p.m. on June 3 Group-Captain Stagg painted a gloomy weather picture at a meeting of the Supreme Commander and his commanders in chief in the library at Southwick House near Portsmouth—the elegant Regency mansion that served as Admiral Ramsay's headquarters and as SHAEF's advance command post. Stagg said that the unexpected breakup of the long period of settled weather was due to the collapse of a high-pressure system over the Azores. The weather forecast for the British Isles and northeast Atlantic was "very disturbed and complex," he informed the commanders.

It was, in fact, the worst weather picture for that time of year in 40 or 50 years. "A series of three depressions were strung out across the Atlantic from north Scotland toward Newfoundland," noted Stagg. There would be strong winds in the Channel until June 7, he predicted, with ten tenths

Douglas A-20 attack bombers of the American Ninth Air Force stage a preinvasion raid on German defenses at Pointe du Hoc, a tiny peninsula jutting out from Normandy's checkerboard of fields and hedgerows. In the five weeks preceding D-Day, this command alone flew approximately 53,800 sorties against the enemy's coastal defenses and communication targets and dropped a total of about 30,700 tons of bombs.

cloud down to 500 or 1,000 feet. Under such weather conditions neither the sea bombardment nor the airborne assaults could take place. Eisenhower and his commanders decided to delay their decision until 4:15 the next morning, Sunday, June 4, but in the meantime gave orders to the flotillas that had the farthest to go to set sail.

The next 24 hours was a time of enormous strain for Eisenhower. The whole vast edifice of *Overlord* now rested on the expertise of a British meteorologic team and their assessment of a vague complex of pressure systems and cold fronts hundreds of miles away.

At 15 minutes past 4 o'clock on Sunday morning the commanders met again. The tension in the room was overpowering. Stagg confirmed his previous forecast. Admiral Ramsay was prepared to go ahead, though he did not like the prospect. So was General Montgomery. But Air Chief Marshal Leigh-Mallory said that his bombers could not operate in the heavy cloud that was forecast, and Air Chief Marshal Tedder agreed with him.

General Eisenhower said that since the Allied ground forces had no overwhelming superiority over the Germans, *Overlord* was not a sound operation without Allied air supremacy and could not be risked if that supremacy was taken away by the weather. He therefore postponed D-Day by one day. Further sailings of the invasion fleet were called off, and convoys already at sea were turned back. "When we went out into the quiet and still, almost cloudless morning," Stagg wrote in his diary, "the enormity of the decision we had just heard was borne in upon us." But he added: "There was still an element of doubt in what we had done."

At 11 a.m. the Admiralty issued a gale warning for the Irish Sea. All through Sunday the storm grew in fury, driving white breakers onto the beaches of Normandy. The bombarding warships that had sailed from the distant ports in Scotland and northern Ireland battered their way back to port through rough water in the Irish Sea. Part of one force was halfway to France before it was turned back by a seaplane. In the crowded harbors of southern England the barrage balloons danced on their wires, the landing craft tossed at their anchors and the multitude of soldiers, many of whom had been packed on board for three or four days, waited seasick and anxious.

When the commanders met again at 9:30 that Sunday evening of June 4, the wind was still blowing hard, and it was raining out of an overcast sky. The commanders sat informally in easy chairs and couches in the long oak-paneled library, now used as a senior officers' mess. They stared at Stagg solemnly. It was, they all knew, a desperate moment. The invasion could not really be postponed for another 24 hours—the tide would be at its lowest point, the troops could not be kept cooped up and exposed on the decks of the landing craft any longer.

If D-Day had to be postponed, it would have to be postponed by two weeks, and then there would not be any moonlight for the airdrops. But such a postponement would cause untold chaos to the movement of troops and matériel. Follow-up units were already moving into marshaling camps evacuated by the assault units that had embarked on the ships, and it was virtually impossible to reverse the movement without jamming the *Overlord* machinery. The men had been briefed; if they were disembarked, there would be a tremendous risk to security as well as morale. There was further risk: Stalin had been promised that the Second Front would be opened in the first week in June and

RAF Group-Captain J. M. Stagg, the gloomy Scot whose last-minute forecast of a break in the bad weather launched the invasion, was none too happy with the demands of his job as chief meteorologist to SHAEF. He was frequently asked to predict weather five days in advance. This feat was impossible, he said gloomily, for "all the meteorological brains of the U.S. and British (and any other) weather services put together."

had timed his big summer offensive on the Eastern Front to coincide with it.

"The inescapable consequences of postponement," Eisenhower wrote afterward, "were almost too bitter to contemplate." It made little difference that a girl in the London office of Associated Press had accidentally and unwittingly sent out a flash on the teletype machine: "URGENT A.P. NYK FLASH EISENHOWER'S HQ ANNOUNCE ALLIED LANDINGS IN FRANCE." Though this news was broadcast in America and Moscow before it was killed, it had no bearing on Eisenhower's dilemma Sunday evening. Only the weather could decide. He therefore listened intently to Group-Captain Stagg, and what Stagg said surprised him.

"Gentlemen," said Stagg, "since I presented the forecast last evening some rapid and unexpected developments have occurred over the north Atlantic." A cold front was coming through faster and farther south than expected, he explained. After it had passed through the Channel area there would be a brief period of improvement starting on the afternoon of Monday, June 5, and lasting till late on the evening of Tuesday, June 6. At that time the weather would again become unsettled.

Stagg was offering the commanders the unexpected gift of a hole in the weather—and hole just big enough for the initial assault force to pass through.

A prolonged silence greeted Stagg's statement. There was the danger that though the short break in the weather might allow the first few assault waves to land, the bad weather due to follow could delay the build-up and leave the assault waves isolated onshore and an easy prey for the Germans.

General Eisenhower turned toward Montgomery and put the question to him: "Do you see any reason why we should not go on Tuesday?"

"No," Montgomery answered. "I would say—Go."

"The question is," Eisenhower said, "just how long can you hang this operation out on the end of a limb and let it hang there."

The decision of whether to launch or to abort the Second Front was for the Supreme Commander to make, and he had to make it alone.

At 9:45 he announced that decision: "I don't like it but there it is . . . I don't see how we can possibly do anything else. I am quite positive we must give the order."

Outside the door at the end of the meeting, Eisenhower came over to Stagg. "Well, Stagg," he said, "we're putting it on again. For heaven's sake hold the weather to what you told us and don't bring any more bad news." Then he smiled broadly and went out.

And yet, the final, irrevocable decision to launch the assault had to be delayed for one last weather report at the commanders' meeting scheduled for 4:15 on Monday morning, the 5th of June. "Our little camp was shaking and shuddering under a wind of hurricane proportions," Eisenhower wrote of that time, "and the accompanying rain seemed to be travelling in horizontal streaks. It seemed impossible in such conditions that there was any reason for even discussing the situation."

The meeting convened. "Gentlemen," Stagg began, "no substantial change has taken place since last time but as I see it the little that has changed is in the direction of optimism." He said that the fair-weather interval would extend through all southern England during the night and would probably last into the afternoon of Tuesday. Stagg subsequently wrote: "Immediately after I had finished the tension seemed to evaporate and the Supreme Commander and his colleagues became as new men. General Eisenhower had sat, turned sideways, facing me, taut and tense. Now a broad smile broke over his face."

"OK," Eisenhower said finally. "We'll go."

With those words the die was cast. The signal was flashed to the fleet: "PROCEED WITH OPERATION NEPTUNE."

Dawn was breaking as the commanders made their way to their tents and quarters, and the woods were loud with the song of birds. The planners, having done all they could, went to bed. The Second Front now belonged to the men who would do the fighting.

THE BIG BUILD-UP

U.S. P-51 fighters, their wing tips removed to provide clearance, are trucked through Liverpool on their way to an air base to be prepared for invasion duties.

"THE GREATEST MILITARY BASE OF ALL TIME"

In April 1942, when the Allies decided to invade Europe from England, the U.S. War Department set in motion an unprecedented plan, called Operation *Bolero*, to build up a million-man American force in the British Isles. The American Army's SOS (Services of Supply) was charged with the herculean task of arranging for the troops' transportation to Britain, the establishment of their camps and training grounds, and the building of additional airfields and storage facilities. Immediately SOS officers went to work in concert with British military men and civilian agencies.

The transatlantic shipments got off to a slow start in May, adding only 24,682 troops to the 11,962 already based in the British Isles, and the build-up lagged during the winter of 1942-1943, when 153,000 GIs were diverted to support the Allied invasion of North Africa. But thereafter, American troop landings in Britain rose sharply, to a monthly peak of 216,699 in April 1944. Meanwhile, cargo shipments peaked at nearly 500,000 tons a month, so overtaxing Britain's venerable ports and small labor force that the influx of war matériel had to be curtailed. All together, in little more than two years there arrived in Britain 1.5 million servicemen and five million tons of invasion supplies and equipment, including 8,000 airplanes, 1,000 locomotives and 20,000 railroad cars.

The Americans were quartered in 398,666 prefabricated huts, in 279,204 tented camps and in 111,590 British buildings of all kinds, ranging from thatched cottages in the countryside and warehouses in industrial towns to fashionable hotels in London's bustling West End. Hundreds of square miles of Britain—from the moors of Scotland to farmland along the southwest coast—were crowded with American supply depots, ammunition dumps, repair shops, truck and tank parks, camps and air bases. By the eve of the invasion in June 1944, after the expenditure of 400 million man-hours of labor and $644 million for new construction alone, Operation *Bolero* had transformed England into what General Eisenhower called "the greatest operating military base of all time."

A message pinned to a church door in a town evacuated for the GIs asks them to treat the building with the same respect shown it by the villagers.

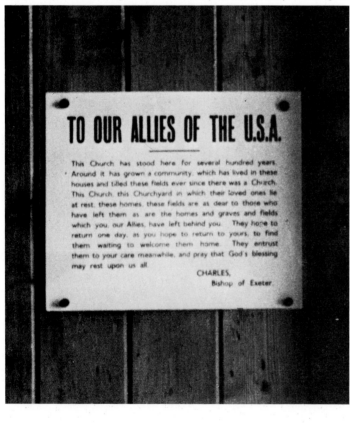

TO OUR ALLIES OF THE U.S.A.

This Church has stood here for several hundred years. Around it has grown a community, which has lived in these houses and tilled these fields ever since there was a Church. This Church, this Churchyard in which their loved ones lie at rest, these homes, these fields are as dear to those who have left them as are the homes and graves and fields which you, our Allies, have left behind you. They hope to return one day, as you hope to return to yours, to find them waiting to welcome them home. They entrust them to your care meanwhile, and pray that God's blessing may rest upon us all.

CHARLES,
Bishop of Exeter

Long rows of steel bays, each one holding 32 tons of artillery shells, flank an English country road concealed by trees from German reconnaissance planes.

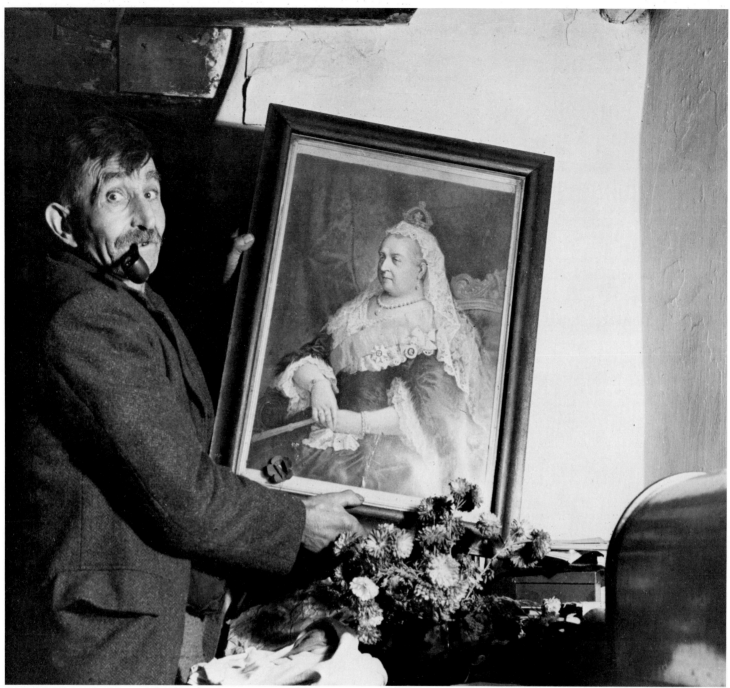

Preparing to move, a citizen of Slapton takes down a portrait of Queen Victoria. Residents were reimbursed by the British government for moving expenses.

MANEUVERS HELD IN QUAINT COUNTRY VILLAGES

As invasion preparations speeded up in the autumn of 1943, American officers toured the English countryside looking for terrain that resembled Normandy so that the GIs could stage maneuvers under realistic conditions. One area chosen for a series of crucial maneuvers lay in southwest England. It consisted of 26 square miles of varied terrain surrounding Slapton Sands, a steeply sloping beach, and included a cluster of picturesque Devonshire villages that dated back several centuries.

Because the troops would be using live ammunition, the 3,000 inhabitants of the area were evacuated, and historic buildings were clearly marked with white tape, warning the troops not to fire on them. Between exercises on the beaches, soldiers practiced house-to-house fighting in the towns, swarming around empty pubs, post offices, schools and shops.

Two months after D-Day, the local inhabitants were permitted to return home. They found every window shattered and the old church in Slapton village badly damaged by an errant artillery shell. The townspeople complained to their government but received only partial compensation for the damage.

A white-coated Slapton butcher helps a moving man carry his chopping block out to a van. All businesses and households were cleared out within six weeks.

A dog gazes down an empty street of an evacuated Devonshire town. The British Women's Volunteer Service found temporary homes for most evacuees.

Acting as casualties, soldiers lie on a Cornwall beach, waiting for medics and landing-craft crews to evacuate them.

Preparing for soggy terrain in Normandy, men of the 8th Infantry Division cross a swamp on an infantry footbridge.

Burdened with battle gear, members of an airborne infantry unit scale fences and embankments in an attack drill designed to test their speed and stamina.

FINAL DRILLS FOR THE ASSAULT

At the start of invasion drills in January of 1944, each branch of the U.S. Army staged separate maneuvers to practice its own specialty in simulated combat. Then all of the branches—infantry, engineers, signal corps, tanks—joined Naval units in large-scale maneuvers that were designed to improve their teamwork and timing in Normandy-like amphibious operations.

Two huge joint maneuvers climaxed the arduous preparations. In one of these exercises, known as *Fabius*, selected American units spent two weeks training with British and Canadian forces. The majority of the Americans took part in *Tiger*, an exhausting nine-day operation. Both big maneuvers were marred by traffic jams and confusion, but the troops had little time left to smooth out the rough edges. It was May, and D-Day was only a month away.

In a gun park at Ashchurch village in southern England, 105mm howitzers are tended by GI maintenance men, who regularly cleaned the barrels and then

American fighter planes and bombers wait for their preflight servicing by busy Air Force mechanics.

A peaceful farmer walks his horse past invasion-bound half-tracks in the Ashchurch ordnance depot.

re-covered the muzzles to prevent corrosion.

A SUPERABUNDANCE OF EVERYTHING

As early as 1942, when only a trickle of armaments was reaching Britain, the Allied invasion planners realized that their toughest problem would be to find room in the tight little isles to stash the huge quantities of war matériel that American factories were beginning to produce. The U.S. Services of Supply promptly gave highest priority to a program of establishing adequate storage facilities. Gradually, the SOS officers acquired or built 73.5 million square feet of storage space, and they laid 170 miles of railroad trunk lines to route the goods to dozens of collection points.

The depot program proved to be the most successful part of the big build-up.

It provided the U.S. Ordnance alone with enough room to stockpile 320,000 different kinds of items, some of them as large as 10-ton wreckers. It set up ammunition dumps wherever unused space could be found—including public parks. It located farmers' fields and the green lawns of baronial estates that could be used as parking and storage space for 450,000 tons of ammunition and 50,000 vehicles.

By the eve of the invasion, the 1.5 million U.S. troops were supremely confident that they had more than enough supplies and equipment for the task ahead. They even had tons of chewing gum to combat seasickness on the voyage to France. But some supplies reminded them that the invasion would be no picnic: 124,000 hospital beds and, stacked high in a corner of a camp in Dorchester, uncounted coffins.

U.S. supplies and equipment, stored prodigally in depots all over the British Isles, include (clockwise from top left) stacks of construction lumber, barrels of motor

oil, sections of prefabricated Nissen huts, bundles of brooms, boxes of dried eggs and tiers of pontoons to form the bridges that would span France's rivers.

Neat ranks and files of American armored vehicles stretch across an English plain as far as the eye can see. The half-tracks (right), used to transport combat troops and to drag artillery pieces, and the Sherman tanks were a small fraction of the 50,000 military vehicles shipped to Great Britain for the invasion of Normandy.

SUPREME COMMANDER

Roosevelt's message (below) to Stalin names Eisenhower as commander of the invasion force, whose personnel wore a flaming sword insignia (above) symbolizing the liberation of Europe. U.S. Chief of Staff George C. Marshall drafted the message and sent it to Eisenhower as a souvenir.

From the President to Marshal Stalin

The appointment of General Eisenhower to command of Overlord operation has been decided upon.

Roosevelt

Cairo, Dec. 7. 43

Dear Eisenhower, I thought you might like to have this as a memento. It was written very hurriedly by me as the final meeting broke up yesterday, the President signing it immediately.

G.C.M.

A GIFTED TEAM WORKER FOR A PRESSURE POST

On Christmas Eve of 1943, after operating without a leader for nearly a year, the Allied forces assembling in Britain learned who was to have the momentous task of completing their preparations for the invasion of France and launching the assault. That day in Washington, President Roosevelt announced over the radio that the chief of the Supreme Headquarters of the Allied Expeditionary Force (SHAEF) was to be General Dwight D. Eisenhower.

Two years earlier, Eisenhower had been so little known even in America, that a newspaper had called him "Lt. Col D. D. Ersenbeing"; now, he was so famous that King George VI of England requested his autograph for a relative. Eisenhower's swift rise—first to commander of the North African invasion and then to chief of U.S. troops in the European theater—was due primarily to his ability to weld leaders with assertive personalities and differing national interests into a winning team. That talent had impressed German spies and they noted it in their reports. But some Allied observers considered Eisenhower unqualified for his new job. They pointed out that he had never personally commanded troops in battle and they accused him of being indecisive and overly conciliatory—more an arbitrator than a dynamic leader. Eisenhower's consideration for the British prompted several U.S. officers to grumble, "Ike is the best commander the British have." Alert to the charge, Eisenhower stopped carrying his swagger stick—an old habit that his critics might have condemned as too British.

Eisenhower assumed his manifold new duties in England on January 15, 1944. His most crucial and time-consuming work was discussing problems of strategy, tactics and supply with members of his high-powered American and British staff. But—contrary to his critics' beliefs—he never flinched at making the tough decisions. It was Eisenhower who decided to use paratroopers in Normandy despite predictions of 70 per cent casualties. And on June 5, when some SHAEF officers argued that the Normandy operation should be postponed because of bad weather, Eisenhower ordered the assault anyway.

On duty in England, Ike inspects Winston Churchill's "siren suit", a garment the Prime Minister designed to permit air raid wardens to dress in a hurry.

Always short on time, the busy Supreme Commander checks his watch in his London office a week after taking charge of SHAEF.

At SHAEF's Southwick House headquarters near Portsmouth, Eisenhower gave the final go-ahead for the invasion in the library.

At an American air base, Eisenhower goes over invasion plans with Major General Lewis H. Brereton and Lieut. General Carl Spaatz (center) of the Air For

LONG DAYS OF TAXING DUTIES

As Supreme Commander, General Eisenhower followed a man-killing schedule of routine duties and special assignments. He spent hours at SHAEF meetings and many

logbook, which contained top-secret cables, intelligence reports and staff summaries. He received diplomats, attended business lunches with Churchill at least two times every week, and made frequent trips to examine new weapons and to review combat units.

Ike felt that the most important part of his job was visiting the troops. "It pays

big dividends in terms of morale," he e plained, "and morale is supreme on t battlefield." He set for himself a nea impossible goal: to speak to every unit troops that would take part in the invasio Once he gave so many speeches that at t end of the day he was hoarse. Almost ways, he spoke without written notes a finished to cheers of "Good ol' Ike!"

ttending graduation exercises at the Royal Military Academy, the Supreme Commander reviews the newly commissioned officers.

Visiting U.S. troops at target practice, Eisenhower and Churchill try
out new Winchester carbines while SHAEF Lieut. General Omar N. Bradley
loads his weapon. Though the GIs fired at a range of 200 yards, the VIPs
got handicaps: Bradley's target was set up 75 yards away, Eisenhower's 50
yards, Churchill's 25 yards. They fired 45 shots and scored only 29 hits.

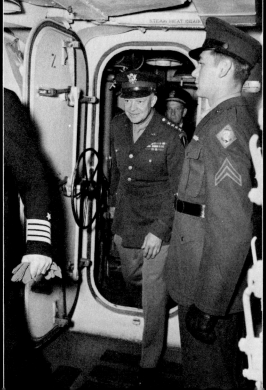

Flashing his famous grin, Eisenhower inspects the Quincy, an American
cruiser, in Belfast, Ireland. The Quincy later joined the warships that

Ike examines aerial photographs of the damage done by Allied bombers to soften up enemy defenses.

Our landings in the
Cherbourg — Havre area
have failed to gain a
satisfactory foothold and
I have withdrawn the
troops. (This particular
operation) My decision to
attack at this time and place
was based upon the best
information available,
The troops, the air and the
Navy did all that
Bravery and devotion to duty
could do. If any blame
or fault attaches to the attempt
it is mine alone.

——————

July 5

n this accidentally misdated note scrawled by Eisenhower before D-Day,
he assumes full responsibility for the decision to launch the invasion.
The message, to be made public in the event the landings failed, proved
unnecessary. Eisenhower later gave the note to one of his aides.

Paratroopers of the U.S. 101st Airborne Division, their faces camouflaged
with night paint, chat informally with Eisenhower before departing from
their base near Newbury to attack heavily fortified positions in Normandy.
Ike, worried about the paratroopers' perilous assignments, spent part
of the evening moving among them, listening to their jokes and stories.

3

In the gray predawn light of June 5, while the airborne troops who would spearhead the D-Day invasion were still asleep, the ground forces were already starting their slow seaborne journey to Normandy. Nearly 5,000 ships of all kinds—battleships and cruisers, frigates and sloops, tank landing craft and gunboats, troop transports and assault boats, repair ships, hospital ships, ammunition ships, ships to lay smoke screens, to direct aircraft and to be sunk as tide breakers off the Normandy coast—put out to sea that blustery morning. From the overcrowded harbors of the English south coast, from as far west as Falmouth and as far east as Felixstowe, the components of the greatest fleet that ever sailed butted through wind and swell toward the assembly point, Area Z, off the southern tip of the Isle of Wight.

No one who saw this panoply of overwhelming might could doubt that the Allies would triumph in the battle to come. An English Coastguardsman in his lookout high up on the Dorset cliffs at Saint Alban's Head watched in disbelief as more than a thousand ships streamed by. Below him were soldiers and tanks in landing craft; above were barrage balloons; on the horizon were flotillas of landing craft to the east and lines of battleships to the west and a whole fleet silhouetted against the white cliffs of the Isle of Wight to the south. When the last of the ships had disappeared southward over the horizon, the Coastguardsman turned for home. "A lot of men are going to die tonight," he told his wife. "We should pray for them."

The armada drove on through a moderate sea, with the wind blowing 16 to 20 miles per hour. Aboard the bouncing, heavily laden vessels, many soldiers and sailors were prostrated with seasickness. But the men did little complaining. On the decks and in the holds they cleaned their weapons, received briefings and learned for the first time exactly where they were going to land. Afterward, they spent most of their time "standing about looking out to sea, talking now and then and thinking," reported BBC war correspondent Robin Duff, who was aboard a U.S. troop transport. "When they spoke they were self-conscious. There was a tenseness and a sense of good humor and good fellowship that were impossible to translate into words."

The armada plowed forward, its ships flashing signals to one another. The troop transports were preceded by minesweepers, which cleared 10 lanes through the Germans' mid-Channel minefield. The fleet was protected against German U-boats and torpedo boats by Navy and Air Force patrols and by a day-and-night umbrella of fighter planes. The ships took up their final order of battle as the sun began to dip in the sky. By 8 p.m. the leading minesweepers were off the Normandy coast at Cap Barfleur. At 10 p.m. the crewmen could pick out houses on the dark shore. Not a single German gun had been fired.

That afternoon, as the seaborne armada built up at its assembly point, the men of the Allied airborne forces spent their final hours in England in compulsory rest. Their last letter home had been written, their last briefing attended, their last check made, their parachutes fitted, their heavy equipment loaded on the planes and gliders that were to take them to Normandy to open the Second Front. Late in the afternoon, in sealed camps all over southern England, they lined up for their last hot meal. Then the paratroopers, British and American alike, loaded themselves up with 85 to 100 pounds of gear to meet every imaginable contingency.

As the evening light began to fade, nearly 20,000 men of the British 6th Airborne Division and the U.S. 82nd and 101st Airborne Divisions were driven out to 22 scattered airfields, where almost 1,200 transport aircraft (mainly C-47 Dakotas) and more than 700 gliders were assembled for the greatest airborne assault in history. General Eisenhower drove out to watch some units of the 101st prepare to take off from their base near Newbury. Ike's old friend and aide, Captain Harry Butcher, later wrote: "We saw hundreds of paratroopers, with blackened and grotesque faces, packing up for the big hop and jump. Ike wandered through them, stepping over packs, guns, and a variety of equipment such as only paratroops can devise, chinning with this and that one." Going the rounds at other airfields, British Air Marshal Leigh-Mallory found the troops "grim and not frightfully gay," but he had no doubt of their determination to do the job. Last-minute prayer services were held at every base.

Between 10 p.m. and midnight on June 5, paratroopers at English airfields stubbed out their cigarettes, drained their mugs of coffee or tea and took their seats in the aircraft. "Now the whole field is shaking with the roar of motors," wrote Private First Class David K. Webster of the American 506th Parachute Infantry. "Our tail swings around. We

wheel about and head up the runway. My legs are weak and my throat is dry and I can only talk in a stuttering whisper. With a soft rush we leave the ground."

Transport planes, bombers and gliders began to fill the night sky, their red and green navigation lights blinking fitfully. An American paratrooper peered out the open door of his transport; "I could hardly see the sky for the planes," he said later "—there just was not room for more." For hours the stream of aircraft droned above the darkened towns and fields of southern England, and sleeping people were awakened by the throaty rumble of the mighty air armada as it passed overhead.

Aboard the leading British planes flew the pathfinders who would mark the way for the main airborne forces. In addition to the normal heavy load, each man carried a 60-pound kit bag attached to his leg containing lights and beacons with which to define the glider landing zones (LZs) and paratroopers' drop zones (DZs). The pathfinders were scheduled to drop at 15 minutes past midnight. At the same time, the first British combat forces, in six gliders, would go into action. These were five platoons of the 2nd Battalion Oxfordshire and Buckinghamshire Light Infantry (known as "the Ox and Bucks") and a company of Royal Engineers. They had been assigned the task of capturing the bridges of the Caen Canal and Orne River, which guarded the eastern flank of the invasion beachhead.

The gliders carrying the Ox and Bucks ran into gusty wind on reaching the English Channel, and they began to pitch and yaw on the ends of their towropes. They were flying through ragged clouds, and at times the pilots could see nothing but the taillights of the towplanes and the rain spattering on the cockpit windows. But occasionally the clouds parted to reveal a scudding full moon and, far below, the dark, stormy Channel, flecked with the white arrowhead wakes of innumerable ships. The seaborne armies were right on schedule for their landings, to begin at 6:30.

Soon after midnight, the British pathfinders and glider troops saw below them the white, curving shore of France and two ribbons of water mirrored in the moonlight—the Orne River and the Caen Canal. At 12:18 a.m. the six aircraft carrying the pathfinders came over their targets beyond the east bank of the Orne. The first planeload of paratroopers jumped into space. At the same time, 5,000 feet above the mouth of the river, the leading glider pilot cast off his towrope and lifted up the glider's nose to reduce speed. The roar of the wind on the hull died down, and in the eerie silence the craft glided smoothly through the darkness toward enemy territory. The copilot opened the forward door and cold air streamed in. The leading glider leveled out from the dive, then made a 90° turn to the right.

Peering out into the darkness, Major John Howard, commanding the six-glider attack on the bridges, glimpsed for a second the dimly gleaming ribbon of the canal. His glider straightened up for the final approach to the canal bridge. At 3,000 feet the pilot dived steeply and the land rose up; fields and trees were rushing past below at 90 miles an hour. "Hold tight!" the pilot shouted. The platoon linked arms, lifted their feet off the floor and sat locked together, waiting for the impact of the soil of German-occupied France.

As the first airborne invaders were descending on their targets, the German defenders below remained supremely confident that no such thing could happen. The weather was too poor for an invasion. It was windy, cloudy and drizzly, with poor visibility and a rough sea. The weather —and the conviction that everything depended on it— obsessed the 58 German divisions west of the Rhine. By the evening of June 5, the weather was so marvelously bad that

men guarding the northwest coast of France looked forward to a quiet night off after weeks of constant alert.

In Cherbourg, Rear Admiral Walther Hennecke, Naval Commander Normandy, had already received a reassuring signal from the head of his meteorological station at Cap de la Hague at the tip of the Cotentin Peninsula. "Rough sea, poor visibility, force 5 to 6 wind, rain likely to get heavier." Assuming that the weather was too bad for even the usual air raids, the admiral had canceled the customary torpedo-boat patrols for that night. Major General Max Pemsel, chief of staff at Seventh Army headquarters in Le Mans, had received the same forecast from the meteorological section at Naval Group Headquarters in Paris. He came to the conclusion that the invaders could not come that night and, therefore, that they would not come for several weeks—not until the next favorable combination of tide and moon. He so informed Colonel General Friedrich Dollmann, commanding the Seventh Army, and Dollmann ordered his divisional and regimental commanders to leave their units and attend a *Kriegspiel,* a staff war game, in Rennes at 10 a.m. on June 6. The subject of the exercise: "Enemy landings in Normandy, preceded by parachute drops."

To get to the *Kriegspiel* on time, the Seventh Army commanders whose positions would be assaulted by the American airborne forces had left their posts before the first

American planes approached the Normandy coast. One of the last to depart was Major General Wilhelm Falley, commanding the 91st Air Landing Division located near Sainte-Mère-Eglise. As he set off, Falley told his chief of operations, "Nothing's going to happen in this lousy weather."

Field Marshal Rommel, whose Army Group B defended the coasts of France and the Netherlands, was out of touch. That morning he had left his headquarters at La Roche-Guyon between Paris and Le Havre and had started for his home at Herrlingen on the Danube in Germany. June 6 was his wife Lucie's birthday. He intended to celebrate with her, then drive on to Berchtesgaden to ask Hitler to transfer two armored divisions to Normandy. Rommel had labored tirelessly for months to improve his defenses, and he meant to make them invulnerable before any invasion came.

Rommel's superiors spent June 5 dealing with routine problems. Hitler was only concerned that day with Portuguese tungsten imports, diesel truck construction and a fecal examination by his doctor. At Berchtesgaden in Upper Bavaria, OKW—the Supreme Headquarters of the German Armed Forces—kept busy with normal staff work. "OKW had not the slightest idea that the decisive event of the war was upon them," later wrote the deputy chief of operations at Supreme Headquarters, General Walter Warlimont.

And yet on June 5, OB West—the Paris-based headquarters of all German ground forces in Western Europe—was in possession of evidence that the invasion was on its way. The headquarters had been warned in advance by a double agent working in the French Resistance movement.

According to the spy, the British Special Operations Executive, the agency in charge of underground activities throughout occupied Europe, had arranged with the Resistance to carry out extensive sabotage operations to coincide with D-Day. To alert the Resistance, the French-language service of the BBC would quote two lines from Paul Verlaine's poem "Autumn Song." The first line—"The long sobbing of the violins of autumn"—would be broadcast to indicate that the invasion date had been tentatively set. The second line—"Wound my heart with monotonous languor"—would mean that the attack was to begin within 48 hours and that sabotage instructions would follow in code.

Acting on the spy's tip-off, OB West arranged for all BBC transmissions to France to be monitored by the signal center of the Fifteenth Army at Tourcoing, on the Belgian border. On June 1 and 2, the BBC transmitted—and the German monitors received—the first line of the Verlaine poem. Then at 9:15 p.m. on the 5th of June, during a broadcast of many meaningless phrases such as "The doctor buries all of his patients," the signal center heard the vital second line of the poem.

The officer in charge quickly passed on the D-Day warning to his superiors. Within two hours the information had reached Supreme Headquarters at Berchtesgaden, the Commander in Chief West in Paris, Rommel's headquarters and the headquarters of the three big units that made up his Army Group B: the Seventh Army, the Fifteenth Army and the Netherlands Forces.

Incredibly, nothing happened. The warning was not relayed to any of the German troops guarding the invasion coast. In Normandy the Seventh Army's 84th Corps and the divisions of that corps were ignorant of the Allied plans until the invasion hit their coastal positions. Rommel was not recalled from Herrlingen.

The blame for this failure lay with the Commander in Chief West, Field Marshal von Rundstedt. That aged and inflexible officer did not believe that the invasion could take place in such foul weather, and he did not believe that the Allies would be so stupid as to announce their plans on the BBC in advance. In short, he did not believe the report of his own military intelligence, which had previously sounded false alarms, and for hours he did nothing to prepare his armies to meet the invasion.

The commanders in Normandy began finding out about the danger from local reports. One of the first to be informed was Admiral Hennecke, ensconced in his villa overlooking the sea at Cherbourg. Around midnight, the admiral was entertaining a group of musicians who had given a concert for the men at the Naval base. One of Hennecke's guests, a young woman, had seated herself at the piano and was playing Schumann's *Papillons* when the music was interrupted by a lieutenant. He reported to the admiral, "Very heavy air raids on towns and roads in the coastal area." Hennecke went down to his underground command post. The duty officer passed him reports from several observation posts. "Loud engine noise of approaching bomber formations . . . light reconnaissance aircraft penetrating over a broad front . . . target markers being dropped behind the front." The admiral was not alarmed—just puzzled. Something was happening, but he was not sure what it was.

The planes whose presence overhead had been reported to Hennecke were more than 1,000 RAF bombers, beginning all-night attacks to soften up German coastal defenses in preparation for the morning seaborne landings. Soon the admiral's uncertainty, and the confusion of German radar operators all along the northern coast of France, would be compounded by a ruse.

The Allied invasion planners, realizing that their airdrops would tip the Germans off to the invasion area, had carefully prepared a series of deceptive D-Day maneuvers, part of Operation *Fortitude*. Several plans were designed to convince the Germans that the activity in Normandy was merely a diversion for a much larger assault on the Pas-de-Calais area, well to the northeast.

The deceptive operations got under way at about the same time that airborne landings commenced in Normandy. To make the airdrops look like a feint, RAF bombers began dropping hundreds of life-size dummies by parachute all over Normandy. To mask the approach of the invasion fleet, powerful radio transmitters in England began jamming German radar stations along the Normandy coast. To point out the Pas-de-Calais as the Allies' objective, RAF bombers began flying hundreds of sorties throughout that area, and German-language broadcasts from England began ordering Luftwaffe planes away from Normandy to defend the Pas-de-Calais. Meanwhile, acting on coded instructions, the French Resistance began sabotaging German communications centers all over France.

The main feature of Operation *Fortitude* on D-Day was a massive electronic conjuring trick. Two small groups of British motor launches headed across the Channel toward the Pas-de-Calais. Each boat towed two 29-foot-long balloons, one floating in the air overhead and the other bobbing behind tethered to a raft. Each balloon was fitted with a nine-foot reflector that produced a radar echo resembling that of a 10,000-ton troop transport. Above the launches, two squadrons of RAF bombers flew in precise patterns, dropping strips of aluminum foil to simulate more planes on radar screens. Aluminum foil had been previously dropped

in bombing raids primarily to jam the German fighter control apparatus; this time, the bombers' precise flight pattern, together with the scattering of foil cut to a special length and shape, created the radar image of a huge air fleet. German radar stations—those that were not knocked out by jamming or bombing—soon began reporting an enormous sea and air armada bound for the Pas-de-Calais.

With all but a few Luftwaffe fighters now heading for the Pas-de-Calais, the Allies owned the air over Normandy. The 1,000 RAF bombers pounding the invasion coast had to contend with nothing but wind, bad weather and antiaircraft fire; their uninterrupted all-night sorties would drop nearly 6,000 tons of bombs on German coastal defenses

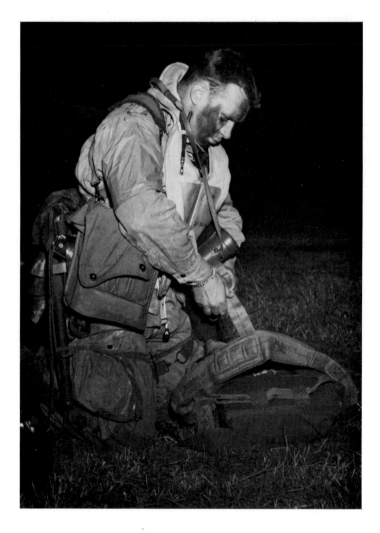

Saddled with 100 pounds of supplies and equipment, an American paratrooper adjusts his parachute before departing for Normandy. Each paratrooper was a walking arsenal: he carried two fragmentation grenades, one smoke grenade, one antitank mine and one antitank Gammon bomb made of plastic explosives in a cloth bag. He also had at least one personal weapon—rifle, carbine, pistol or submachine gun plus ammunition. Other gear included a pocketknife, flashlight, razor, spoon, maps, compass, first-aid kit, rations, entrenching tool, main and reserve parachutes, gas mask, jump knife, helmet and spare clothing.

between Cherbourg and Le Havre. To German troops on duty along the coast, the night was alive with enemy planes and the crump of their bombs. The soldiers could not understand why their Luftwaffe fighters did not rise to challenge the enemy.

On the bridge over the Caen Canal at Bénouville, Private Helmut Römer, a young German on sentry duty, heard bombs exploding in the direction of Caen and antiaircraft guns pounding in the region of Troarn. Suddenly he saw the dim shape of an aircraft swooping silently toward him at treetop height. At first he thought it was a bomber with its engines dead, and he watched transfixed as it hit the ground with a tremendous crash, careered across the tiny field on the far side of the canal, knocked over a cow and came to a splintering halt with its crumpled nose in a barbed-wire barrier less than 50 yards from the far end of the bridge. It was not a bomber, it was a huge glider, and for a moment no sound came from it.

Then Private Römer heard English voices calling their platoon's rallying signal: "Able-Able." Almost at once, another glider crash-landed 10 yards behind the first, then a third only 15 yards farther away. "Baker-Baker," called the Englishmen in the second glider, and the soldiers in the third replied, "Charlie-Charlie."

The Englishmen came rushing from their gliders, and one of them hurled a phosphorus grenade against the pillbox on the bridge. A machine gun in the pillbox opened fire but was immediately silenced by another English soldier who popped a grenade through the gunport. Römer had no time to call out the guard or even his own platoon. Some Germans appeared and began manning the trenches on the near side of the canal, but they could not stop the English invaders charging toward them across the bridge, firing as they ran. Römer flung himself into the trenches on the western side of the bridge. The British soon broke into the trenches and the Germans—Römer among them—ran off.

Thanks to the glider pilots' precise landings, the three platoons led by Major Howard secured the Caen Canal bridge less than 10 minutes after the first glider landed (page 99). Howard's other three gliders, attacking the Orne River bridge, did not land so accurately but were just as successful; the first platoon rushed to the attack and found that the German defenders had already fled. Thus, within minutes the glider-borne strike force of the 6th Airborne had secured the first objectives of the invasion—the two bridges carrying the main road leading inland from the beachhead on the eastern flank of the 59-mile invasion front. The force's radio operator sent out his report using two code words for the bridges to announce their capture: "Ham and jam." The platoons settled into defensive positions to await reinforcements. Not far away, pathfinders for the 6th Airborne were setting out navigation lights and radar beacons to mark the paratroopers' drop zones east of the bridges and north of the village of Ranville.

The second wave of the 6th Airborne roared over the coast at 12:50, and some 2,000 paratroopers of the 5th Paratroop Brigade began their drop over the DZs marked by the pathfinders on the outskirts of Ranville. Guy Byam, a reporter for the BBC, jumped with the paratroopers and later recorded his impressions for broadcast: "Out, out, out fast into the cool night air, out, out, out over France." His parachute opened, and in about 10 seconds, "I find myself in the middle of a cornfield. I look around and even with a compass I can't be sure where I am—overhead hundreds of parachutes and containers are coming down. The whole sky is a fantastic chimera of lights and flak, and one plane gets hit and disintegrates wholesale in the sky, sprinkling a myriad of burning pieces all over the sky."

The paratroopers came down in a strong wind and many of them drifted wide of their DZs. The scattered men were rallied by the mellow calls of English hunting horns, and the reassembled units set about their assignments without delay. One battalion hurried off to reinforce the soldiers at the bridges. A second went to secure the eastern approaches to the bridges. The third battalion went to work clearing the landing zone for the third wave of the 6th Airborne, due to land by glider at 3:20 with the divisional headquarters and the brigade's heavy equipment—the all-important antitank guns, heavy mortars, machine guns and jeeps.

Then, shouting their war cry, "Tallyho," the paratroopers left the LZ and drove enemy infantrymen of the 21st Panzer Division out of Ranville—the first village in France to be liberated from German rule. As the invaders slipped by in the streets below, townspeople whispered from bedroom windows. *"Bonjour!"* Inevitably, the paratroopers caused some confusion. "We are the British Army of Liberation," a lieutenant announced to the matron of a maternity home near Ranville. "What!" exclaimed the matron, glancing in bewilderment at the lieutenant and his tiny party of nine disheveled young men. "All of you?"

At 3:30, as planned, 68 gliders of the 5th Parachute Brigade came in for their landings at the Ranville LZ. Some of them crashed into heavy poles implanted by the Germans to prevent such landings (pages 100-101). Two gliders collided and were destroyed. One slammed through a cottage and came out the other side carrying a bed. But 50 gliders landed accurately, on time and with only light casualties.

Cursing and cheering, the men struggled out of their gliders onto the plowed field. One soldier sang out, "I told yer we wouldn't 'ave to swim." Then, hacking their way into broken gliders, the men salvaged a number of jeeps and 10 of their 18 precious antitank guns. In small groups they

stumbled toward the dark outline of their rendezvous point, the square-towered Norman church in Ranville. At the edge of the field, the groups were halted by their advanced guard, who challenged them with the call "V for" and let them pass when they gave the countersign "Victory."

Beyond the landing zone, on a road near the Ranville church, everything was in a state of confusion. A hot little skirmish was being fought as the soldiers assembled and formed a column. Somewhere nearby German voices were heard; a burst of submachine-gun fire silenced them. Then some British soldiers, who had taken shelter in a ditch, protested an order to get back on the road. Above the clamor the familiar booming voice of the commander of the 6th Airborne Division could be heard: "Don't you dare argue with me! Get on, I say, get on."

Major-General Richard Gale, who had just landed with the main glider force, established order and got the column moving toward his preselected headquarters, a château in Ranville. Gale, a flamboyant six-footer described by an associate as "a bit of a buccaneer," set out on foot but soon called to his aide-de-camp for a handsome chestnut horse that he had found grazing in the landing zone. He mounted and completed the trip on horseback.

At the château, Gale drove the troops hard; there was much to do and little time to do it in. The men implanted their antitank guns, dug trenches, fought skirmishes, rounded up stragglers. Dawn was just two hours away. Then the Germans would come—the heavy tanks and crack troops of the 21st Panzer Division. Gale and his troops would have the difficult task of keeping the enemy from attacking the invasion beaches to the northwest.

Meanwhile, some six miles to the east, Gale's 3rd Parachute Brigade was running into trouble. Two of the brigade's three battalions were assigned to blow up the five

bridges across the Dives River and to occupy the high ground between the Dives and the Orne, thereby establishing a defensive position on the eastern flank of the invasion. There they expected to meet a counterattack by German panzers from the direction of Caen. But several of their drop zones had been inaccurately marked by the pathfinders. Many of the transport pilots found it hard to tell the Dives from the Orne and came in too fast and too high. Inexperienced pilots disobeyed orders and began dodging antiaircraft fire, tossing the overladen paratroopers about, delaying their jumps. The result was that the men were scattered over a wide area.

Even those who managed to jump over their appointed DZs were carried off course by the high wind. Hundreds of paratroopers came down in the swamps of the Dives and many died there. Some of them floated to earth many miles off course and took three or four days to rejoin their units. Several landed so far behind enemy lines that they were obliged to fight alongside members of the French Resistance for months before linking up with the British Army.

The paratroopers made the best of a bad situation. Singly and in small groups, challenged and sniped at by Germans, embraced by excited French civilians who loaded them with brandy, bread, strawberries and fresh milk, the men joined their skeleton units and set off for their objectives. They blew up four of their five target bridges over the Dives with little difficulty. But the fifth and most important bridge—the southernmost one at Troarn, which carried the main road from Caen to Rouen—would have remained intact but for the verve of a nine-man demolition team.

Landing about five miles from the bridge, the soldiers commandeered a medical-corps jeep and trailer and roared off to Troarn, only to crash into a barbed-wire barricade at the edge of the town. After struggling for 20 minutes to cut themselves free, they raced into Troarn and swerved up the main street with headlights on and their guns returning a barrage of German fire. Finally, they reached the bridge and swiftly blew it up. They then abandoned the jeep and made their way cross-country to their headquarters. The destruction of this bridge and the other four was to delay the expected German counterattack by several vital hours.

The last and toughest mission of the British airborne division had been assigned to the 9th Parachute Battalion, under 29-year-old Lieut. Colonel Terence Otway. The 650 men of the battalion were to storm the seemingly impregnable German battery at Merville, whose outer defenses consisted of a minefield, a barbed-wire entanglement 15 feet across and an antitank ditch. If they got that far, they would face a ring of machine-gun nests manned by more than 130 soldiers, and they would have to assault the heavy guns housed in a blockhouse with heavy steel doors and concrete walls six feet thick.

Nothing had been left to chance. Before Otway's attack, 100 RAF Lancasters were to drop enormous bombs on the position, and during the assault three gliders full of troops were supposed to crash-land on top of the battery to help out. If the attack failed, a British warship would shell the battery at dawn. But it was absolutely essential for Otway and his men to succeed, for the battery commanded the left flank of the British landing beaches. The battery would wreak havoc on the seaborne invaders if its four big guns were still in working order at daybreak.

Otway's mission seemed to be doomed even before he landed. The Lancasters dropped their two-ton bombs a half mile wide of the Merville battery, killing some cows and flattening the village of Gonneville-sur-Mer. On the way over, the five gliders carrying Otway's antitank guns and jeeps broke their towropes and crashed into the sea. And the battalion's parachute drop was nearly as calamitous. As the transport planes came over the French coast, the pilots began swerving violently to escape the flak. The parachutists, lined up for their jumps, were thrown to the floor in struggling heaps.

"Hold your course, you bloody fool!" Otway shouted out to his pilot.

"We've been hit in the tail!" a crewman yelled back.

"You can still fly straight, can't you?" Otway retorted. When his turn came to jump he handed a half-empty bottle of Scotch to the RAF dispatcher. "You're going to need this," he said, and then threw himself into space.

As Otway descended tracer bullets tore through his parachute, and he saw that he was falling straight toward a farmhouse that he instantly recognized from intelligence reports as a German headquarters. Otway bumped into the house at 15 miles an hour, and as he landed in a garden a

German stuck his head out of an upstairs window and fired a pistol at him. One of Otway's men threw a brick at the German, and the head ducked back inside. Then Germans began pouring out of the front door, and Otway and two other men ran for their lives.

As Otway prowled around in the dark, he realized that he had a disaster on his hands. His battalion, instead of being concentrated on a field one mile long and a half mile wide, was widely scattered. It later turned out that his men had landed over 50 square miles of Normandy. About half of them had dropped into the swamps of the Dives, some as far as 30 miles away. Many had drowned. Otway himself saw one paratrooper up to his shoulders in mud, struggling and crying out as he sank inexorably and vanished from view beneath the slimy surface of a bog. "The drop's a bloody chaos," said Otway's second-in-command. "There's hardly anyone here."

Gradually, Otway assembled 155 men. About 400 were missing. The mortars, antitank guns, jeeps, heavy assault equipment and mine detectors were lost; the engineers and doctors were not to be seen. Otway had only one machine gun and scarcely enough explosives to blow up the German guns. But at 2:57 he gave up waiting for more troops and marched off with the men he had.

Nearly an hour later, they reached the outskirts of the Merville battery and got ready for the attack. Then the battalion suffered more bad luck: at 4:30, when two of the gliders that were supposed to crash-land on the battery appeared overhead, Otway's men could not find the flares to signal that they were present and ready for the carefully synchronized assault. One glider soared over the battery 100 feet up, then turned away and landed in a field four miles off. The other, set ablaze by tracer shells from the battery, crash-landed without casualties in an orchard 200 yards from Otway's position. The third glider never appeared; it had broken its towrope shortly after takeoff and had come down safely in England.

In desperation Otway gave the order to attack. The paratroopers moved through the minefield along a trail marked earlier by pathfinders. They blew two gaps in the barbed wire, charged through and swarmed across the antitank ditch. Then they attacked furiously in two groups. One group engaged the German machine gunners in savage hand-to-hand fighting in the trench network. The other group headed for the guns, fighting to within 30 yards of the steel doors in the concrete blockhouse. Two of the doors were open, and the paratroopers emptied their guns into the interior. Then they raced inside and grappled with the gun crews. The Germans battled fiercely but they were soon overwhelmed.

Otway's men blew up the guns in the blockhouse and then took a toll of their casualties. Around the battery lay more than 175 dead and wounded, 65 of them British. Of the 155 paratroopers Otway had led into battle some 20 minutes earlier, only 80 were now fit to march besides him.

Someone found a flare and fired a signal, announcing the destruction of the guns to a spotter aircraft circling overhead. The plane relayed the signal to the Royal Navy just 15 minutes before its big guns were scheduled to shell the position. Then Otway's signals officer took a carrier pigeon out of his blouse and sent it winging back across the Channel—above the approaching armada and below the incoming waves of bombers—with news that the major objective of the British 6th Airborne Division had been achieved.

At a quarter past midnight on D-Day, at almost the same

Three British gliders, commanded by Major John Howard (inset), lie within 50 yards of one another after a near-perfect landing that led to the capture of the Caen Canal bridge (partly visible at upper right). Air Chief Marshal Leigh-Mallory called the feat the War's finest piece of airmanship.

moment that the British pathfinders were landing on the eastern flank of the invasion beachhead, the American 82nd and 101st Airborne Divisions were dropping their pathfinders on the western flank of the beachhead 50 miles away. The pathfinders marked four DZs and one LZ with lights and radar beacons. One hour later, the main American paratroop force crossed the coastline in a huge aerial armada of some 800 planes.

The chief objectives of the American airborne divisions were to secure the west flank of the invasion beachhead and to spread inland across the neck of the Cotentin Peninsula, cutting off the port of Cherbourg so it could be captured once the Allied invasion forces had built up their strength. These tasks were vastly complicated by the terrain. The airborne target areas were all flooded, either by nature or by the Germans. Behind Utah Beach lay a long, mile-wide lagoon crossed by four narrow causeways. Ten miles farther inland, the Merderet and Douve River valleys, which were also airborne objectives, had been allowed to fill with water by the German forces.

Unless the causeways leading off Utah could be secured by airborne troops, the seaborne forces might be trapped on the beach under German guns. And unless the bridges across the Merderet were secured, a large part of the American invasion force might be bottled up between the lagoon and the flooded rivers, dangerously exposed to German counterattacks from the north, west and south.

From the outset, the American airborne operations were more confused than the British ones. The planes of the transport fleet, flying in formations of nine behind a screen of fighter planes, drifted apart in haze and clouds as they neared the French coast from the west. By the time the scattered formations broke out of the cloud banks over Normandy, many planes were too far off course to start looking for the pathfinders' drop zones—most of which, it later turned out, had been marked in the wrong places. To make matters worse, many pilots who came under German antiaircraft fire began dodging the flak bursts, heaving their passengers about and forcing them to jump in wild disarray.

For all these reasons, more than three quarters of the 6,500 men in each division were widely scattered and took no meaningful part in the action that occurred in their sectors. Thousands of paratroopers were simply lost. Individually and in small groups, they wandered about in fields cut up by impenetrable hedgerows and hiked along country roads between farming villages, fighting brisk skirmishes with German patrols along the way. And yet the drifters' erratic movements inadvertently helped some American units to win crucial engagements; they kept the Germans as bewildered as they were themselves.

The 101st Airborne, assigned to take the causeway exits behind Utah Beach and to throw up a defensive perimeter on the American southern flank, had to land with pinpoint accuracy to avoid falling in the mile-wide lagoon or in the 82nd Airborne's territory along the flooded Merderet valley a few miles inland. But the 101st's drops were a shambles. The paratroopers came down over an area 25 miles long and 15 miles wide, with a few stray groups even farther away. The division commander, Major General Maxwell

Field Marshal Rommel's own design (right) shows the tall, thick poles—known as "Rommel's asparagus"—that he ordered implanted in inland fields so that "enemy aircraft and gliders will break up while landing." The wires were designed to be connected to shells, which were never installed, and only 10 percent of his proposed 50 million stakes were in place by D-Day. But the wreckage of a Waco glider (far right) in a Normandy field is testimony to the effectiveness of these obstacles.

Taylor, landed all alone in a field and scouted around for half an hour before he found the first of his men, a private. In sheer relief the general and the private embraced like long-lost brothers.

The 101st paratroopers assembled as best they could in flattish terrain that offered few landmarks to guide them. Every man in the division had been issued a small metal toy that made a cricket-like click-clack sound when snapped between the thumb and the forefinger, and everywhere in fields and marshes lost soldiers were using the gadgets to signal their presence. The sharp signals also betrayed many men to German snipers. (For this reason the 82nd Airborne, which had suffered heavy losses using the sound makers in Sicily and Italy, had abandoned the devices and was using instead the whispered password "Flash" and the counter-sign "Thunder.") Gradually, the small groups of 101st Airborne men got larger. But by dawn General Taylor would have at his disposal only one sixth of his men. (A day later about half of the division was still missing.)

Nevertheless, several makeshift units of a dozen to 100 men began to function effectively. Troops of the 502nd and 506th Parachute Infantry Regiments seized two of the causeways leading across the long lagoon. On the Americans' southern flank, men of the 501st Parachute Infantry ran into stiff opposition from the Germans but managed to fling up a line of shaky defenses against counterattacks from the direction of Carentan. These and later objectives were attained less by plan than by good luck and extraordinary personal initiative.

Lieut. Colonel Robert G. Cole, commander of the 3rd Battalion of the 502nd Regiment, was the mainspring in a successful action that typified the fighting. Cole landed practically by himself just to the west of his drop zone, in 82nd Airborne territory, and he wandered still farther off course before he was informed at a farmhouse on the edge of the town of Sainte-Mère-Eglise that he was heading in the wrong direction.

With a handful of his paratroopers and some stray 82nd Airborne men, Cole hiked east toward his battalion's objective, the German gun battery at Saint Martin-de-Varreville. Click-clacking their crickets along the way, he and his men built up a little force of about 75 assorted paratroopers. They bumped into a small enemy convoy of vehicles, killed several Germans and took 10 prisoners. Then, on reaching the coastal battery, Cole was astonished to discover that the position had long since been abandoned—the result of several bombing missions that had damaged the fire-control setup and forced the Germans to remove the guns. So Cole marched his group of men approximately a mile to the southeast and captured the inland end of Exit 3 from Utah Beach. There the paratroopers lay in wait, and when an enemy force came toward them from the beach, Cole's men shot down 50 to 75 Germans.

About a mile due west of Cole's position, in the general area of the 1st Battalion of the 502nd Regiment, one enlisted man put on a remarkable display of reckless courage. Staff Sergeant Harrison Summers was a member of a small group of paratroopers who were advancing toward the western edge of the town of Mésières. In front of them lay a row of stone houses that served as the barracks for German coast artillerymen; the position had been given the designation "WXYZ" by American intelligence. Summers' battalion commander, Lieut. Colonel Patrick Cassidy, told him to move up and wipe out WXYZ.

The sergeant rounded up 15 paratroopers; he had never worked with any of them before and did not even know their names. The men showed a distinct lack of enthusiasm for the attack, so Summers set out alone, hoping the others would follow him. Eventually a few did.

Summers sprinted for the first building, kicked open the door and dashed inside with his submachine gun blazing. Four German soldiers fell dead and the rest fled through the back door. Then, covered by his reluctant detachment from a ditch along the road, Summers bolted into the next house. It was empty.

Smashing his way into the third house, Summers mowed down six more Germans. Inside the fourth house he killed another six men.

Summers was joined by Private John F. Camien. Armed only with the Tommy gun and a carbine, Summers and Camien went from house to house, each taking a turn attacking with the Tommy gun while the other covered him with the carbine. Between them they gunned down 30 more Germans in the next few houses.

Then they came to a big building at the end of the line. It was the Germans' mess hall. Incredibly, 15 enemy soldiers were eating breakfast oblivious to Summers' private war outside. Summers burst through the door and cut down all 15 as they rose from the table.

In a few minutes of actual combat, Staff Sergeant Summers had personally accounted for more than 50 enemy dead. He was later awarded a battlefield commission and a Distinguished Service Cross for his action at WXYZ.

West of the 101st Airborne sector, the men of Major General Matthew Ridgway's 82nd Airborne Division encountered worse troubles but eked out no less vital successes. Most of the division made terrible drops. Two of the three regiments discovered to their horror that the flooding of the Merderet and Douve River valleys was far more extensive than they had anticipated; great tracts that looked like solid land in reconnaissance photographs, and that were described as safe landing areas by American intelligence, were in fact overgrown with tall grasses that hid flooded terrain. Some paratroopers drowned, dragged down into the muck and water by their 100-pound loads of gear. Many more men wallowed around aimlessly and learned where they were only by blundering upon the elevated roadbed of a railroad that ran from Caen to Cherbourg. By the time that they extricated themselves from the morass, they were too late to carry out their missions—to blow up the bridges over the Douve and to establish a defensive line to the west of the Merderet.

Farther east lay the 82nd Airborne's primary objective, the thriving crossroads town of Sainte-Mère-Eglise, whose capture General Ridgway had assigned to the 505th Parachute Infantry Regiment. To the German garrison holding the town, the American airdrop seemed to be a small, quick failure. About 30 paratroopers landed right in town, which was lit up by the lurid glare of a fire set by preattack bombers. One trooper landed in the main square and was immediately captured. Another fell on the church steeple and hung there from his parachute pretending to be dead for two and a half hours before he was cut down and taken prisoner. Two men plummeted through the roof of a burning house and died instantly when the mortar shells they carried exploded. One German soldier confronted some French civilians and, pointing to the body of a paratrooper hanging from a tree, shouted triumphantly, "All *kaput!*"

But the 505th was far from *kaput;* most of the regiment had landed in a compact area outside of town and quickly organized to attack Sainte-Mère-Eglise and establish defense lines to the north and south. The assault on the town was assigned to the 3rd Battalion, under Lieut. Colonel Edward Krause, who started out with 108 men. Banking heavily on speed, Krause wasted no time on a cautious house-to-house search. To keep his men from accidentally shooting each other in the dark, he ordered them to use only knives, bayonets and grenades; anyone who fired a gun would clearly be marked as an enemy.

The Germans were caught off balance after their effortless early victory in town. The little fighting they did took place on the outskirts. The mayor of the town, Alexander Renaud, violated the German curfew and went to find out what was going on. He found a lone American paratrooper who had landed in a pond and he pulled him out by his parachute. Then Mayor Renaud slipped back into town and watched for developments at his front window. In the first light of dawn, he saw that the Germans were gone and that American soldiers were strolling about.

The liberation of Sainte-Mère-Eglise had been that easy. In fact, it had been too easy. The real battle for the town started three hours later, when the Germans counterattacked in regimental strength. The Americans had to fight hard all day, but they kept the town and with it command of the vital main road between Cherbourg and Carentan. The capture of Sainte-Mère-Eglise, together with the successes of the 101st Airborne, meant that the Americans had accomplished most of their major missions.

All through the dark morning hours of June 6, while thousands of Allied paratroopers were scrambling toward their Normandy objectives and while thousands of Allied ships were closing in on the Normandy coast, the German commanders failed to take concerted action. Their disastrous indecision was due partly to the fact that they had been taken by surprise and partly to their own incompetence. But to a large degree, the Germans were befuddled by the Allies' brilliant plans of deception.

The main part of Operation *Fortitude*—the two small groups of balloon-toting motor launches—was an unqualified success. Shielded from enemy reconnaissance planes by a curtain of RAF fighters, the launches proceeded sedately toward the Pas-de-Calais. All night long, the image of an immense invasion armada covered German radar screens in the area; the radar operators did not learn of the deception until dawn, when the launches headed back to England and the ghost fleet suddenly disappeared from their screens. Meanwhile, the real invasion fleet was steadily sailing toward Normandy, but for hours it was masked by the intense radio jamming that, with the heavy Allied aerial bombardment, knocked out all but 18 of the 92 radar stations along the Normandy coast. Even after the 18 radar crews spotted the fleet, their hectic reports seemed far less convincing than the many seemingly solid reports of the ghost invasion fleet aimed at the Pas-de-Calais.

The other *Fortitude* operations worked exactly according to plan. The dummy parachutists dropped in Normandy persuaded German commanders to disregard reports of real paratroopers nearby. All through the early morning hours, Allied bombers continued plastering the Pas-de-Calais— and drawing Luftwaffe fighters away from Normandy. Many of the German pilots were misdirected by the British operator who was broadcasting from England on Luftwaffe frequencies. The German ground controllers soon noticed that the British operator mispronounced German words, and they warned their pilots, "Don't be led astray by the enemy." But the warnings did no good; pilots continued to follow the spurious orders—along with wrong orders from their real controllers. At one point, an exasperated German controller swore into the microphone. At this, the British operator deftly told the Luftwaffe pilots, "The Englishman is now swearing!" In despair, the German controller shouted, "It is not the Englishman who is swearing, it is *me!*"

Confused by this barrage of deception, the German generals did little all night long, while they waited for the murky situation to clarify. Even after a few commanders began to sense that the real invasion was beginning in Normandy, they could not persuade their superiors to share their alarm much less to speed reinforcements.

The hour after midnight, when the chaotic airborne landings were at their most vulnerable, passed calmly in nearly all important headquarters throughout Normandy. General Erich Marcks, in his 84th Corps Headquarters at Saint-Lô, about 20 miles from the coast, was perhaps the first key officer to realize that the threat to Normandy was genuine and urgent. An officer on Marcks' staff later recalled that "at 0111—unforgettable moment—the field telephone rang. Something important was coming through; while listening to it the General stood up stiffly, his hands gripping the edge of the table." The message being read to him told of British operations: "Enemy parachutes drop east of the Orne estuary. Main area Breville-Ranville and the north edge of the Bavent forest. Countermeasures are in progress." Then Marcks was informed by an aide of unusual air activity in and around Cotentin Peninsula—the area of the American airdrops.

Putting together the two alarms, Marcks acted swiftly. He flashed a command to the 352nd Infantry Division west of Bayeux: "State of readiness 2." Marcks also called back the divisional commanders who were on their way to the *Kriegspiel* in Rennes. General Falley of the 91st Air Landing Division, who had departed too late to get far, returned in a hurry and soon ran into a group of American paratroopers. They opened fire, and Falley's car crashed. As the general reached for his pistol, the Americans shot him dead.

At 2:15 a.m., General Pemsel, the Seventh Army chief of staff, telephoned his commander, General Dollman. "General," he said, "I believe this is the real invasion. Will you come over immediately?"

At about the same time, Rommel's chief of staff, General Hans Speidel, was awakened with reports of the paratroop landings. Speidel was skeptical, concluding only that a few men might have been air-dropped to link up with the French Resistance; nevertheless, he telephoned Rundstedt at OB West in Paris. Soon thereafter Speidel was called by Pemsel, who said: "Engine noise audible from sea on east coast of Cotentin. Admiral, Channel Coast, reports ships located by radar off Cherbourg." All of this, Pemsel said, pointed to a major operation. Speidel still was dubious but he dutifully relayed Pemsel's report to Rundstedt. At 2:40 a.m. Pemsel was informed that Rundstedt did not consider this scattered Normandy activity to be a major operation. In any case, the Seventh Army was ordered put on the highest state of alert.

By 2:55, after Rundstedt had pondered Pemsel's report of enemy ships, he told his OB West operations officer, General Bodo Zimmerman, to telephone Hitler at Berchtesgaden to let the Führer know what was happening. Rundstedt was beginning to think that a major attack was in progress. But would the main blow hit Normandy or the Pas-de-Calais?

By 4:15, when American landing craft were setting out on their long run to Omaha Beach, the field marshal had finally made up his mind. He announced that the airborne landings were "definitely the opening phase of a sea landing to be expected at dawn." A quarter of an hour later he issued a command that required Hitler's approval; he ordered the available Strategic Reserves—two crack German armored divisions, the 12th SS Hitler Youth and the Panzer Lehr—to move up to the Normandy coast at once.

Had Rundstedt's order deploying the Strategic Reserves

been implemented even at that late hour, a prompt German counterattack in strength might have pushed the Allied invasion back into the sea. But Rundstedt's order was not implemented. His message to Supreme Headquarters in East Prussia requesting approval of his order was ignored for two vital hours while Colonel General Alfred Jodl, Hitler's chief of operations staff, who had to act on it first, was allowed to go on sleeping. Nor did anyone awaken the Führer, who had only recently retired to bed with a sleeping draft; his Naval aide-de-camp, Admiral Karl Jesko von Puttkamer, feared "that if I woke him at this time he might start one of his endless nervous scenes which often led to the wildest decisions." And no one disturbed Field Marshal Rommel at his home in Herrlingen until shortly after 6 a.m.

At about 6:30, as the Allied seaborne landings were beginning, Jodl finally woke up. He was furious to learn of Rundstedt's "arbitrary employment" of the Strategic Reserves without Hitler's approval. Jodl maintained that it was wrong to commit the Strategic Reserves before the Allies' intentions were known; the airborne landings in Normandy, he said, might be a trick to divert German attention from what appeared to be a much larger assault aimed at the Pas-de-Calais. Jodl countermanded Rundstedt's order deploying the Strategic Reserves.

Jodl's command marked one of the decisive moments of the War. It meant—as Rundstedt's operations officer, General Zimmerman, later declared—that "the first critical day was lost! The success of the invasion was already decided!"

In Normandy dawn was coming. The survivors of the British 6th Airborne lay quiet in their positions between the banks of the Dives and the Orne. They turned their blackened faces to the south and the east, toward the advancing enemy. At Ranville the last antitank guns were manhandled into place. On the grounds of General Gale's château headquarters, the paratroopers carved out their last trenches with plastic explosives. The general, who had left for a quick inspection of the captured bridges, came bowling back in his jeep. As he strode inside, Gale was overheard muttering to himself, quoting lines from Shakespeare spoken by King Henry V before the battle of Agincourt: "And gentlemen in England now a'bed / Shall think themselves accursed they were not here."

Some 50 miles to the West, the men of the 101st Airborne were still fighting scattered skirmishes beside hedgerows and along the coastal roads. In and around Sainte-Mère-Eglise, the isolated regiment of the 82nd Airborne was preparing to defend the town against counterattack. But many American paratroopers heard nothing more important than the kick start of a German motorbike and the occasional crack of a sniper's rifle in the distance.

Then, in the faint first light of dawn, the British paratroopers and later the American paratroopers heard a new sound. The entire 50-mile invasion front was rocked by a rumbling, concussive roar as the guns of Allied warships opened up a continuous bombardment of the German coastal defenses and artillery batteries. At Ranville, the earth trembled and women screamed. Huge 15-inch shells were roaring their way overhead heading for targets 10 miles inland. At the Caen Canal, a British soldier exclaimed, "Cor, what next? They're firing jeeps!"

At German strong point W5 above Utah Beach, naval shells rained down incessantly in a deafening barrage. They blew up the minefields, filled the trenches with sand, battered the concrete bunkers and covered the Germans inside with fine white dust. The soldiers lay helpless with their hands pressed over their ears.

Suddenly a soldier cried, "Ships!" Second Lieutenant Arthur Jahnke, the strong-point commander, grabbed his telescope and, peering through the gray haze, saw innumerable black hulks—like the silhouettes used in lectures on enemy ship identification. Jahnke gasped at the sight. The sea was full of ships and the air was full of barrage balloons.

Unlike their High Command, the German soldiers along the beaches of Normandy had no doubt about what was happening. The day of invasion had come.

YANKS IN BRITAIN

American servicemen, based in Britain for the long-awaited invasion of France, amble past Buckingham Palace on a sightseeing tour through fogbound London.

THE GI OCCUPATION OF ENGLAND

Dear old England's not the same,
The dread invasion, well it came.
But no, it's not the beastly Hun,
The G-- D--- Yankee Army's come.

This rude anti-American verse, from a wartime British ballad titled "Lament of a Limey Lass," embarrassed many proper Englishmen, who had no desire to offend their allies. Yet the verse—and the others on the following pages—contained more than a kernel of truth. By May 1944, Britain had been inundated by some 1.5 million U.S. soldiers brought over for the invasion. They were billeted in more than 100,000 British buildings in some 1,100 locations, mainly—the Scots were relieved to note—in southern England. The Yanks were frightfully brash by British standards, and without a by-your-leave they turned staid London into the boisterous GI capital of the world. "On some streets," said American war correspondent Ernie Pyle, "an Englishman stood out as incongruously as he would in North Platte, Nebraska."

Even on their best behavior the Yanks caused tensions. An American private earned nearly five times more than his British counterpart, and he spent his pay freely (and often successfully) on British women. British soldiers considered this unfair competition, and their resentment was presently captured by a Cockney comedian who coined a phrase that swept the country. There were only three things wrong with the Yanks, he said: they were "overpaid, oversexed and over here."

But the problems caused by the collision of two cultures proved to be much less serious than the Allied commanders had feared. Most Englishmen genuinely liked the Americans and welcomed them into their homes. They appreciated the Americans' generosity in handing out candy bars and chewing gum to sweets-starved British youngsters. They enjoyed the free-and-easy air that the Americans brought to British pubs, dance halls and quiet country towns. The infectious gaiety of the GIs was "as good as tonic," one Englishman said, and "for a while the people forgot about the war."

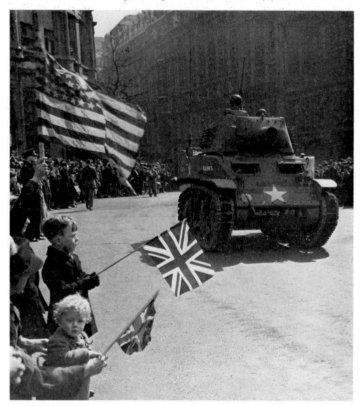

In a show of Allied solidarity, children in a crowd of English civilians wave American and British flags during an American military parade in London.

U.S. airmen and a British woman pose unsubtly for a publicity picture, flaunting favors from a British party thrown to promote Anglo-American relations.

In front of a country pub, GIs cultivate a taste for British beer. At first some American soldiers found the brew so tasteless that they added salt for flavor.

A LIBERAL EDUCATION IN FOREIGN FOLKWAYS

They moan about our lukewarm beer—
Think beer's like water over here,
And after drinking three or four
We find them lying on the floor.

Flat, warm British beer was only one of many local peculiarities that the Americans taught themselves to put up with—if not to like. They learned to drive on the left side of the road and to eat fish and chips out of last week's newspaper. They also learned British English: e.g., that a copper was a penny, not a policeman, that a vest was not an outer garment but an undershirt. And the GI billeted in a boarding-house learned not to laugh when his land-lady promised to "knock him up"—i.e., waken him—in the morning.

The GIs never did learn to like the British wartime diet of mutton, boiled kidneys, Brussels sprouts, tea, and coffee that tasted like mud. This fare depressed the Americans so much that steaks, bananas, tomatoes and other solid American food had to be imported from the States. A GI sergeant later said, "I think the first shipment of peanut butter saved our lives."

An English hostess introduces a visiting American soldier to a British institution: afternoon tea.

An adventuresome GI tries his hand at darts, which was new to most Yanks. The soldiers' interest in the classic British pub game was heightened by betting.

At Tussaud's, GIs and WACs admire wax figures of famous Americans.

A Yeoman warder points out sections of interest in the Tower of London.

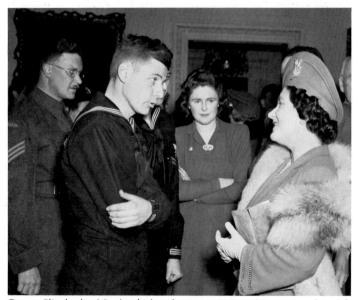

Queen Elizabeth of England plays hostess to U.S. sailors at a London club.

At Stonehenge in southern England, American servicemen take a lesson in local prehistory from a British guide during a break in their training maneuvers.

SEEING THE SIGHTS IN A WAR ZONE

They swarm in every train and bus,
There isn't room for both of us.
We walk to let them have our seats,
Then get run over by their jeeps.

Off-duty GI sightseers overcrowded all of the British transportation facilities as they spread out through the country individu-ally, in small groups or on large, orga-nized tours. Some of them visited quaint old English towns. A few made pilgrimages in search of ancestral homes or the haunts of famous English authors. Swarms of GIs visited London landmarks—and were of-ten admitted first, to the dismay of British tourists already waiting in line. In London, Madame Tussaud's Wax Museum was the Americans' favorite, and to repay their pa-tronage the museum added to the exhibit the figures of 14 U.S. Presidents, Generals Eisenhower and MacArthur, and Admiral Harold Stark *(top left).*

Some GIs were insensitive to Britain's historical sites. One sergeant, unimpressed by Scarborough Castle, an imposing ruin overlooking the sea, told a British family that "it was a waste of a marvelous site for a hotel" and ought to be pulled down. But every American was moved by one tour set up by the Army to introduce newly arrived GIs to the realities of war: they were taken to see Britain's bomb-ravaged areas.

113

"Don't forget, Beryl—the response is 'Hiya, fellers!' and a sort of nonchalant wave of the hand."

"They won't let on who the camp is for."

"Those guys just don't know there's a war on!"

"TAXI!"

"Dear Momma, in England they drive on the left side of the road . . ."

"Doris sends her love and has asked me to play 'Deep in the Heart of Texas' as a reminder of them all at Shepherd's Bush."

"DOING ANYTHING TONIGHT, BABY ?"

"Making it look like home"   STRUBE in *Daily Express*

During the War, British cartoons on the subject of ubiquitous American GIs ranged in tone from good-natured joshing to barely suppressed bitterness.

JAUNDICED VIEWS OF THE BOISTEROUS ALLIES

Yanks say they've come to shoot and fight,
It's true they fight . . . yes—when they're tight.
I must admit their shooting's fine,
They shoot a damn good Yankee line.

To British cartoonists, the GI seemed more interested in winning a woman than in winning the War. However, the newspaper editors culled cartoons that seemed offensively anti-American. It was just as well, for some that got printed were biting enough. One cartoon (*left, bottom right*) attacked the Yanks' un-British aggressiveness: U.S.

airmen forced down in Germany hail a cab and start operating just as if they own the place. In another cartoon that was unkind to the soldiers of both nations (*top, left*), British overseas troops, listening to a BBC program, hear an English girl ask the disc jockey to play an American song for her conveniently located GI boyfriend.

London's Rainbow Corner, the largest American service club in England, attracted thousands of fun-seeking GIs and also brigades of Piccadilly prostitutes.

COURTSHIP AMERICAN STYLE

And you should see them try to dance,
They find a partner—start to prance.
When we're half dead, they stop and smile,
How'm I doin', Honey Chile?

Many an English "Honey Chile" wanted to go out with GIs and engage in a form of athletic dancing they called jitterbugging. The young couples did this terpsichore to the music of visiting USO bands: Cab Calloway's, Artie Shaw's and Glen Miller's.

They did it in crowded British pubs, American Red Cross clubs and especially in London's GI club, Rainbow Corner, near Piccadilly Circus.

But what the GIs really liked to do best was make time with British women. They flattered their dates incessantly and plied them with nylon stockings, bottles of perfume and scented soap—wartime luxuries that were obtainable in England only at the American post exchanges. "We felt like queens," recalled one English woman. The GIs were notoriously vigorous in pressing their suit. When a new panty appeared on the market it naturally inspired the

popular joke: "One yank and they're off!"

The results of the American-British affairs became conspicuous. So many British women were put in a family way that clinics and welfare organizations found it difficult to keep accurate statistics. Uncounted GIs pestered their commanders for permission to marry, and thousands actually applied for marriage licenses (70,000 British women eventually went to the U.S. as war brides). But whether an affair was serious or casual, it came to a sudden pause when the camps were sealed and the GIs were denied communication with their women. D-Day was about to begin.

Inside Rainbow Corner, GIs found a dance hall, game room, library, jukeboxes, barbershop, lounges, an American snack bar and attractive British volunteers.

A GI and his date embrace in London's Hyde Park, one of many public places where American soldiers and their British girl friends tried to find a little privacy.

And then he leaves you broken-hearted,
The camp has moved—your love departed.
You wait for mail that doesn't come,
Then realize you're awfully dumb.

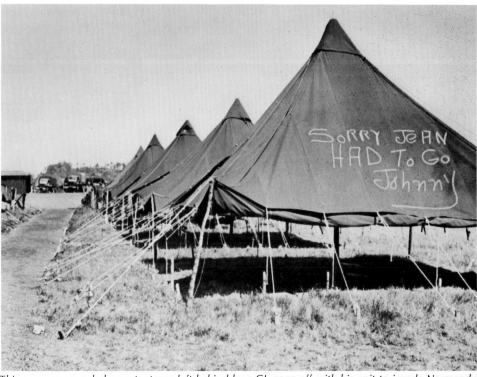

This message scrawled on a tent was left behind by a GI, gone off with his unit to invade Normandy.

THE INVASION ARMADA

At an English port, a motorized artillery unit bound for Normandy rolls up ramps into cavernous landing ships. The invasion fleet was ready days ahead of time.

UNLEASHING THE COILED SPRING

By June 1, 1944, at ports and beaches all around the British Isles, the more than 170,000 soldiers of the assault wave and the 5,000 ships of the D-Day armada were braced for the invasion of Normandy. To the Allied Supreme Commander, General Eisenhower, the mighty expedition was like a "great human spring, coiled for the moment when its energy should be released and it would vault the English Channel in the greatest amphibious assault ever attempted."

In fact that moment lasted three days, starting on June 3, when the first ships pulled out of their ports. By nightfall on June 5 the fleet had assembled 13 miles southeast of the Isle of Wight for the journey across the Channel. Minesweepers led the armada, followed by warships, freighters, landing vessels, swarms of tugs and, among the troop transports, converted yachts and luxury liners.

For the soldiers on board, the choppy voyage was tense and interminable. Seasick men groaned at railside while belowdecks troops with strong stomachs enjoyed hearty preinvasion feasts that included roast beef, steak, chicken à la king, peas, plum pudding and ice cream. Some of the men tried in vain to read or sleep; others visited chaplains or wrote last letters home. To dispel somber thoughts, soldiers improvised sports and other types of entertainments. On one ship, men of the 3rd Canadian Division put on a talent show. On H.M.S. *Ben Machree*, U.S. Rangers strung heavy ropes from the masts and amused themselves by swinging across the deck.

The waiting came to an end shortly before dawn on June 6, when the first troops scrambled down cargo-net ladders into landing craft and began the 8- to 11.5-mile run to the beaches. Troops huddled underneath blankets to get out of the cold spray. Many soldiers were now so seasick that they filled their issued vomit bags and began using their steel combat helmets. As the men bobbed about miserably in their assault craft, one of the officers said, "I'll bet they'll be glad to hit the beach." His companion, looking toward the bristling shore, replied: "The poor sons of bitches, they're lucky to be where they are."

Members of the RAF fill barrage balloons with helium before turning them over to the Navy to protect D-Day convoys from German air attack.

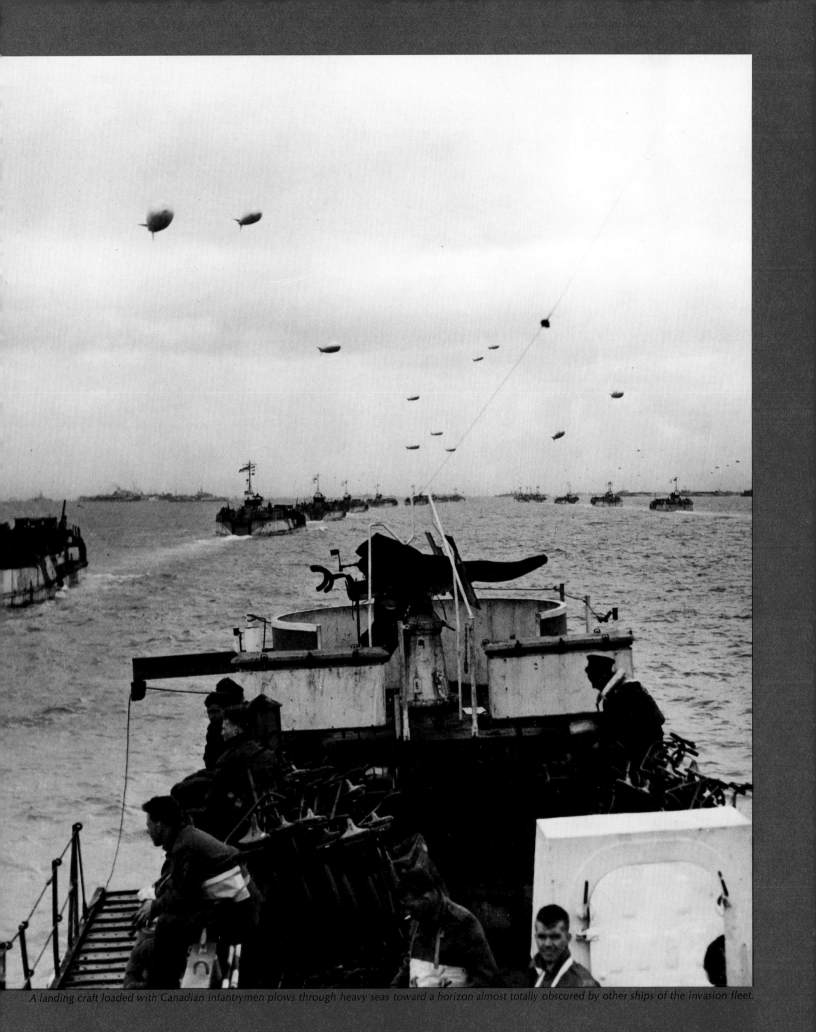

A landing craft loaded with Canadian infantrymen plows through heavy seas toward a horizon almost totally obscured by other ships of the invasion fleet.

Killing time aboard ship en route to Normandy, soldiers relax, ready grenades, play shuffleboard and card games, and even study French from pocket dictionaries

Troops on an invasion barge squeeze in between trucks, cranes and command cars. All told, the fleet ferried 20,111 vehicles to France for the D-Day operation.

In the predawn darkness of D-Day, a Royal Navy cruiser blasts German coastal guns and fortifications. The warships that provided covering fire for the amphibious assault were stationed from three to 14 miles offshore. The long-range guns began their attack two hours before the landings.

Framed by two Americans in steel helmets and life jackets, infantrymen wade through the chest-high surf between landing craft, closing in on Omaha Beach at H-Hour, 6:30 a.m. The skippers of many landing craft were unable to see through the heavy smoke of the bombardment, and they failed to go aground on their assigned sector of the beach.

4

In salvo after salvo, the American and British warships in the Bay of the Seine pounded away at the German fortifications along the 59-mile stretch of Normandy shore. Orange fire from the gun muzzles of fighting ships flashed in the dawn. The battleships and cruisers were standing about six miles out, the smaller, more agile destroyers were less than four miles offshore; and the thunder of their fire rolled up and down the coastline.

Adding to the barrage, thousands of Allied fighters and bombers, flying in over the bay in wave after endless wave, strafed and bombed beaches code-named Utah and Omaha, Gold, Juno and Sword.

As the shells from the battleships and cruisers roared overhead, the spray-soaked and seasick U.S. assault troops surged toward shore. The Americans were leading off the seaborne attack with landings by the 4th Division at Utah, the westernmost of the D-Day beaches, and by the 1st Division at Omaha, the next target beach down the twisting coastline. They would hit the beaches, coded into sections (e.g., Easy) and subsections (e.g., Red and Green), at 6:30, H-Hour, one hour after low tide, when the obstacles would be exposed and easier for the engineers to demolish. Farther east on the British beaches, where the tide came in later, H-Hour at Gold, Juno and Sword was set for 7:30.

In the clumsy U.S. landing craft plunging and bucking through choppy seas toward the Normandy shore, soldiers heard the reassuring drone of the bombers and the snarl of the fighters, and through holes in the low cloud cover they caught glimpses of massed formations of warplanes. From the distant shoreline came the rumble of exploding bombs. These sights and sounds gave hope to the men about to face the defenses of the Atlantic Wall. It seemed inconceivable to them that either the enemy or his weapons could survive such a monumental bombardment.

Over Utah Beach, 269 Marauder medium bombers of the U.S. Ninth Air Force, flying low beneath the clouds, took visual aim on seven German defenses on the beach and dropped 4,404 two-hundred-fifty-pound bombs on them.

At one of these defenses, German strong point W5 on the dunes at the southern end of the beach, Second Lieutenant Arthur Jahnke and his men huddled in their shelters as the American bombs hit the dunes and buried them in sand. The lieutenant had barely dug himself out when a

AMERICAN LANDINGS

destroyer moved out of a line of U.S. warships and began shelling the strong point with murderously accurate salvos. Jahnke's world exploded and flew apart, and when the bombardment moved inland, he found that many of his men were dead and that his guns, flamethrowers and telephone switchboard were all destroyed. Against the landing craft already streaming shoreward in a long line abreast, Jahnke's shattered strong point could muster only two machine guns, one mortar and the soldiers' rifles. Half stunned by the bombardment, the survivors took up their positions. Behind the first wave of landing craft they could see many others speeding toward the shallows. The Germans of W5 waited for the storm to break.

Among the American assault troops was the oldest man and the only general to land on the beach in any of the initial waves on D-Day. Fifty-seven-year-old Brigadier General Theodore Roosevelt, assistant division commander with the U.S. 4th Division, was an extraordinary soldier by any standard. Eldest son of President Teddy Roosevelt, and a cousin of Franklin D. Roosevelt, the general had already participated in landings in North Africa, Sicily and Corsica. A small, wrinkled man with a fibrillating heart, an arthritic shoulder and a raucous voice, General Roosevelt was renowned for his courage under fire and his easy-going, affectionate relations with his men. Though too old for amphibious combat, Roosevelt had persuaded General Bradley, the commander of the U.S. First Army, to let him take part in the D-Day landings "to steady the boys." Armed with only a pistol and a walking stick, the little general had a reassuring effect on the scared and seasick young soldiers of the first assault wave, and he was to be an inspiration to everyone under fire that morning.

The first wave of 20 landing craft approached the southern end of Utah Beach at full speed. To the men of the 4th Division the straight, featureless shore was almost invisible under the clouds of smoke and sand raised by the naval barrage. When the first wave was only 300 to 400 yards from the beach, the assault company commanders fired smoke signals into the air, and instantly the support craft raised their fire from the beach. There was a brief period of uncanny quiet. At 6:31, almost exactly on H-Hour, 10 landing craft lowered their ramps and the 300 men of the 2nd

Battalion of the 8th Infantry Regiment—the first amphibious assault troops to land in France on D-Day—walked off into the waist-deep water and waded through 100 yards of the surf to the dry sand beyond. A few minutes later the 10 landing craft carrying the 1st Battalion of the 8th Infantry Regiment touched down to the right. The tide was a long way out, and in front of the soldiers lay a stretch of firm, gently shelving yellow sands 500 yards wide, strewn with beach obstacles and surmounted by a 100-yard belt of low dunes. The men were elated. They brandished their rifles in the air and shouted to one another. To the surprise of everyone, there was little response from the Germans.

There were several reasons for the sparse opposition. Many of the Germans had been killed and their guns destroyed by the preliminary bombardment, and the survivors were too numbed and demoralized to man their posts when the Americans landed. And the Americans, to their good fortune, had landed in the wrong place. The smoke and dust of the naval bombardment had obscured landmarks on the shore, and a strong lateral current running off the beach had forced the boats off course. Instead of landing at their intended site, where the Germans happened to have two powerful batteries, the assault boats came ashore some 2,000 yards farther south, in an area where the enemy defenses were much weaker.

Moreover, 28 duplex-drive (DD), 33-ton Sherman tanks floated ashore in their inflatable canvas covers with the first waves. The Germans had not expected armor to rise out of the sea against them. When Lieutenant Jahnke first saw the tanks, they seemed like immense floating boxes several meters high, drifting slowly toward the land. Only when they climbed out of the water and moved up the beach, deflating their canvas covers and revealing their turrets and guns, did the horrified Jahnke recognize them for what they were.

The tanks opened fire on strong point W5. They knocked out one machine-gun nest and a mortar. A German lance corporal named Friedrich, in an old French tank, shot up a landing craft of Army engineers and kept the American infantry pinned down at the waterline with his machine gun. Then his tank was hit in the turret, with a sound like a church bell cracking. As a last resort Jahnke decided to launch a secret weapon against the advancing American tanks: remote-controlled, unmanned miniature tanks about

three feet high and capable of carrying 200 pounds of dynamite a distance of 600 yards before being detonated by radio. But the bombardment had upset the delicate electronic circuitry of the Goliaths, as they were known, and they could not be directed near their targets. The little tanks crawled about aimlessly and then lay still on the shore. The Americans found the tanks amusing oddities, but when a group of them wedged a hand grenade in one it blew up like a bomb and tore them to pieces.

To the invaders the lightness of the German opposition was gratifying but the configuration of the beach was puzzling. Where were they exactly? Their maps and plans did not check with what they saw. General Roosevelt, who made a reconnaissance of the rear beach area, was the first to find out their true position and quickly helped the two assault battalion commanders improvise an attack plan to conform with the terrain confronting them.

To the Americans the W5 strong point, which guarded the beach road running inland to the village of Sainte-Marie-du-Mont, was the most troublesome of the German defenses on Utah. Led by General Roosevelt, they launched a 600-man charge across the beach toward the strong point. Crouched in the lee of the antitank wall at the back of the beach, they blew holes in the wall to let the tanks through. To Lieutenant Jahnke the next few minutes were like a dream. Out of the corner of his eye he was aware of the flash of a shell nearby. He felt a blow in the small of his back, and then passed out. When he recovered consciousness he found he was buried under sand and someone was tugging at his legs. Suddenly he was pulled out into the air and light. He looked up and saw that his rescuer was an American soldier.

Wounded, bloody and dusty, Jahnke was taken behind a tank for interrogation. It did not last long. From a grass-covered hill 10 miles away, a German battery began a counterbombardment of Utah Beach. The Americans flung themselves down into the hollows in the sand or against the sides of their tanks as the shells landed among them and shot up great spouts of sand and metal. Jahnke was hit by a piece of shrapnel that tore open his side; his American guard crawled up to him and gave him a cigarette and a gauze dressing from his first-aid kit.

Jahnke was smoking his cigarette, in a state of some shock, when he was ordered to get up. An American general was standing opposite him. Jahnke raised his hand to his bare head in salute. The general half raised his hand to salute him back, then changed his mind. He lowered his hand and gave an order that Jahnke did not understand. Then the young German lieutenant was led away from the war, down the beach to a waiting landing craft and captivity in England.

After he ordered Jahnke to the rear, General Roosevelt stomped up and down, oblivious to the shellfire, his cane in his hand, waving a map as if he were looking for land to buy. He had a tough decision to make. He could divert all succeeding waves of the 4th Division to this new, relatively calm stretch of beach. But only one road led inland. Thirty thousand men and 3,500 vehicles were scheduled to land at Utah during the day. If the road could not be kept open, the beach would become hopelessly glutted with men and machines—easy prey for a German counterattack. Roosevelt could, on the other hand, march his troops up the beach to the original assault area. But there the exit road inland was fiercely defended by German strong points. Troops landing there, according to plan, were being cut to pieces by enemy fire.

Roosevelt conferred briefly with his battalion commanders and made his decision. He would try to capitalize on the felicitous error and commence the invasion of France from the wrong place. He would, in his own words, "start the war from here."

Roosevelt's gamble paid off. His rapid move inland deepened the beachhead and cleared the area for the fresh assault waves piling up on the shore. (On July 12, just after General Eisenhower appointed him commanding general of the 90th Division, General Roosevelt suffered a heart attack and died. He was buried at Sainte-Mère-Eglise, just six miles from Utah Beach, and was posthumously awarded the Medal of Honor.)

By the time that the Germans were able to adjust their fire to the more southerly beach, the landings on Utah Beach had gathered uncheckable momentum. Four hundred men from the Naval-demolition and Army-engineer teams had come in on the heels of the assault waves and within an hour had blown up the German beach obstacles and bull-

In this aerial view of Utah Beach, American infantrymen swarm ashore during the first minutes of the invasion. On the beach (bottom), men sprawl in the sand, some already dead or wounded, while others wade in through the surf. The two large vessels at top right, some 300 yards offshore, are LCTs that have just unloaded the tanks seen nearing the shore in an irregular line. The other vessel is a troop-carrying LCI.

dozed a route through them for landing craft to follow.

By 9 a.m. the leading regiment, the 8th Infantry, and the tanks had broken through the Atlantic Wall on a two-mile front between the sea and the lagoons at the back of the dunes. By 10 a.m. the main body of the follow-up regiment was landing with so little trouble it seemed almost like routine training. An endless stream of men, tanks, guns, vehicles and supplies poured onto Utah from the sea. There was little opposition at this end of the beach. The distant German guns kept up a sporadic fire, but they did not loosen the American grip on the beachhead. Noticing that the German guns seemed to be ranging on the barrage balloons that protected the landing craft, one landing-craft commander ordered his balloons cut loose, and as they floated out to sea they were pursued by salvos from the puzzled German artillery. After that, all of the other balloons were released.

Some of the assault troops at Utah, instead of immediately driving straight inland, swung north and south along the beach to attack the positions that should have been occupied in the initial landing. The Americans desperately needed more routes off the beach, and during the morning they got them. One by one the strong points guarding roads inland, north and south of the original beachhead, fell to the assault troops, and by the end of the morning three exits from the beach were in American hands.

Still, progress was painfully slow. The Germans had made good use of the terrain behind the sand dunes of Utah. There they had flooded a stretch of meadowland usually kept dry for cultivation, thus confining the American flow of men and matériel to the three causeways that traversed the marshy ground. As the Americans pushed westward and southwestward over the causeways, aiming to link up with the hard-pressed 101st and 82nd Airborne forces then struggling to capture key coastal villages, German shells knocked out vehicles, creating massive traffic jams and slowing the American surge to a crawl. But American casualties remained remarkably light. By the end of the day, only 197 soldiers who landed on Utah had been killed or wounded; 60 were missing, presumed drowned.

Just southeast of Utah, a much fiercer battle was under way on the wild, four-mile-long crescent beach between the towns of Vierville-sur-Mer and Colleville-sur-Mer. What happened there early on June 6, 1944, made Omaha one of the immortal names of American military history, as valiant and as terrible as Guadalcanal, Tarawa and Iwo Jima. On Omaha Beach was fought the bloodiest and the most desperate battle of D-Day. It was there that the Germans came nearest to throwing the invaders back into the sea.

Omaha Beach was not a good place for an amphibious assault. At either end it was dominated by sheer cliffs 100 feet high. The beach, 300 yards across at low tide, shelved gently up to a steep bank of coarse pebbles, impassable to vehicles in most places. The pebble bank was backed by a combination of sand dunes and sea wall, also impassable to vehicles.

Behind the dunes lay a level shelf of sand, marsh and coarse high grass. From there the ground sloped up to a farmland plateau 150 feet high. Only four exits led inland from Omaha Beach—three were cart tracks, the fourth a paved roadway; all wound through deep, thickly wooded

The ill-starred infantrymen of A Company, 116th Regiment, 29th Division gathered for a group picture at Fort Meade, Maryland, in 1941. Three years later, within 10 minutes of their D-Day landing on Omaha Beach, an estimated 96 per cent of the company's 197 men were killed or wounded—one of the highest casualty rates of the Normandy invasion. Particularly hard hit was a group of 35 men from the small town (total population 3,800) of Bedford, Virginia. Twenty of them perished.

ravines in the plateau (usually referred to as "draws" in American military reports because of their resemblance to the dry watercourses of the American West). Each track led to one or another of the stout little stone villages on the Isigny–Port-en-Bessin coast road, which ran along the cultivated edge of the high plateau approximately one mile inland. The westernmost track led to Vierville, the easternmost to Colleville, the two in the middle to Saint-Laurent-sur-Mer. Fortified by the Germans, each village blocked the Americans' only routes off Omaha.

The Germans had made the geography of Omaha even more difficult for the Americans. The beach between the low and the high watermark had been thickly planted with mined obstacles: upright iron frames called Belgian Gates, a 10-foot-deep line of heavy wooden stakes angled toward the sea and steel hedgehogs angled to stave in the bottoms of landing craft. Thus the troops of the first waves, who landed at low tide, would have to advance on foot up a beach that offered no cover from fire other than the mined obstacles until they reached the relative shelter of the pebble bank at the top of the beach.

Immediately above the pebble bank the Germans had constructed a thick barricade of coiled barbed wire. Beyond this, the flat shelf of sand and marsh between the beach and the escarpment beneath the high plateau was heavily mined and crosscut with antitank ditches. The Germans had sited their weapons so that no inch of Omaha Beach was left uncovered by fire. From the cliffs at either end of the beach, high-velocity 75mm and 88mm guns, protected by concrete walls three feet thick, could pour flanking fire over the entire beach. Defensive strong points were sited on the slope above the whole stretch of the beach, especially near the entrance to the draws.

Each strong point was a complex system of pillboxes, gun casemates, mortar pits, firing trenches and open positions for light pieces of artillery and antitank guns, surrounded by wire and minefields and connected to one another and to underground bunkers and magazines by tunnels and deep trenches. The machine gun was the basic weapon of the German emplacements at Omaha Beach, but the defenders could also bring to bear multibarreled rocket launchers, obsolete French tanks sunk flush with the ground and heavy infantry mortars in concrete pits.

The German defenses at Omaha were among the worst encountered by the Americans in the entire War. And the beach defenses were only the first line. The string of villages behind Omaha formed a second line of defense. The flooded valley of the River Aure, about four miles farther inland, formed a third line, which the Americans would have to traverse if they were to avoid being bottled up in the narrow coastal strip. The Americans would never have dreamed of landing at Omaha if there had been anywhere else to land. But along the 20-mile stretch of coast between Utah and the British beaches there was nowhere else—only sheer cliffs and rocky offshore reefs.

Along with the unfriendly terrain and formidable defenses, a sudden shift of German troops had worsened the prospects of the invaders. Up until a week before D-Day, the Americans had not been particularly worried about the quality of the Omaha defenders. Their intelligence reports indicated that the beach lay within a 45-mile stretch of coastline held by the 716th Infantry Division—a nonmobile outfit equipped only for a static role, low in morale, 50 per cent of them foreign conscripts, mostly Polish or Russian. Only 800 to 1,000 men actually manned the beach defenses against the 34,000 Americans who were to land there on D-Day. Those were promising odds. But in the week preceding D-Day Allied intelligence confirmed that the crack German 352nd Infantry Division, a mobile unit battle-hardened on the Eastern Front, had moved up from Saint-Lô to stiffen the crust of the coastal sector that included Omaha Beach. This information was received too late to pass on to the American assault troops already on their way to the area. They went into action believing that Omaha was weakly manned, even if strongly fortified.

To make matters worse, the Americans committed costly errors in their D-Day planning. The commander of the American task force, Rear Admiral Alan G. Kirk, rejected the advice of Admiral Sir Bertram H. Ramsay, the overall Allied Naval Commander in Chief, to anchor the American transports within eight miles of the shore. Anxious to keep his transports out of range of German coastal batteries, Admiral Kirk instead anchored them 11 to 12 miles offshore—where the wind-whipped seas were running far too rough for the clumsy landing craft.

Furthermore, the U.S. Army ignored lessons learned by the Canadians during the Dieppe raid—the need to avoid frontal attacks on fortified objectives and the need for close armored support for infantry in the first minutes of a landing. The American commanders also rejected as unproven the specialized armor—the mine-clearing tanks, the flamethrower tanks and the pillbox-busting tanks—developed by the 79th British Armored Division to deal with beach obstacles and fortifications while under fire. And though some floating DD tanks were allocated for the Omaha assault, they were too few in number and were cast afloat too far from the shore. The unfortunate soldiers of the 1st Division, one of the Army's toughest and most experienced outfits, were in effect required to carry out a frontal assault on a fortified position with little but light weapons to help them. And the engineers were expected to clear gaps, dismantle obstacles, demolish roadblocks and lift mines by hand while defenseless and under fire. Under such circumstances it is not surprising that Omaha threatened for a while to develop into an even greater tragedy than Dieppe.

The plan for the Omaha landing called for two regimental combat teams in the initial assault: the 116th Infantry Regiment on the right between Vierville and Saint-Laurent, the 16th Regiment on the left between Saint-Laurent and Colleville. As soon as the teams had gained a foothold on Omaha, the remainder of the 1st and the 29th Divisions of the U.S. V Corps would land. The 29th would clear the area between the coast and the River Aure as far west as the Vire estuary, while the 1st Division would wheel left to link up with the British Second Army at Port-en-Bessin and then drive south to secure a bridgehead over the Aure to the east of Trévières. By nightfall on D-Day the V Corps hoped to have established a beachhead 16 miles wide and six miles deep. Such was the plan.

Almost from the moment of their descent into the sea nearly 12 miles offshore, the troops of the early assault waves ran into trouble. Ten landing craft carrying more than 300 men were swamped by the steep waves, some within a few minutes after launching. Others remained afloat only because their occupants bailed water furiously with their steel helmets. The artillery, transported in DUK-Ws, went wholesale to the bottom. Another tragedy occurred 6,000 yards from the shore when 29 DD tanks were launched from their LCTs to make their own way to the eastern side of Omaha Beach. These tanks could operate in only relatively calm and protected waters, and very quickly their inflated canvas covers began to collapse in the choppy seas. The tanks sank like stones.

Some crewmen managed to escape through the hatches, and they thrashed about in the waves, choking on the salt water. Others sank inside the tanks. Of the 29 tanks, only two reached the shore. Three others, their flotation bags deflated, were beached from an LCT whose damaged ramp could not be lowered at sea. Thus the 16th Infantry landed with almost no armor support. The remaining 32 DD tanks, destined for the 116th Infantry flank on the western sector of Omaha, were not launched because the Army officer in charge wisely considered the sea too rough. He decided to go in and beach them instead.

For those whose landing craft stayed afloat, the approach to the beaches was absolute misery, and for many the only note of encouragement in an otherwise dismal dawn was the booming sound of the battleships flailing away at the enemy shoreline. Novelist and war reporter Ernest Hemingway, who was on board a landing craft bound for Omaha, later described the scene: "As the LCVP rose to the crest of a wave, you saw the line of low, silhouetted cruisers and the two big battlewagons lying broadside to the shore. You saw the heat-bright flashes of their guns and the brown smoke that pushed out against the wind and then blew away.

"Those of our troops who were not wax grey with seasickness, fighting it off, trying to hold onto themselves before they had to grab for the steel side of the boat, were watching the Texas with looks of surprise and happiness.

"There would be a flash like a blast furnace from the 14 inch guns of the Texas, that would lick far out from the ship. Then the yellow brown smoke would cloud out and, with the smoke still rolling, the concussion and the report would

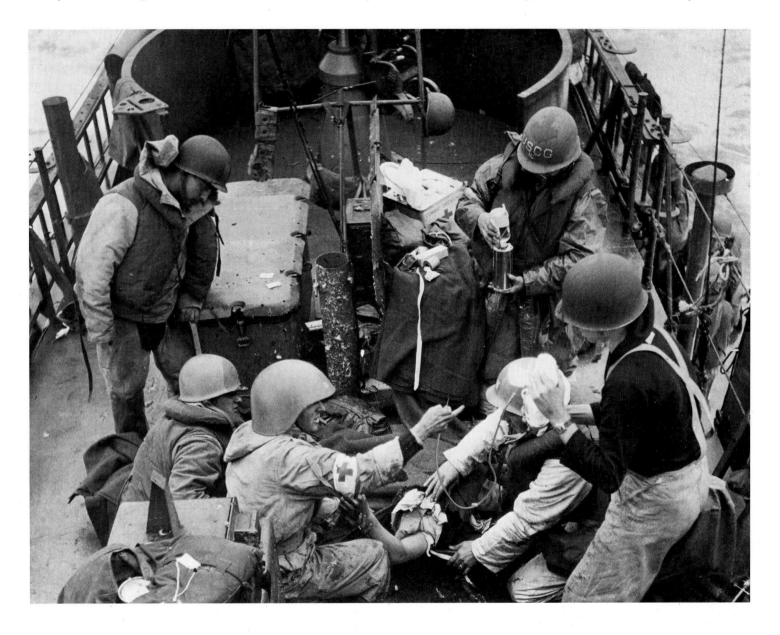

On a shell-battered landing craft off Omaha Beach, a medic gives a blood transfusion to an American crewman wounded too severely to be transferred to a hospital ship. Scattered on the deck around them are fragments from the kapok jackets of other crewmen killed by a shell blast.

hit us, jarring the men's helmets. It struck your ear like a punch with a heavy, dry glove.

"Then up on the green rise of a hill that now showed clearly as we moved in would spout two tall black fountains of earth and smoke.

" 'Look what they're doing to those Germans,' I leaned forward to hear a GI say above the roar of the motor, 'I guess there won't be a man alive there,' he said happily.

"That is the only thing I remember hearing a GI say all that morning."

The men were deceived by the aerial and naval bombardment. The low cloud cover, the dust and the smoke made it impossible to pinpoint targets on the beach. Few bombs or shells fell near German positions, and the salvos from the rocket craft burst in the water short of the beach. The German batteries and strong points came to life as soon as the bombardment lifted, and as the first wave of American assault troops ran in to the shore, they met increasingly heavy fire from enemy guns and artillery. Over the last quarter of a mile it was clear to everyone that enemy fortifications had not been knocked out.

At defensive strong point WN62, located among the sand dunes beside the track that led to Colleville, the German soldier manning the observation post watched carefully as

On Utah Beach after the battle, U.S. Navy demolition experts dismantle German dynamite-laden, radio-controlled dwarf tanks, not one of which had managed to reach its target. This was not the first failure for the minitanks. They had been used against the Allied landing at Anzio, Italy, in February 1944, and 14 had been destroyed by Allied gunners in one day.

the first line of landing craft from the awesome invasion fleet neared the waterline directly in front of him. Lance Corporal Hein Severloh, 21, a farmer from Metzingen, had his fingers curled around the trigger of his machine gun. In the trench on the slope to the left, three more machine guns were manned by the men from the strong-point garrison. In front of the strong point was the mortar pit. Behind the observation post were two more mortar positions. The infantry were dug in forward. Inside the bunker the commander of the site, a Lieutenant Frerking, was on the telephone giving firing instructions to the battery officer at Houteville, five miles inland, where the regiment's 105mm howitzers were positioned. "Wait for the order to fire," he finished. They waited in silence.

The tide had ebbed a long way out and not yet begun to turn. The landing craft sped toward the shore, then lurched to a halt on the sandbars a little beyond the beach. The range was 400 yards.

"Target Dora," Lieutenant Frerking shouted into his telephone, "Fire!"

At 6:30, as their landing craft touched down, the American soldiers heard a prolonged tattoo of machine-gun bullets beating on the ramps, and when the ramps were lowered they saw the surf in front of them whipped by a hail of bullets. Lance Corporal Severloh had squeezed off a long burst that traversed the advancing Americans from one end of the line to the other. An instant later, the howitzer shells from the 1st Battery at Houteville came screaming over, exploding in showers of sand on the beach.

The six boats of Company A of the 116th Infantry tried to land in a cauldron of fire delivered by the German strong point guarding the Vierville exit and by the gun emplacement on the bluff at the western end of the beach. One landing craft foundered 1,000 yards out. Another craft, hit by four shells, disintegrated. The other four boats grounded on a sandbar 30 yards short of the nearest beach obstacles and several hundred yards short of the sea wall, their nearest effective cover. Then the ramps were lowered and the men leaped into water up to six feet deep.

"As the first men jumped," runs the official report of A Company, "they crumpled and flopped into the water. Then order was lost. It seemed to the men that the only way to get ashore was to dive head first in and swim clear of the fire that was striking the boats. But, as they hit the water, their heavy equipment dragged them down and soon they were struggling to keep afloat. Some were hit in the water and wounded. Some drowned then and there. . . . But some moved safely through the bullet-fire to the sand and then, finding they could not hold there, went back into the water and used it as cover, only their heads sticking out. Those who survived kept moving forward with the tide, sheltering at times behind under-water obstacles and in this way they finally made their landings.

"Within ten minutes of the ramps being lowered, A Company had become inert, leaderless and almost incapable of action. Every officer and sergeant had been killed or wounded. . . . It had become a struggle for survival and rescue. The men in the water pushed wounded men ashore, and those who had reached the sands crawled back into the water pulling others to land to save them from drowning, in many cases only to see the rescued men wounded again or to be hit themselves. Within 20 minutes of striking the beach A Company had ceased to be an assault company and had become a forlorn little rescue party bent upon survival and the saving of lives."

The assault on Omaha Beach was a shambles. The Army and Navy engineers who had the crucial task of clearing and marking boat lanes through the beach obstacles suffered appallingly. German shells detonated the explosives packed tightly on the landing-craft decks, blowing the engineers to pieces. Few of the surviving teams landed in the right places, and as a result several of them had no tank or infantry support. Burdened with equipment and explosives, they made easy targets as they struggled ashore, and much of their equipment, especially the buoys and poles for marking the cleared lanes, was lost. Some of the obstacles could not be destroyed because the rising tides had covered them, others because infantrymen were taking shelter behind them. One blew up prematurely when its charges were set off by mortar shells, killing engineers and nearby infantry. In half an hour the engineers could clear only six gaps through the obstacles and just one of those could be marked. In their heroic effort during this bloody day, they suffered 41 per cent casualties.

Meanwhile, the assault troops were being mowed down

at the water's edge or pinned down behind the sea wall or pebble bank at the top of the beach. Some of their personal weapons, and many of their support weapons—bazookas, flamethrowers, mortars—were lost in the chaotic landing. When the subsequent waves came in, German fire was tornadic, and the new arrivals simply contributed to the chaos, augmenting the heaps of dead and the huddles of living soldiers. The losses in the first hour of the assault, particularly opposite the Vierville exit, were awesome.

As the tide crept remorselessly in, the press of men became more concentrated, and along the pebble bank the bodies of the living and the dead eventually formed a solid, motionless belt seven yards wide. Too exhausted and too shocked to move, their units scattered or broken, many of their officers and noncoms killed or wounded, uncertain of their bearings, unsure of where to go or what to do in the face of the unrelenting German fire that hammered around them, the bewildered troops were slow to rally and even slower to move off the beach and advance inland. Succeeding waves of men, support weapons and transport were arriving now, but as there was only one marked channel through the obstacles, some boats blew up when they hit mined stakes underwater, or they were impaled on steel obstacles, where they foundered or became easy targets for the German guns, which blew them out of the water.

Ernest Hemingway, in his landing craft, came into the eastern end of Omaha. The battle was at its height; Hemingway noticed that the tanks were still on the beach. "Just then," he wrote, "one of the tanks flared up and started to burn with thick black smoke and yellow flames. Farther down the beach, another tank started burning. Along the line of the beach, they were crouched like big yellow toads along the high water line. As I stood up, watching, two more started to burn. The first ones were pouring out grey smoke now, and the wind was blowing it flat along the beach. As I stood up, trying to see if there was anyone in beyond the high water line of tanks, one of the burning tanks blew up with a flash in the streaming grey smoke.

"On the beach on the left . . . the first, second, third, fourth and fifth waves lay where they had fallen, looking like so many heavily laden bundles on the flat pebbly stretch between the sea and the first cover. To the right, there was an open stretch where the beach exit led up a wooded valley from the sea. It was here that the Germans hoped to get something very good and later we saw them get it.

"I saw three tanks coming along the beach, barely moving, they were advancing so slowly. The Germans let them cross the open space where the valley opened onto the beach, and it was absolutely flat, with a perfect field of fire. Then I saw a little fountain of water jut up, just over and beyond the lead tank. Then smoke broke out of the leading tank on the side away from us, and I saw two men dive out of the turret and land on their hands and knees on the stones of the beach. They were close enough so that I could see their faces, but no more men came out as the tank started to blaze up and burn fiercely."

On the bridge of the U.S.S. *Augusta* 12.5 miles offshore, General Bradley, commander of the U.S. First Army and overall commander of the American landings on D-Day, watched and waited anxiously. A desperately worried man, he had heard almost no news of the Utah landings, and the few signals he had received from Omaha indicated an impending disaster: wrecked landing craft, burning vehicles, exploding ammunition and continuous German shelling. By 9:00 a.m. the situation looked so bad that Bradley considered abandoning Omaha and transferring the follow-up waves to the British beaches on the Allies' left. Shortly afterward he sent an urgent message to SHAEF, asking permission to use that alternative. This message did not reach SHAEF until so late that it was no longer relevant.

In the midst of all this confusion a few small, isolated groups began to move out of the lee to the pebble bank, and with infinite pains they found a way over the marshy flat behind the beach and up the bluff to the plateau. Several units of the 1st Battalion, 116th Infantry had been set down farther to the east than intended. There the beach was less heavily defended and was obscured from German view by the smoke of vegetation set on fire by the naval bombardment; under cover of this screen they were able to rush off the beach and work their way through the barbed wire and minefields and up the ridge to Vierville, almost half a mile inland. They were joined by a company of the 1st Battalion, which had also landed too far east and had probed an unmined gap between the German strong points.

THE RANGERS' ATTACK ON A CLIFFTOP BATTERY

Early on D-Day morning, 225 Americans of the 2nd Ranger Battalion landed below the cliff at Pointe du Hoc, three miles west of Omaha Beach. Their mission was to scale the 100-foot-high precipice and destroy a coastal battery that Allied intelligence said contained six 155mm German howitzers. These powerful guns had to be prevented from wreaking havoc on the Americans landing at Omaha and the fleet offshore.

The Rangers, defying enemy fire pouring down from above, used rocket guns to shoot grapnels with ropes attached to them into the cliff face. Then they started climbing hand over hand up the face. One by one, they were picked off by German snipers and fell into space. One wounded Ranger slid down his rope, careening off rocks, before he lost his grip. It was, a buddy said later, "a lifetime before his body hit the beach." Other men managed to struggle into crevices in the cliffside.

But more and more Rangers reached the clifftop, and soon they routed the enemy. Only then did they learn—with dismay and outrage—that the howitzers were not in the battery. The Rangers found them hidden a mile inland and destroyed them.

The Rangers paid dearly for their herculean attempt to silence the nonexistent battery. At the end of the day, after the unit had fought off three German counterattacks, only 90 out of the 225 Rangers who had started the climb up the cliff were still able to bear arms.

Rangers occupy a former fortification at Pointe du Hoc, as German defenders are taken captive. The draped flag serves as a marker to prevent Allied shelling.

Before midmorning there were 200 Americans in Vierville—just enough to drive off a German counterattack designed to overrun what was left of the troops pinned down on the beach by the formidable German strong points.

Farther to the east, parts of the 2nd and 3rd Battalions of the 116th Infantry also landed under cover of the unintended smoke screen of burning grass near the draw at Les Moulins. The smoke there was so thick that some troops, in order to reach the crest of the beach, had to put on their gas masks. Others made little progress until they discovered a minefield that had been detonated by the bombardment, and several groups from both battalions were able to work their way over the bluff toward Saint-Laurent before the Germans closed in with shellfire.

On the left flank of Omaha Beach part of the 16th Infantry had been similarly assisted by navigational errors that had set them down half a mile or more east of their planned objectives. They thus side-stepped the formidable German strong points still guarding the entrance to the Colleville draw, which the decimated first wave was to have stormed, and instead found a way up the steep but weakly defended gully in the cliffs that bound Omaha Beach at its eastern end. By 9:30 a.m. they had breached the German defenses at this point and were moving steadily eastward along the top of the cliffs toward Port-en-Bessin, where they were supposed to link up with the British invasion force.

On their right, men of the 1st and 2nd Battalions of the 16th had enjoyed no such good fortune. Most of them had been chopped to pieces by the guns of the Colleville draw. Some lay motionless beneath the crest of the beach, pinned down by the German fire.

A courageous lieutenant and a wounded sergeant eventually got the men up and moving. Standing up under fire, the lieutenant and the sergeant walked over to inspect the barbed-wire entanglement above the pebble bank, then walked back and looked down at the men, hands on hips. "Are you going to lay there and get killed," the lieutenant asked, "or get up and do something about it?" No one moved. So the lieutenant and the sergeant went back to the wire, still under fire, and blew a gap through it themselves. This rallied the men, and in single file they followed their officer over the ridge along a narrow, mined track where a false step meant death or injury. Many were the false steps, and the wounded lay where they fell, for fear of setting off other mines, while the rest of the column stepped over them and moved on. Through this dangerous gap, which claimed many casualties, 300 men eventually passed through the German defenses en route toward Colleville.

The bulk of the American troops were nevertheless still stuck on the beach when at 9:50 a.m., on board his headquarters ship, Major General Clarence R. Huebner, commander of the 1st Division, received a message from them: "There are too many vehicles on the beach; send combat troops. 30 LCTs waiting off shore; cannot come in because of shelling. Troops dug in on beaches, still under heavy fire." If Huebner's troops did not break out from the beach quickly, further reinforcements from the German 352nd Division might tip the balance and overrun the American positions. Huebner took drastic measures at once. He interrupted the meticulous flow of material to the beach and ordered the follow-up regiment, the 18th Infantry, to go in and more DD tanks to be put straight down on the beach. At the same time he called on the Navy to punch out the German strong points and batteries even at the risk of hitting his own men.

On board the battleship *Texas*, Rear Admiral C. F. Bryant, acting on Huebner's request, exhorted gun crews on his ships over the radio: "Get on them, men! Get on them! They're raising hell with the men on the beach, and we can't have any more of that! We must stop it!" The destroyers swept in close to the beach, some coming into waters so shoal that only a few inches separated keel and bottom. All morning they fired, and well into the afternoon. Their sterns occasionally touched the sandy bottom as they came in and turned to deliver their salvos. Their fire was almost the only artillery support most of the troops saw that day, and it filled the gap caused by the loss of many of the DD tanks and the DUK-Ws carrying the Army guns.

By 11 a.m. the battle was beginning to go in the Americans' favor. Colonel George A. Taylor, commanding the 16th Infantry, yelled across the beach: "Two kinds of people are staying on this beach, the dead and those who are going to die. Now let's get the hell out of here!" He then led his troops forward to attack the German positions. At 1:30 p.m. General Bradley on board the *Augusta* received a report from V Corps: "Troops formerly pinned down on beaches Easy Red, Easy Green, Fox Red now advancing up heights beyond beaches." Overwhelming reinforcements of men and matériel began to wear the German defenders down. At the main exits fresh troops and new tanks captured the German strong points weakened by bombardment from the destroyers, and the engineers were clearing the minefields. But the Americans still had to advance inland and deepen their front before the day was won.

As it turned out, they were assisted by the German 84th Corps' lack of detailed information about the Omaha engagement. Communications had been broken by the bombardment, and the paltry information that General Marcks, the 84th Corps commander, received from the invasion front indicated that his troops in the British sector were more hard pressed than the 352nd Division at Omaha. The armored reserves that might have made all the difference to the outcome at Omaha were consequently pitched against the British, who in the meantime had landed on the beaches code-named Gold, Juno and Sword. At 1:35 p.m. General Marcks was erroneously informed by the 352nd Division's chief of staff that the invasion had been thrown back into the sea, and Rommel's headquarters were therefore informed that "the situation in the area of 352nd Division is now restored."

The available 352nd Division reserves were squandered during the course of the day on repeated counterattacks against three companies of U.S. Rangers, around 200 men in all, who at 7:00 a.m., in a bold stroke, had scaled the 100-foot sheer cliffs at the Pointe du Hoc (page 139) and had captured the German battery whose big guns, it was thought, would have commanded both the Utah and Omaha fleet anchorages. The guns, some damaged by the bombardment, were found to be unmanned and were put out of action by a Ranger patrol of two men. But the Rangers, hard pressed for the rest of the day, successfully held out against German forces that otherwise might have inflicted serious reversals on the main American assault force at Omaha.

Ninety minutes after landing on Omaha's left bank, the follow-up regiment, the 18th Infantry, reached the seaward edge of Colleville to reinforce some companies of the 16th Infantry that were fighting a house-to-house battle in the village. It was late afternoon before vehicles could move off the beach, and not until the evening did a few tanks and howitzers arrive in Colleville to support the infantry. Shortly before nightfall the resolute troops of the U.S. 1st Division penetrated the Germans' second line of defense along the Colleville–Saint-Laurent road, pushing their front line to the south and east of the coast road and extending their beachhead to between one and one and a half miles inland—a remarkable achievement for men who had been so badly drubbed in the morning. A short way down that coast road to the west, two infantry regiments and an artillery battalion of the 29th Division, after clearing Vierville, hung on grimly to the outskirts of Saint-Laurent.

By dark, V Corps held a beachhead six miles long and not even two miles deep. Its hold was precarious. The minefields were not completely cleared; German mortars and artillery still harassed the beach; there was a grave shortage of tanks and guns and the troops were in a seriously weakened condition after a bloody and exhausting day in which they had sustained some 3,000 casualties.

Whether the Americans were at Omaha to stay depended on what the German defenders could throw against them in the night and in the days to follow. And that, in turn, depended on the fortunes of the British battling it out on Gold, Juno and Sword.

ORDEAL AT OMAHA

A GI, his form blurred by photographer Robert Capa's movement, crawls under fire toward Omaha Beach. Poking up at rear are German antiboat obstacles.

STALKING DEATH WITH A CAMERA

These 10 historic D-Day pictures, taken at Omaha Beach by LIFE photographer Robert Capa, survived an accident that destroyed many more.

"If your pictures aren't good," Robert Capa often used to say, "you're not close enough." Certainly Capa got close enough to the action on June 6, 1944. The veteran combat photographer, who had covered the Spanish Civil War and the World War II campaigns in North Africa and Italy for LIFE, was in the first wave to head for the Easy Red sector of Omaha Beach.

At 6:31 a.m., when Capa left his landing craft with a rifle company of the 16th Infantry Division, he knew that he was risking his life. But he did not have death on his mind. He was thinking "very much of getting the best pictures of the day." His first impression was that "my beautiful France looked sordid and uninviting." The Germans' invasion obstacles had turned the pleasant shoreline into "the ugliest beach in the whole world." To reach the sand, he and the riflemen had to traverse some 100 yards of tidal flats in the face of machine-gun fire. As the bullets "tore holes in the water" around him, Capa kept shooting pictures furiously. He headed for the protection of a burned-out amphibious tank and reached it "between floating bodies." Then as the tide came in, he made it to the beach and threw himself on the sand.

Now began a savage mortar bombardment that pinned down the Americans. Capa felt "a new kind of fear shaking my body from toe to hair, and twisting my face." He attempted to reload his camera, but could not, his hands were trembling so. "I did not think and I didn't decide it," he wrote later. He stood up and he ran toward an incoming landing craft. "I knew that I was running away. I tried to turn, but couldn't face the beach." As he climbed on board, he felt an explosion. "The skipper was crying. His assistant had been blown up all over him, and he was a mess." Capa turned and took one more photograph of the beach. He had made 106 pictures in all.

His three rolls of film were rushed to LIFE's London office for processing. There a darkroom technician, eager for glimpses of the landing, dried the film too fast. The excessive heat melted the emulsion and ruined all but 10 frames.

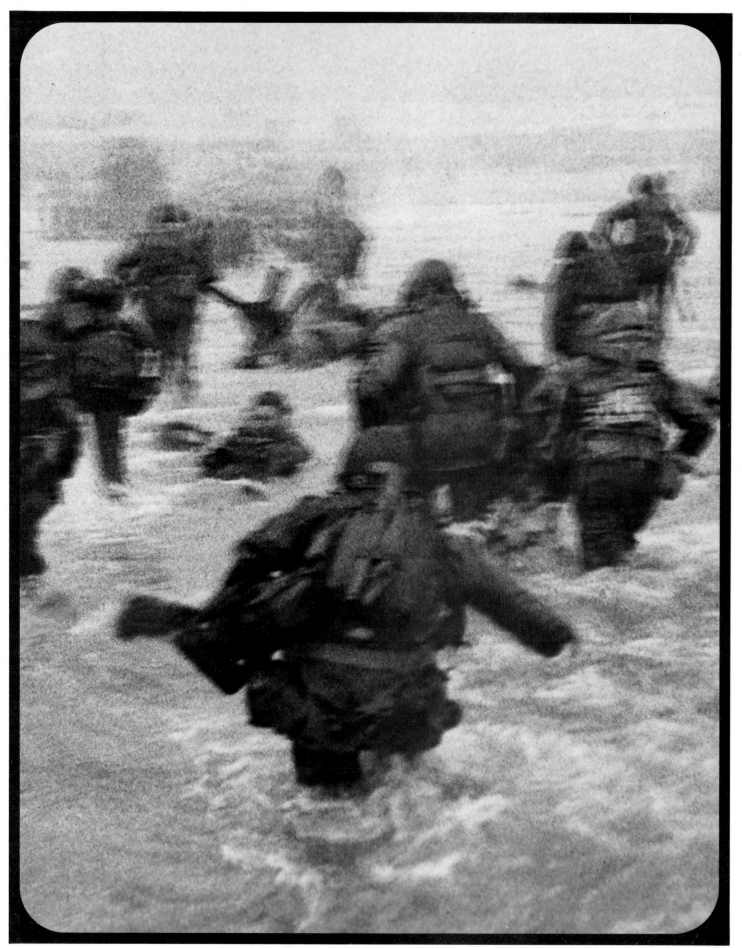

Slogging through the surf past a fallen comrade, a company of American riflemen struggles toward the beach between bursts of enemy machine-gun fire.

Stopped by deadly fire from bluffs overlooking the beach, invaders in the first wave take shelter behind German barriers and a disabled American tank.

Men in the first wave trade fire with the enemy from behind a jumble of long logs implanted in the sand to prevent invasion craft from reaching the beach.

Pinned down by enemy gunfire at H-Hour-plus-1, riflemen in the second wave huddle behind German obstacles. By 9:30 a.m. the Americans had won a foothold.

5

The Americans who had landed on Utah and Omaha Beaches had been pinned down and shot up for a whole hour on D-Day before the first British soldiers set foot on their invasion beaches to the east—Gold, Juno and Sword, in that order. The difference in the H-Hours was only the beginning; the British were going to do things differently all day long. They had to.

British strategy had been dictated by a powerful threat that the Americans did not have to face: German tanks. By the end of D-Day, the British Second Army under General Miles Dempsey would have to clash with at least one panzer division, the crack 21st, in order to achieve its two primary objectives, the capture of the city of Caen and the securing of the eastern flank of the Allied invasion front. This meant that Dempsey's 75,000 British and Canadian troops had to move inland far and fast in order to set up defenses deep enough to contain the expected assaults by masses of counterattacking German tanks. The beachhead would be none too safe even if it extended 20 miles into France by nightfall, but General Montgomery, the chief strategist for the British, believed that his troops should push inland as far as possible.

To make reasonably sure that the Second Army was not detained on the beaches, Montgomery had arranged for the 137 warships with the British invasion fleet to lay down a pulverizing two-hour preliminary bombardment, starting 20 minutes before the American shelling and lasting 80 minutes longer. Moreover, Montgomery had the British transports positioned three or four miles closer to the coast than the U.S. vessels to give the troops a shorter ride shoreward. The Americans had set their H-Hour at 6:30 because the tide was near its lowest point, exposing the Germans' underwater invasion obstacles. But Montgomery and Dempsey had set theirs at 7:30, not only to ensure the longer bombardment but also to enable the landing craft to ride in with the tide and place the men higher up on the beach.

At about 6:15, after 45 minutes of thunderous naval shelling, the first wave of landing craft set out for the shore four or five miles away. The seas were rough, and many men became seasick. But visibility was good, and the troops, crowded together shoulder to shoulder, could see up ahead beaches that were entirely different from the American ones. Nowhere on their 24 miles of beaches from Ouistre-

BRITISH BEACHHEADS

ham west to Le Hamel were there natural terrain features as formidable as the high bluffs overlooking Omaha or the flooded lagoon behind Utah. The British faced only low beaches, a sea wall close by, small summer resorts and ugly villas *(page 156)* along the coast road, and beyond, flat, open country—good tank terrain. It seemed a civilized scene to the soldiers who watched its details materialize before them. But the tankmen saw nothing. They were buttoned up and ready to go in their Churchills, Shermans and specialized tanks *(pages 172-181)*, including those equipped to swim ashore at the head of the first wave.

Awaiting the assault along the shoreline, the German defenders braced for action. Their forces consisted of 10 beachside companies of infantry, 50 mortar teams, 500 machine guns and 90 artillery pieces. Behind the beaches, in defensive positions four to six miles deep, stood another 14 companies of infantry and 22 batteries with more than 100 guns. And behind them waited another five infantry battalions and more gun batteries.

As the Germans swung into action, landing craft a few hundred yards from the shore began catching shells and machine-gun fire. But the British and Canadians sat still under the barrage, steeled by at least one motive the U.S. Army lacked: revenge. They were the avengers of Dunkirk and Dieppe, and now was the time to repay the Germans.

Shortly before 7:30 the gates of the landing craft clanged open, and the soldiers in their hobnailed boots clanked down the ramps into the surf. For a time after that the British attacks bore less resemblance to a crucial military action than to a traveling road show. From aboard rocket barges and close-in destroyers, loudspeakers blared forth two songs of the day, "Roll Out the Barrel" and "We Don't Know Where We're Going." Some of the Commando units, which were assigned the difficult task of filling the gaps between the infantry beachheads, were led ashore by bagpipers playing martial Highland airs. Australian newsman Alan Moorehead, covering the invasion for the London *Daily Express,* said that "the whole scene looked at from this distance was toy-like and unreal. It lacked the element of danger or excitement, even of movement."

The landings were easier than the British had dared hope, certainly much easier than those on Omaha. But they were not really easy. Landing craft struck mines and foundered, or were shelled into floating wrecks. Shells set tanks on fire in their LCTs at sea. Many men were killed aboard landing craft. The bodies could not be taken back to England—they would delay the reembarkation schedule—so the landing-craft crewmen heaved them overboard, weighted down with any heavy objects they could spare.

On the shore, tanks lumbering up the beaches ran over screaming wounded men. Soldiers hurt at the water's edge were dragged up the beach by their comrades, who feared that they would otherwise be drowned in the still-incoming tide. The infantrymen on the tide-narrowed beaches had only to run about 100 yards to reach the German positions or the shelter of the sea wall. But in several German pillboxes and bunkers, the defenders recovered quickly from the nerve-shattering bombardment, and they kept the invaders pinned down on the beach longer than the demanding British timetable allowed.

The French seaside villages made a strange battlefield. Weeping civilians appeared at garden gates to pour wine for the advancing soldiers. In the rubble of Saint-Aubin-sur-Mer, Commando mortar men wheeled their weapon around in a purloined ice-cream cart, while in a Ouistreham café a Frenchman in pajamas danced about crying joyously, "It is the day! The day of liberation!" And the weird tanks that the soldiers called Funnies were everywhere: flail tanks beating lanes through minefields; Churchills armed with huge mortars, blasting gaps in the sea wall to let other tanks and trucks inland; floating tanks swimming ashore, casting off their flotation gear at the water's edge and immediately going into action, crashing through barbed-wire thickets and knocking out bunkers with point-blank fire.

Death on the British beaches was a random harvest rather than the grim reaping of Omaha. How a soldier fared often depended on where he landed. Some units came ashore in undefended areas. Others landed near positions whose defenders instantly surrendered; some Germans came over the dunes with suitcases already packed. But British units that were set down before resolute defenders or caught in murderous crossfires suffered greatly. Men arriving in the second wave found scattered concentrations of bodies lying where they had fallen, their blood clotting the sand.

In a few vital areas, the British and Canadians were held up on the beaches for an hour and more. But generally they maintained the initiative and carried the fight to the Germans in the streets of the villages and in the open fields beyond. One by one, most of the units with inland objectives fought their way off the beaches and began advancing on or close to their assigned schedules.

All through the morning landings, the key German commanders were virtually out of touch with the front; their communications had been so severely damaged by aerial bombardment, naval shelling and French Resistance sabotage that Seventh Army headquarters did not learn of the first British landings until 8:45 a.m., an hour and 20 minutes after they occurred, and it did not receive first word of the American landings at Utah until 11 a.m. In Germany itself, at nearly every headquarters, generals knew by midmorning —at the very moment the news of the invasion was breaking in the Allied countries—that something was up in Normandy, but the size and objectives of the operation were unclear to them throughout the day. Far away at OKW, the Supreme Headquarters in Germany, the prevailing opinion was that the Normandy attack was a feint for a larger strike at the Pas-de-Calais. For this reason, OKW Chief of Operations Staff Jodl, who carried out Hitler's orders while the Führer was sleeping nearby, refused to release the strategic panzer reserves despite urgent appeals from Field Marshal von Rundstedt, Commander in Chief, OB West, Paris.

British crewmen make final checks on their midget submarines before heading to Normandy on June 2, 1944. The two 57-foot vessels positioned themselves off the invasion coast on the 4th of June. At daybreak on D-Day the submarines surfaced and transmitted radio and sonar signals that accurately guided the British fleet to its appointed anchorage.

At La Roche-Guyon, to the west of Paris, the Army Group B headquarters of Field Marshal Rommel desperately telephoned the same request, but was told by OKW: "The landing operation in Normandy will certainly not be the only attempted major landing by the Allies. A second attack must be expected definitely in the Pas-de-Calais and therefore the withdrawal of troops from that sector to assist in Normandy cannot be allowed." When Rommel's staff officers protested, OKW sharply informed them that they "had no data whatever on which to base any judgment."

Rommel himself, at home in Herrlingen in southern Germany, had been told at 6:30 a.m. of the airborne activity in Normandy and was not unduly alarmed. But shortly after 10 a.m. his chief of staff, General Speidel, phoned to tell him that some sort of amphibious invasion was also taking place there. This news hit Rommel hard. "How stupid of me," he said quietly as he hung up the phone. "The call had changed him," his wife Lucie later said, "there was a terrible tension." Rommel was, said his aide, Captain Helmuth Lang, "terribly depressed," and the field marshal canceled the planned meeting with Hitler at Berchtesgaden. Rommel prepared to leave for his headquarters at 1 p.m.

Finally, at around 10 a.m.—by which time all of the 1,600 German tanks in northwestern France were fueled up and awaiting orders to move toward the British beachhead—Hitler woke up. In his pajamas he listened to a briefing by his adjutants. Then he sent for Jodl and OKW Commander in Chief Wilhelm Keitel. It was his view, the Führer said, that Jodl was right and that the Strategic Reserves should not be committed to Normandy until the battle picture clarified.

Then, before bathing and dressing, Hitler told Jodl to issue orders starting the bombardment of London with Germany's secret weapon: the long-range V-1 rockets. Some 60 launching sites were being built, most of them in the Pas-de-Calais area, and nearly 12,000 of the huge flying bombs had been stockpiled in northern France, Belgium and Germany. Jodl issued the appropriate code word, "Junkroom." (In fact, by the time the V-1 campaign actually began on the night of June 12, only seven launching sites were operative; the rest had been damaged by Allied bombing raids or delayed by shortages of equipment and matériel.)

The Führer did not hold his usual noontime conference with his generals. Instead he entertained the new Hungarian Premier, Döme Sztójay, at Klessheim Castle near Salzburg, an hour's drive from OKW headquarters in Berchtesgaden. Reports continued to come in from Normandy, and Hitler told his deputy chief of operations, General Warlimont, that he would think about the situation during lunch. After his usual vegetarian meal, the Führer emerged and announced his decision: Rundstedt could bring up the two elite panzer divisions of the Strategic Reserves, the 12th SS Hitler Youth from south of Rouen and the Panzer Lehr from near Chartres. (It would be 4 p.m. before the two divisions received their marching orders.)

Meanwhile, all through the echelons from OKW on down, the German fighting forces were suffering severely from the elaborate chain of command that Hitler had installed to keep tight personal control over his armies. No frontline general had clear authority to act on his own initiative, nor did any general know which of several superior headquarters would issue him orders. And no general in Normandy was more disastrously shackled than the commander of the vital division that anchored the whole German line. He was General Edgar Feuchtinger, and his 21st Panzer Division, a veteran force that had served with distinction in North Africa, would be chiefly responsible for defending the primary British objective, Caen.

In the dark morning hours of D-Day, Feuchtinger could be certain of only two things. First, he knew that British paratroopers were landing a few miles from his territory along the Orne River and that his panzers, nearest the scene, should act at once. But second, he knew that without orders from Army Group B he could not move his tanks. As he later wrote, "I could do nothing immediately but warn my men to be ready. I waited impatiently all that night for some instructions. But not a single order from a higher formation was received by me."

Finally, at 6:30 a.m. Feuchtinger acted on his own: "I ordered my tanks to attack the British 6 Airborne." Then, at 7:00, "I received by first intimation that a higher command did still exist. I was told by Army Group B that I was now under the command of 7 Army." But two hours later, "I was informed that I would receive any future orders from 84th Infantry Corps." It was not until 10 a.m. that "I was given my first operational instructions. I was ordered to stop the move of my tanks against the Allied Airborne troops, and turn west and aid the forces protecting Caen."

Feuchtinger followed his orders from 84th Corps and tried to disengage his panzers from combat with the British 6th Airborne. This was no easy maneuver under the best of circumstances, and the tanks, which had to cross from east to west over the Orne, were impeded by rocket-firing fighter-bombers and streams of refugees. Finally, late in the afternoon, most of the panzers broke free of traffic and advanced in two long columns. Despite all their problems, Feuchtinger's tank crews would give the British all the fight they could handle in the most important battle of D-Day.

Before the struggle for Caen developed, many battles were fought to a decision all along the British beaches. With few exceptions, the Germans fought courageously. But they had little knowledge of what was going on around them and, for all their elaborate fixed positions, they enjoyed only a slight advantage fighting in the flat and open terrain. They were widely dispersed, their attackers sharply concentrated, and they could only hope to hold fast in islands of resistance until mobile reinforcements came to their aid.

Gold Beach, on the British right, near the Americans on Omaha, was assigned to two British units, the 50th Division and the 8th Armored Brigade, with tanks in the van. The main defenses facing them were two well-fortified villages at either end of Gold: Le Hamel in the west, nine miles from Omaha, and La Rivière in the east at the juncture of Juno Beach. The attack on Le Hamel was led by the 231st Brigade, whose mission was to capture the town of Bayeux and to link up with the Americans at Port-en-Bessin.

On landing near Le Hamel, one battalion of the 231st ran

Tanks of the 27th British Armored Brigade splash ashore from a landing craft near the village of Hermanville on Sword Beach. The unit spent one hour battling to break out of the beach, during which 50 per cent of its tanks and bulldozers were disabled by mines, obstacles and enemy guns.

into stiff defenses and was held up until midafternoon by troops of the same 352nd German Division that was inflicting such heavy casualties on the Americans at Omaha. But a second battalion landed out of range of the Le Hamel guns, overran the defenders on its front in 40 minutes and headed inland. Later in the day, this battalion seized the high ground overlooking Arromanches, the anchorage point for Mulberry B, one of the two immense artificial harbors that were to be built along the beachhead.

At the other end of Gold Beach, one battalion of the 69th Brigade was forced to fight for La Rivière street by street. But another battalion had little difficulty in piercing the defenses and routing the enemy. By 9:30 the brigade owned the high ground one mile inland, and by 12:30 the rest of the 50th Division had landed on Gold and was assembling inland on a beachhead that now measured three miles wide and two and a half miles deep. All afternoon various British units pressed forward to the south, and by evening they were in the outskirts of Bayeux, whose German defenders were already withdrawing. Three miles away, other units reached the road from Bayeux to Caen.

The results of the day's action on Gold were a mixed bag. By cutting the Bayeux–Caen road, the British had put themselves in a good position to prevent German tanks from reaching the vulnerable Americans on Omaha. But they had failed to link up with the Americans; the battalion that had captured Arromanches was stalled there, seven miles away from the appointed rendezvous point, Port-en-Bessin.

To the left of Gold, on Juno Beach, the principal assault force was the 3rd Canadian Division. The Canadians were supposed to make the deepest penetrations of the day, join in the attack on Caen and capture the strategically important airfield at Carpiquet 11 miles inland. Their front was four miles wide, bracketing the small fishing port of Courseulles on their right and the seaside resort village of Saint-Aubin-sur-Mer on their left at the juncture of Sword Beach.

At Courseulles the Canadians ran into serious problems even before they landed. They were scheduled to come in at 7:35 a.m., late enough so that the rising tide would float their landing craft over jagged offshore reefs, but the choppy seas delayed them a critical half hour longer, leaving the demolition teams little time to clear the mined anti-invasion obstacles before the incoming tide covered them. It also gave the Germans plenty of time to recover from the naval bombardment and to prepare a hot welcome. On the way in, 90 of 306 landing craft were knocked out by the mined obstacles or German shells. But the Canadians still swarmed ashore, attacked furiously and refused to be stopped.

The 7th Canadian Brigade landed at Courseulles at 8 a.m. with close armored support from floating tanks swimming ashore from 800 yards out. The bolt assault overwhelmed or outflanked the German strong points, and two battalions—the Royal Winnipeg Rifles and the Regina Rifles—quickly moved inland. But the rising tide had reduced the beach to a narrow strip so crowded with tanks, trucks and guns that a reserve battalion took 90 minutes to get through. By the time the reserves left the beach, the Winnipegs and the Reginas had plunged several miles inland.

To the east of Courseulles, at the village of Bernières-sur-Mer, the 8th Canadian Brigade got into trouble by landing ahead of its tanks, forcing the soldiers to fight without fire support at the most critical moment of their assault. The battalion on the right, the Queen's Own Rifles, was carried to within 100 yards of the sea wall; in the short stretch that remained, half of one company was killed by enfilading enemy fire. The German strong points kept blasting away until the Rifles took them by storm with the support of point-blank fire from a gunship close inshore. Even then, pockets of Germans held out grimly, tying up three battalions of a follow-up brigade until 3 p.m.

Farther east, around Saint-Aubin-sur-Mer, brutal and complex battles raged all day. The Canadians' left-flank battalion, the French-Canadian Régiment de la Chaudière, had to fight for nearly three hours without tank assistance before the determined German defenses could be silenced. At nearby Langrune-sur-Mer, a British Commando unit was bogged down in a bitter fight in the streets and gardens against enemy troops that could be ousted from blocks of fortified houses only after large-scale demolition.

All in all, D-Day action on Juno was a success. The Canadians almost—but not quite—reached their outermost objective; they were within sight of Caen and established on the fringes of both Bayeux and the Carpiquet airfield when darkness halted operations. Other Canadian units had linked up on the right with British troops on Gold Beach, forming a solid beachhead 12 miles wide and at least six miles deep. But the Canadians on the left were still separated from Sword Beach by two and a half miles of enemy-held territory, and several Canadian battalions that had lost valuable time on the beaches could not make it up once they had fought their way into the clear.

Yet the real danger lay farther to the east on Sword Beach. Somewhere behind the beach lurked the tanks of the 21st Panzer Division. Sword was the one place where things had to go right, and all day long the issue was in doubt.

The principal units assigned to take Sword Beach were the 3rd British Infantry Division and two redoubtable Commando brigades (pages 162-171), the 1st and the 4th. The most important objective—the key to the whole Allied invasion—had been assigned to the British 3rd in concert with troops of the 3rd Canadian Division from Gold Beach. They were to capture Caen, which dominated a plateau about seven miles from the shore and permitted access to good tank country all the way to Paris.

The British 3rd, held up by offshore reefs and a tricky tide,

landed on Sword a little late and ran into fully prepared shoreline defenders. It took an hour for the British to win the beach and even longer to unsnarl a massive traffic jam of tanks and trucks that had piled up during the battle.

As the troops started inland, they watched for signs of General Feuchtinger's 21st Panzer Division, whose exact location had not been established by Allied aerial reconnaissance. They did not know that tanks of the 21st had been operating against the British 6th Airborne since dawn, or that other elements of the 21st were scattered in a big arc around Caen. But they knew enough to proceed cautiously. Feuchtinger's division was known to have 16,000 men, 40 mobile assault guns, four motorized infantry battalions and an antitank battalion with 24 guns. But the real danger lay in the 21st's 146 tanks—most of them powerful Mark IVs. The last thing the British wanted was a brawl with those tanks; it might leave them too weak to fight off an attack by the 12th SS Panzer Division, which British intelligence expected to arrive from the Rouen area on D-Day afternoon.

Accompanied by Churchill and Sherman tanks, the 1st South Lancashire Regiment of the 8th Brigade spearheaded

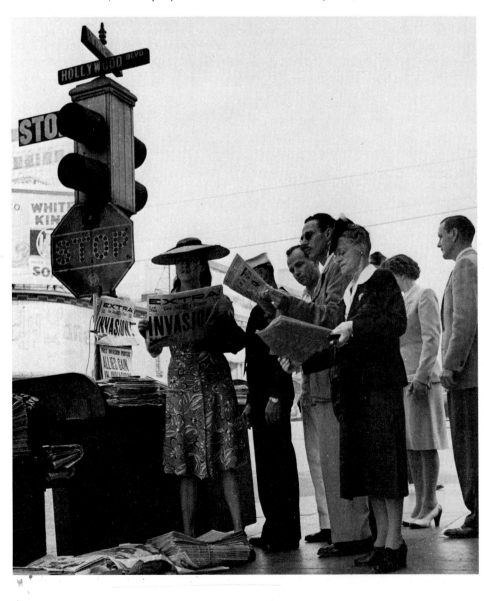

At the corner of Hollywood and Vine, Los Angelenos pore over newspaper accounts of the invasion, announced by Eisenhower while they were asleep. Across the continent in New York City, crowds prayed in the streets for victory. Said Mayor Fiorello La Guardia, "It is the most exciting moment in our lives."

On D-Day morning at a castle near his Berchtesgaden headquarters, Adolf Hitler studies a map while Colonel General Alfred Jodl points out the Allied beachheads in Normandy. The Führer, who had been conferring with Hungarian Premier Döme Sztójay (seated, far left) and Foreign Minister Joachim von Ribbentrop (top left), was so unsettled by the news that he permitted this rare photograph showing him wearing spectacles. Hitler recovered quickly and—to give the impression that he had allowed the invasion in order to trap the Allied army —remarked: "Those Dummköpfe, thank God they have finally made a landing."

the 3rd Division's drive inland. By 9:30 these forces had taken the village of Hermanville, a mile and a half from Sword Beach on the shortest road to Caen. But their drive petered out less than a mile down the road, where they ran into guns of the 21st Panzer's antitank battalion, which were set up on a slope the British called Periers Rise. The South Lancs missed their chance to make a bold strike. Instead of plowing past the antitank guns and some infantry defenders, they dug in below Periers Rise and waited for the 185th Brigade, which was supposed to carry the attack into Caen.

But the 185th had been delayed. Its King's Shropshire Light Infantry battalion (or KSLI) was to lead the way from Hermanville to Caen riding on the backs of the 65 tanks of the Staffordshire Yeomanry. The plan misfired. At the appointed hour, 11 a.m., the 600 men of the KSLI, led by Lieut. Colonel F. J. Maurice, were waiting for the tanks at the appointed rendezvous, an orchard near Hermanville. But the tanks were stuck in the traffic jam on the beach.

Finally Colonel Maurice got tired of waiting and made a daring decision: he would order his troops to start out for Caen on foot and trust that the tanks would catch up soon.

At 12:30, the KSLI set off on its lonely, hazardous march, hiking along in spread-out formation, ready to disperse in case of attack. It was a lovely sunny afternoon. Swallows swooped over the grass, bees buzzed in the flowers along the hedgerows and the yellow corn stood high in the fields.

By about 2 o'clock, when Maurice's men finally started their attack up Periers Rise, the first tanks had finally emerged from the traffic jam on the beach, and 20 Shermans were on hand to join the assault. Almost at once, the tanks and the infantry came under heavy fire from German positions blocking the road to Caen. All but three of the Germans' 24 antitank guns had been removed and thrown into the fighting farther west, but those three were nearly enough: they knocked out nine of the Shermans. Eventually the surviving Shermans and a KSLI company overwhelmed the last German strong point from the rear.

While other units of the 185th Brigade took up defensive positions on Periers Rise, Maurice pressed on toward Caen with his KSLI, his tanks and some antitank guns. By 4 p.m. they were moving through the village of Biéville. They were

159

now only three miles from the northern outskirts of Caen and had high hopes of capturing the city by nightfall.

Those hopes were quickly dashed. About 90 tanks of the 21st Panzer Division had finally broken free of refugee traffic south of Caen—and the first contingent, a strong battle group of about 40 Mark IVs and a battalion of infantry, circled the city and reached the village of Lebisey dead ahead of Maurice and the KSLI.

The leader of the battle group was Colonel Hermann von Oppeln-Bronikowski, and at Lebisey he was met by his commander, General Feuchtinger, and by a distinguished visitor, General Marcks, whose 84th Corps had controlled the 21st Panzers since 10 a.m. To see the battlefront for himself, Marcks had traveled 40 miles from his headquarters at Saint-Lô, and he had reached a sobering conclusion. "Oppeln," he told the colonel, "the future of Germany may very well rest on your shoulders. If we don't throw the British back into sea we shall have lost the war."

Marcks pointed out a serious flaw in the British lines. From Lebisey, a gap several miles wide reached all the way to the coast between Langrune and Lion-sur-Mer. Fierce fighting had been going on around those seaside resorts all day long, and various invading units had failed to clear out the German defenders. If those defenders could be reinforced, the Germans might be able to maintain a wedge three miles wide between the British and the Canadians and, eventually, begin to roll up the beachheads in both directions. As the first step in the counterattack, Marcks and Feuchtinger sent Oppeln-Bronikowski plunging into the gap with his powerful battle group.

The 40 Mark IVs had traveled little more than a mile when they bumped into Colonel Maurice's forces just outside of Biéville. In the opening phase of the first big tank battle of the invasion, the Shermans of the Staffordshire Yeomanry knocked out two Mark IVs, and antitank guns stopped two more. The Germans then veered off into the woods to the west. When they emerged, British pursuers knocked out another six tanks. At this point, the enemy forces disengaged, each going its separate way.

As the battered panzers resumed their drive toward the sea, Maurice's infantry and tanks pressed on toward Caen.

The leading company of the KSLI was only two miles away when it ran into intense enemy fire from a wooded ridge in front of Lebisey. Maurice judged that the German position was too strong to attack without reinforcements. No one had arrived to help, and the other two battalions of the 185th Brigade were strung out along the road to his rear. Reluctantly, Maurice halted his bold push on Caen. He pulled back slightly toward Biéville and dug in there for the night. It would be weeks before any British units surpassed Maurice's high-water mark on the road to Caen.

Meanwhile, at about 7 p.m., Oppeln-Bronikowski and the remnants of his battle group reached Periers Rise and learned to their dismay that it was heavily manned by the British. The panzers' right wing was stopped cold by antitank guns, which knocked out at least seven more Mark IVs. But the German left—a half-dozen tanks supported by a company of infantrymen—slipped through the British lines and drove on to the north. At around 8 p.m. this little force actually succeeded in reaching the coast at Luc-sur-Mer, halfway between Langrune and Lion. There the Germans waited, confident that General Feuchtinger would reinforce them with more tanks as soon as possible.

That was precisely what Feuchtinger had in mind, and he dispatched the rest of his available Mark IVs—perhaps 50 tanks. This battle group was trying to slip past the British defenders on Periers when a tremendous coincidence disrupted their promising counterattack.

Suddenly the sky was filled with planes, and before the Germans' eyes fresh airborne forces swooped past on their way to reinforce the British 6th Airborne along the Orne River a few miles to the east. What the Germans were seeing was the biggest glider force to go into action in Normandy: 250 gliders, towed by 250 transport planes and guarded by a great flight of fighter planes. Aboard the gliders were two infantry battalions of the 6th Air Landing Brigade, the 6th Airborne's artillery, light tanks and reconnaissance regiments. The gliders held a steady course through German antiaircraft fire while the Spitfire and Mustang fighters plunged down to rake the German batteries with cannon and machine-gun fire.

As the gliders neared the Orne, they cast off their tow

cables and slipped silently over the trees and rooftops to their landing zones. At the same time, 600 canisters of supplies and ammunition were dropped by parachute from the transport planes. At one stroke, this massive reinforcement doubled the strength of the besieged and exhausted 6th Airborne, which had been in action nonstop for approximately 20 hours.

To the German tank crews, the enemy planes and gliders seemed to be a huge bridge reaching across the whole horizon. "We looked up," said a lieutenant of the panzer infantry, "and there they were just above us. Noiselessly, those giant wooden boxes sailed in over our heads. We lay on our backs and fired, and fired into those gliders, until we could not work the bolts of our rifles anymore. But with such masses, it seemed to make little difference."

The Germans lost heart. To General Feuchtinger on the outskirts of Caen, it seemed that the great airborne force was landing directly in the path of his northbound tanks. His division had saved Caen for a while, but at a terrible cost; he would end the day with a total loss of 76 out of 146 tanks. Knowing he had done all he could until the reserve panzer divisions arrived, Feuchtinger called off his counterattack toward the coast and reported his failure to Seventh Army headquarters. The Seventh Army report to other commands said simply: "Attack by the 21st Panzer Division rendered useless by heavily concentrated airborne troops."

For the Germans, D-Day ended as it had begun—in confusion or delusion or both. General Marcks of the 84th Corps believed that the American landings on Omaha Beach had been smashed. General Dollmann and his Seventh Army staff thought that the American seaborne landings, whose strength and objectives they could not comprehend, were a sideshow that could easily be dealt with at leisure, and that the British landings were a separate, serious threat against which they should instantly commit all available reserves. OKW in Germany was still waiting for the other shoe to drop—the expected Allied strike at the Pas-de-Calais. Rommel, who had predicted that the War would be won or lost on the beaches, suspected that it had already been lost. In spite of the heavy losses suffered by Feuchtinger's 21st Panzer Division, higher headquarters kept sending him orders to wipe out the invasion beachhead at once.

For the Allies, D-Day had brought a tremendous victory. The much vaunted Atlantic Wall had been breached: seaborne troops had passed through it and secured ground well beyond it; airborne troops behind it, isolated and vulnerable, had held fast. The Allies' mastery of the air was complete: their strategic and tactical air forces had flown 10,585 D-Day sorties; the Luftwaffe had flown 319, and most of those had been shot down or driven off.

The whole vast, complex assault phase of *Overlord* had worked. So effective was the deception program of Operation *Fortitude* that while the German High Command looked toward the Pas-de-Calais, the Allies had landed 152,000 troops and hundreds of tanks in Normandy without receiving a single massed counterattack or suffering anywhere near the serious casualties that even the most optimistic Allied commander had expected. SHAEF's official secret prediction had been for 10,000 dead in the initial assault. In fact, no more than 2,500 men had lost their lives, and total casualties—including wounded, missing and prisoners—were probably fewer than 12,000, of whom 6,600 were American, 3,500 British and 1,000 Canadian.

The Allied commanders were elated, but they were far from complacent. Their beachhead was small, their front thinly held. The American seaborne forces had not yet linked up with the 82nd Airborne, though only a mile now separated them. The Utah beachhead was isolated, the penetration beyond Omaha was tenuous. A seven-mile gap still separated the British and the Americans, and the 3rd British Division was still three miles away from the 3rd Canadian Division. Worst of all, Caen remained in the hands of the Germans, and without Caen as an anchor the whole invasion front was afloat.

On D-plus-1, and for many days thereafter, the battle to expand the Allied beachhead would continue. But another crucial battle was already beginning—the battle to reinforce the bloody invasion beaches. Everything now depended on whether the Allies could land troops and supplies faster than the Germans could bring up their tank divisions from the east.

BRITAIN'S SHOCK TROOPS

Spearheading the British drive inland from Sword Beach, the 1st Commando Brigade advances, under cover of a British tank, past shell-damaged houses.

A PAIR OF BRIGADES IN DUBIOUS BATTLE

Two Commando brigades, both crack units but destined to meet with very different luck, headed shoreward on D-Day morning charged with two of the British Army's most crucial missions. One unit was Brigadier the Lord Lovat's 2,000-man 1st Brigade; it was to land at the eastern edge of Sword Beach. The other Commando force, bound for the juncture of Sword and Juno Beaches, was made up of about 1,000 men from Brigadier B. W. Leicester's 4th Brigade. Trained to hit hard and fast, these units were assigned tasks considered too difficult for the infantry.

Lovat's men, ordered to link up with the 6th Airborne units that had come by parachute and glider during the night, put on a display of casual daring, as befitted their long experience in Commando raids. They wore green berets, disdaining steel helmets. Their bagpiper played as the landing craft came in under heavy fire. Two noncoms sat in full view and shouted mocking advice to the German gunners: "Put your sights up, Jerry," and "Down a little."

On the beach, Lovat found first-wave units of British infantrymen pinned down by enemy fire. His Commandos advanced through the infantry lines and knocked out the German machine guns. To reinforce the paratroopers on schedule, Lovat had to cover six miles in only three-and-a-half hours, and he was determined to be there on time.

Meanwhile, the men of the 4th Brigade, whose mission was to plug the five-mile gap between the Sword and Juno beachheads, had run into trouble even before reaching the shore at Saint Aubin. The preinvasion bombardment had completely missed the beach defenses there, and German mortar shells inflicted heavy casualties on the incoming landing craft. Once ashore, the Commandos' luck was even worse. A German strong point blocked their advance and prevented them from closing the gap. Then a battalion of enemy infantrymen plunged through the opening and reinforced the German positions near Saint Aubin. It was not until the following day that the 4th Brigade, with the blockbusting aid of a Sherman tank, finally overran the strong point and consolidated the two beachheads.

A Commando unit, equipped for speed with light weapons and bicycles, prepares to race inland from a beach congested with tanks and trucks.

Commando snipers, one of them disguised in torn camouflage netting and the other wearing a rain cape, receive instructions from a 1st Brigade officer (right).

Fighting in a haze of gun smoke, 4th Brigade Commandos take cover from German mortar fire on a roadside at Saint Aubin. After two days of savage combat in

the area, the 500-man unit had lost 217 officers and men, including 50 Commandos who were rescued from the water and involuntarily returned to England.

Advancing at last, 4th Brigade Commandos tramp through a village between Sword and Juno Beaches.

Villagers inform 4th Brigade Commandos of

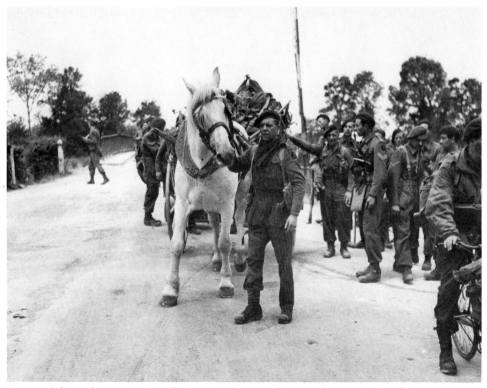

To speed their advance, 1st Brigade Commandos use a horse and wagon to lug their gear forward.

German units deployed near Saint Aubin. A Frenchman also helped the 1st Brigade Commandos, sabotaging power lines to German positions at Ouistreham.

BLAZING A TRAIL BY BICYCLE AND FARM CART

While the hard-luck 4th Brigade was fighting for survival near Saint Aubin, the 1st Brigade was striving valiantly to avoid a fight. In order to reach the 6th Airborne units in time, Lord Lovat could not afford to engage the Germans unless they insisted on impeding his advance.

Following a route carefully selected to avoid main roads and major strong points, the Commandos raced along hedgerows, cut through barbed wire and crossed an antitank ditch using scaling ladders. Confronted with a minefield, they carefully picked their way through it rather than wasting precious time on a long detour. While Commando mortar teams kept the enemy blinded with smoke bombs, the reconnaissance units sped ahead of the main body on lightweight bicycles.

As they advanced, the Commandos im-

provised cleverly to make up for their lack of artillery support. One enterprising officer flagged down a passing British tank, whose obliging crew shelled a pillbox that was blocking the way.

Though the 1st Brigade obeyed orders to avoid the enemy, it left an impressive trail of ruin along its six-mile route. Before the Commandos reached the gliders of the 6th Airborne Division, they knocked out four strong points and destroyed a battery of four field guns.

The Commandos dig in among crash-landed gliders of the airborne troops.

MISSION ACCOMPLISHED, WITH BAGPIPES SKIRLING

Soon after noon on D-Day, Lord Lovat and the men of the 1st Brigade were closing in on the Orne River bridges where they were to link up with the 6th Airborne Division. By then, the paratroopers were in desperate need of reinforcements. The men had been fighting continuously for more than 12 hours; their ammunition was almost exhausted and their casualties were mounting under an unrelenting German mortar barrage. Before too long the paratroopers heard the skirl of bagpipes in the distance and they knew that the Commandos had broken through.

At about 1 p.m. the Commandos came into view and Lovat's bagpipes squealed out the tune of "Blue Bonnets over the Border." The paratroopers raised a cheer and, ignoring German sniper fire, rushed out from cover to greet the Commandos. For a moment the paratroopers mingled boisterously with the Commandos. Then both units went back to fighting again.

Lord Lovat strode up to the paratroop colonel in charge. With a glance at his wrist watch he said nonchalantly, "I'm sorry that we are a couple of minutes late."

On guard in the shadow of a giant Horsa glider, Commandos of the 1st Brigade man their Bren gun and scan the area with binoculars for signs of German troops.

THOSE WONDROUS TANKS

The most spectacular of the British specialized tanks, a Churchill "Crocodile," throws flames 120 yards, using 400 gallons of napalm stored in its trailer.

HOBART'S MENAGERIE OF MECHANICAL MONSTERS

At H-Hour all along the British invasion beaches, weird attack vehicles that looked like canvas-covered bathtubs swam ashore *(right)*. Then they lowered their canvas flotation collars and revealed their true identity as fully armed Sherman tanks. The German defenders were flabbergasted, and one of the tank drivers later said, "I still remember very vividly some of the machinegunners standing up in their posts looking at us with their mouths wide open."

The floating tank, or DD (duplex drive), was only one of an amazing variety of specialized armored vehicles, called "Funnies," that crawled over the supposedly impenetrable Atlantic Wall at Normandy. The British also had modified Sherman and Churchill tanks that exploded mines and laid roadways, as well as some that shot flames. The need for such vehicles had been dramatized by the disastrous British defeat at Dieppe, in which tanks that were supposed to cover advancing infantry failed to break through German obstacles and left soldiers exposed to enemy fire.

The man who developed the Funnies and trained their crews was Major-General Percy C. S. Hobart, a prickly genius personally selected by Churchill to modernize Britain's tank program. As commander of the 79th Armored Division, Hobart and his staff designed, built and tested more than a dozen specialized modifications. Then he saw to it that enough were modified to serve the Allies' D-Day needs.

British General Montgomery, the field commander of all the invasion forces, ordered the Funnies to be distributed among his British, Canadian and American forces. But the Americans accepted only a few swimming DDs; they declined the rest of the Funnies—a decision they later regretted, especially during their bloody struggles on Omaha Beach. For the Funnies did save countless British lives. General Eisenhower wrote after D-Day: "The comparatively light casualties which we sustained on all the beaches except Omaha were in large measure due to the success of the novel mechanical contrivances which were employed. . . . It is doubtful if the assault forces could have firmly established themselves without the assistance of these weapons."

Before taking over the tank program, Hobart was in the Home Guard: the regular Army had forced him to retire because of his eccentric ideas.

THE INVALUABLE DD: A TANK THAT COULD SWIM

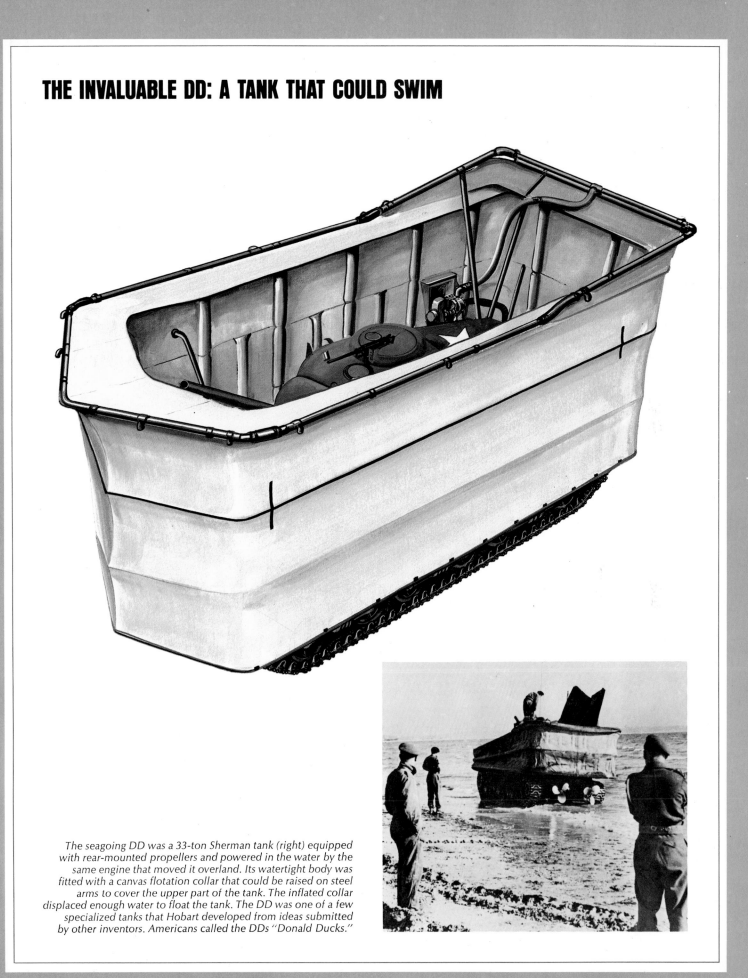

The seagoing DD was a 33-ton Sherman tank (right) equipped with rear-mounted propellers and powered in the water by the same engine that moved it overland. Its watertight body was fitted with a canvas flotation collar that could be raised on steel arms to cover the upper part of the tank. The inflated collar displaced enough water to float the tank. The DD was one of a few specialized tanks that Hobart developed from ideas submitted by other inventors. Americans called the DDs "Donald Ducks."

CLEARING MINES WITH A BATTERY OF FLYING CHAINS

The Sherman flail tank—nicknamed the "Crab" by the British—was designed to clear paths through minefields for the infantry. The flails were massive chains attached to a 10-foot-wide metal drum that was mounted on the front end of the tank. As the tank trundled forward at one and a half miles per hour, its drum was rotated at high speed, slamming the chains against the ground and detonating any mines buried in its path.

176

A CHURCHILL TANK THAT FIRED "FLYING DUSTBINS"

The Churchill AVRE (Armored Vehicle Royal Engineers) was used to destroy enemy strongholds, and to protect and transport demolition teams. It had a short-barreled mortar mounted on the turret in place of the usual long gun. The 290mm mortar fired a 40-pound projectile—called a "Flying Dustbin" because of its square shape—that could demolish most enemy pillboxes and barriers. The tank could fire two or three rounds a minute.

A TOW SERVICE FOR CRIPPLED TANKS

For all their versatility, the Funnies were just as susceptible to breakdowns and enemy fire as their regular cousins. Tanks disabled on the battlefield often blocked advances. To remove crippled tanks, Hobart equipped some Churchills with winches, pulleys and towing equipment at front and back. A crewman from the rescuing tank—known as an Armored Recovery Vehicle (ARV)—attached the towing apparatus to the disabled tank (inset), which was then coaxed, lifted and pulled out of the way.

ROLLING OUT THE CARPET

The "Bobbin" was a Churchill equipped with a giant spool, on which was rolled a 110-yard-long carpet of coir—a coarse material made from the husks of coconuts. This carpet, stiffened by bamboo rods, was unrolled in front of the advancing Bobbin, permitting it and other vehicles to traverse soft, slippery clay. The carpet was first pulled down from the spool and guided by hand until it was caught under the tank treads. Then the forward movement of the tank pulled down more of the carpet. The spool could be lowered (inset) when the tank was on level ground.

A MOVABLE ROADWAY AND BRIDGE

The Armored Ramp Carrier—dubbed "ARK"—was a turretless Churchill tank whose flat superstructure supported two runways. Attached by hinges at both ends of each runway were adjustable ramps. When an ARK reached a sea wall too high to climb, it would push its nose against the wall and lower its rear runways, thus forming a roadway on which other tanks could climb over the wall. ARKs also took up positions in the middle of ditches and streams and, by lowering both sets of ramps, created bridges for other vehicles to cross.

BIGGER BRIDGES FOR BIGGER OBSTACLES

Whenever ARKs (left) proved to be too small to overcome an obstacle, Churchill AVREs equipped with small box girder bridges took over. The 30-foot bridge, mounted on the front of the tank and held in position by cables, was lowered by a hand-operated winch at the rear. To position the bridge for use, the tankmen lowered it to within a few feet of the supports it would rest on. Then they set small charges that cut the cables, and the bridge fell into place. The bridge could support a 40-ton load.

The Allies spent the night of D-Day clinging to their patches of Normandy coastline. Although the Germans mounted no serious thrusts at the beachheads, the invaders got little rest during the hours of darkness. On the beaches they labored to clear away the wreckage, preparing for the incoming flood of men and machines scheduled to resume at first light. Farther inland, infantry patrols padded through orchards and farmyards, alert to enemy movement. Those GIs or Tommies lucky enough to catch a few winks awoke stiff and cold in their foxholes, beside their field guns and tanks, to find the sun rising in a brilliant blue sky, across which buzzed swarms of fighter planes.

At the village of Saint-Aubin-sur-Mer, just behind Sword Beach, Lieut. Colonel James L. Moulton and his men of No. 48 Commando arose to clean up the mess around them. "It was a shocking sight," Colonel Moulton wrote later. "Many corpses, some of them badly dismembered, were lying among the rest of the debris of the assault: wrecked and burnt out tanks, equipment and stores of every sort, scattered on the beach or drifted up along the water's edge; wrecked landing craft broached-to on the beach or in the sea among the beach obstacles. . . . Among all this, several French women were walking about, picking up what tinned food they could find—incredibly they had small children with them, who gazed with indifferent curiosity on the shattered corpses, the broken equipment and the scattered tins of food."

But the Allies had little time to pause and contemplate the death and destruction on the beaches. Their task now was to keep the Germans on the run. General Montgomery, the Allied ground commander, arrived off the invasion beaches on board H.M.S. *Faulknor* early on the morning of June 7. In shipboard meetings with General Bradley, the American First Army commander, and General Dempsey, the British Second Army commander, Montgomery stressed the importance of maintaining the Allied initiative, of shoving the Germans still farther inland to protect the beaches during the vital influx of fresh fighting men, their weapons and supplies. It was also essential, Montgomery told his commanders, to link up the bridgeheads so the Germans could not drive wedges through the gaps between them.

For the moment Montgomery issued no new orders. Operation *Overlord* continued according to plan. The two

6

THE FIGHTING INLAND

Allied armies would strive to complete their D-Day objectives. The Americans were to capture Carentan, thus linking up their Utah and Omaha beachheads, and then thrust across the neck of the Cotentin Peninsula to isolate the port of Cherbourg as a preliminary to its capture. The British were to continue their battles for Bayeux and Caen, deepen their bridgehead southward across the Caen–Bayeux road and, on their right flank, link up with the American V Corps at Port-en-Bessin.

But on June 7 it was clear to the Allies that this was easier said than done. Air reconnaissance showed that German armored reserves were moving up on Caen and resistance was stiffening there. And the Americans were still in trouble on Omaha. German resistance there was so strong that the 29th Division found it almost impossible to expand its beachhead westward, and the beach itself was still under fire by mortars and shells and so cluttered with wreckage that stores could be unloaded only in a few places.

Inland, on the Cotentin Peninsula, the situation was precarious. All through the night General Ridgway's scattered and isolated 82nd Airborne Division—still short of 60 per cent of its infantry and 90 per cent of its artillery—had borne the brunt of the German counterattacks across the Merderet River, one of which had been stopped only 400 yards short of Ridgway's command post. Dawn found the Americans in desperate straits and almost out of ammunition. As the day wore on, however, the picture improved. By noon the 82nd had been reinforced with glider infantry and supply drops and had linked up with the seaborne forces from Utah, where the beach was firmly in U.S. hands.

Although the Germans kept trying, they could not break through the American line along the Merderet. By nightfall the VII Corps at Utah held a bridgehead eight miles deep and nine miles long.

By then even the situation at Omaha had improved. The savage fighting of D-Day had drained the morale of the German defenders, and there were no available resources to reinforce them. The Americans of the V Corps were able to force their way to the River Aure, about four miles south of Omaha Beach, and establish a bridgehead across it. The worst was over, though nobody knew it yet.

While the Americans were struggling to expand their beachheads, their allies to the east defused a German counterattack aimed at the gap between the British and Canadian forces north of Caen. The attack was to be launched with two panzer divisions, the 12th SS and the 21st, which between them had 160 tanks and five battalions of infantry. General Kurt Meyer, commander of the 12th SS, thought this was a force large enough for the assault. General Feuchtinger, commanding the 21st, did not agree with Meyer. Feuchtinger, who had lost nearly half his tanks on D-Day, wanted to wait until both units were joined by a third division, the Panzer Lehr, then on its way to Caen from near Chartres, over 100 miles away. Field Marshal Rommel, who had arrived back at his headquarters, ended the disagreement with an order to launch the attack immediately, aiming at the coast through the gap between the 3rd Canadian and 3rd British Divisions.

But the British and Canadians struck first. The British hit the 21st at Lebisey, north of Caen, while the 12th SS was distracted by a Canadian push toward the Carpiquet airfield west of the city. Meyer was forced to commit nearly all his forces against the Canadians, and though he was able to drive them back with heavy casualties, he was left with only 17 tanks and one infantry battallion to carry out the original attack down the gap that led to the sea. Before he could even start, the Allies had closed the gap.

The Germans were so heavily involved in their struggle to hold Caen against the 3rd British and 3rd Canadian Divisions that they could do very little to check the advance of the 50th British Division northwest of Caen. Consequently, most of the Caen–Bayeux road fell into British and Canadian hands, and on June 8, Bayeux was captured by the British—the first important town in France to be liberated from German occupation.

The German intelligence officer at the 84th Corps headquarters bunker in Saint-Lô, Major Friedrich Hayn, was told of this loss by a German woman auxiliary on the Bayeux telephone exchange:

"Herr Major, British tanks are now passing the Soldiers' Club," she coolly informed him. "They are right in the middle of the town. . . . I'm the last one here."

Then she added: "Now the Tommies are driving past the building outside. You can hear for yourself, Herr Major."

She held the telephone out the window and the intelligence officer in Saint-Lô heard the clanking of the enemy tanks. It was unbelievable.

The tanks belonged to a squadron led by Lieut. Colonel Stanley Christopherson. "We were the first troops into the town," the colonel recalled. "We were given a most enthusiastic and spontaneous reception by the inhabitants who demonstrated their joy by throwing flowers at the tanks and distributing cider and food among the men.

"One enemy machine gun post concealed in a house held out in the south of the town, which caused the building to catch fire as a result of our gunfire. After a very short space the clanging of a bell heralded the arrival of the Bayeux fire brigade, manned by a full team all wearing shiny helmets. Regardless of the machine gun fire, they held up the battle, entered the house, extinguished the fire, and brought out the German machine gun section."

Unlike other towns in Normandy, Bayeux had suffered no war damage. The shops were full of Calvados and wine; there were evening gowns for sale in the shop marked haute couture. The Lion d'Or, an old inn, was open for business as usual, and correspondent Alan Moorehead was astonished to discover that he could have lunch there. "The proprietress was a round little woman dressed in black," he wrote, "and she accepted our arrival with aplomb. We watched the lunch arrive. Soup, omelettes, steak, vegetables, cheese. The wine was a dry Sauterne, 15 shillings a bottle. The Armagnac was a genuine Armagnac."

With the capture of Bayeux the liberation of France had truly begun. "While we ate," said Moorehead, "there was a commotion in the square outside. A crowd came yelling up the Rue St. Jean, driving an old man in front of them. His shirt was torn off to the waist. There was blood running down his face, his eyes were wide with fright. Every now or then a man or a woman would run forward to beat him or scratch him. They did this viciously, with an evident sense of gratifying some pent up desire for revenge. It was difficult to get much sense out of the crowd. They merely shouted, 'Collaborateur.' Presently more victims were brought out and beaten in the square in front of the hotel. It was the first of many such incidents we were going to see through France and Belgium."

The invasion had not simply liberated a few Frenchmen on the Normandy coast: it had fired Frenchmen every-

U.S. gliders sit in a patchwork of Normandy fields after landing two miles south of Sainte-Mère-Eglise on June 7 with infantry, artillery and vehicles—reinforcements for the isolated and hard-pressed 82nd Airborne troops. C-47 tow ships circle over the landing zone on their way back to England.

where. Fearful of massive German reprisals, Eisenhower on D-Day had asked the civilian population of France not to rise against the German Occupation authorities. This appeal was largely ignored. The Resistance emerged en masse and in strength, and France was soon in a state of open rebellion. Sabotage spread through the factories. Guerrillas blew bridges and ammunition dumps, cut telephone lines and harassed German road convoys. The French railway network used by the Germans for supplying and reinforcing their armies in the west was devastated. On D-Day night alone there were 950 interruptions on the railways; after D-Day every train leaving Marseilles for Lyons was derailed at least once. All lines to the busy junctions of Troyes, Lille and Tourcoing were cut within a night or two after D-Day and were kept cut until the end of the month. The main line between Toulouse and Paris was cut 800 times in June.

Normandy villagers welcome an advancing British unit. The invasion brought local inhabitants hardships as well as freedom. Many villages were destroyed, food distribution was disrupted and for a few months after D-Day life was harder than it had been during the German Occupation.

While the French were crippling German transport on the ground, the British and Americans were doing the same from the air. On D-Day, OKW had ordered up reinforcements from the south—the 2nd SS Panzer from Toulouse, the 17th SS from the Loire Valley, the 77th Infantry from Saint Malo, the 3rd Parachute from Brest and battle groups from three other divisions in Brittany. The 2nd SS in Toulouse was so hampered by air strikes on the railway that it could not entrain its tanks for 11 days.

Rundstedt reported that Allied planes controlled not only the battlefield but also the approach route, to a depth of more than 100 miles. The warning cry "Low flying aircraft!" was constantly heard down the marching troop columns. A staff officer of an SS division recalled his journey to the Normandy front on June 7:

"Our motorized columns were coiling along the road toward the invasion beaches. Then something happened that left us in a daze. Spurts of fire flecked along the column and splashes of dust staccatoed the road. Everyone was piling out of the vehicles and scuttling for the neighboring fields. Several vehicles were already in flames. This attack ceased as suddenly as it had crashed upon us fifteen minutes before. The men started drifting back to the column again, pale and shaky and wondering how they had survived this fiery rain of bullets.

"The march column was now completely disrupted and every man was on his own, to pull out of this blazing column as best he could. And it was none too soon, because an hour later the whole thing started all over again, only much worse this time. When this attack was over, the length of the road was strewn with splintered antitank guns (the pride of our Division), flaming motors and charred implements of war.

"The march was called off and all vehicles that were left were hidden in the dense bushes or in barns. No one dared show himself out in the open any more. Now the men started looking at each other. This was different from what we thought it would be like."

General Fritz Bayerlein, who had been chief of staff of Rommel's Afrika Korps, was himself attacked from the air as the 260 tanks of his crack Panzer Lehr struggled to reach the front after having been ordered up from Chartres. With Bayerlein in the staff car was his driver, Corporal Kartheus,

and his orderly officer, Captain Alexander Hartdegen. Hartdegen described what happened at dawn on June 8:

"We were bowling along the road when we saw three fighter bombers in the dawn sky. They had evidently spotted us, for they were streaking along the straight road at low altitude, straight at us. The brakes screeched. As a dozen times earlier that day, General Bayerlein let himself drop into the roadside ditch out of the moving car. I caught sight of a concrete culvert, raced toward it, and dived into the pitch-dark pipe head first. Kartheus also managed to get out of the car just before the aircraft cannon spat out their first shells. In an instant the BMW staff car was ablaze. The next plane streaked right along the ditch, opening up at us as it dived. The 20mm shells burst immediately in front of my concrete pipe. The corporal had just called out to Bayerlein: 'Crawl away from the car, Herr General, get away from it'— then he was silent."

Hartdegen was saved by the concrete culvert, but Corporal Kartheus lay dead in the ditch. Bayerlein suffered only a few cuts and shrapnel wounds, but the staff car was a smouldering pile of scrap metal on the road.

"Ten such attacks in succession," commented Hartdegen, "are a real foretaste of hell."

Incidents like these taught the Germans to move only at night. No motor vehicles were allowed within a radius of 500 yards of any military headquarters by day, and all tracks and tire marks had to be painstakingly obliterated. Tanks and other vehicles had to stay still and hidden in the shade of the dense, leafy woods.

The paralysis of German troop and tank movements caused by Allied air strikes and Resistance sabotage meant that the Allies were gaining the advantage in the crucial battle of the build-up—even though high winds, shelling and congestion on the beaches had put them 50 per cent behind schedule in unloading men and matériel. In those days just after the landings, work was proceeding on the two Mulberry harbors, but they would not be functional until D-plus-12. Blockships sunk as temporary breakwaters off the beaches provided some shelter for landing craft, but it was not until the Allies decided to run the ships right up on the beach to unload—waiting for the next high tide to float them off if necessary—that the disembarkation of men, vehicles and supplies could begin to catch up. As seen on the beaches, the logistics of *Overlord* were staggering.

"Almost as though on conveyor belts, a regular steady stream of DUK-Ws was moving," a BBC announcer reported from the British beaches. "Hundreds of them, they went out empty from the shore, changed from wheel drive to propeller a few yards out, and made tracks, or rather wakes, for the merchantmen lying out to sea. They were coming inshore, reversing the process, and driving their piled cargoes of crates, tires, petrol, shells, up the coast roads to the depots . . . 2,000 tons. they brought in on this small sector alone yesterday, and it will be nearer 3,000 tons today. That's only the DUK-Ws, mind you; there are LCTs, Rhino ferries, and innumerable other craft piling in supplies for our armies ashore. The beaches are alive with vehicles and men. There's a stream of traffic coming off the craft and going away up the roads and into the interior. As you come in towards the beaches, it's rather like driving in on the roads towards an industrial town; it's like a great, enormous industrial area—a remarkable sight."

From the crowded beaches endless columns of men and vehicles moved inland. "I think that one of the things I shall never forget," an RAF officer, Wing Commander L. A. Nickolls, recalled of the days immediately following the invasion, "is the sight of the British infantry, plodding steadily up those dusty French roads towards the front, single file, heads bent down against the heavy weight of all the kit piled on their backs, armed to the teeth; they were plodding on, slowly and doggedly towards the front with the sweat running down their faces and their enamel drinking mugs dangling at their hips; never looking back and hardly ever looking to the side—just straight in front and down a little on to the roughness of the road; while the jeeps and the lorries and the tanks and all the other traffic went crowding by, smothering them in great billows and clouds of dust which they never even deigned to notice. That was a sight that somehow caught at your heart."

Although the Allies were clearly winning the battle of the build-up, they had failed to expand their bridgehead as swiftly as the *Overlord* strategists had hoped. By June 10 the Americans of the VII Corps were locked in an inch-by-inch struggle to cut the neck of the Cotentin Peninsula. To the east the Germans clung doggedly to the key road center of Carentan—an Allied D-Day objective—and thus maintained a dangerous gap between the V and VII Corps. On the eastern flank of the Normandy bridgehead, the British and Canadians were still frustrated in their attempts to take Caen and its vital system of roads, some of which led to Paris, only 120 miles away.

Amazingly, the German High Command continued to believe that the Normandy landings were a diversionary

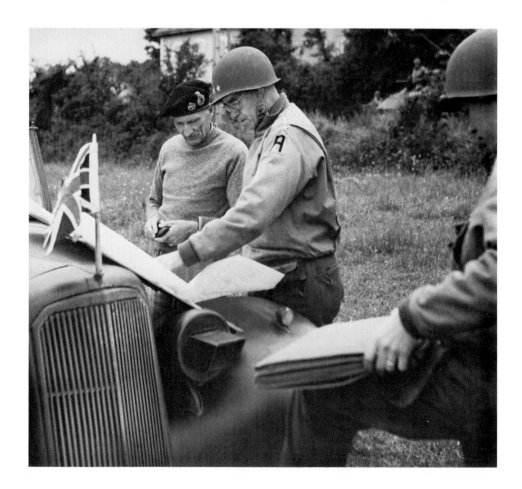

In their first postinvasion meeting on D-plus-4, British General Bernard Montgomery (left), commander of all Allied ground forces in France, and Lieut. General Omar Bradley, U.S. First Army commander, discuss troop movements in a quiet field near Port-en-Bessin.

feint. The Allies maintained their deception program after D-Day, convincing the Germans that a large force under General Patton—whom they considered to be a tank commander second only to their own brilliant General Heinz Guderian—would form the main body of the real invasion in the Pas-de-Calais. The intention of the Allied forces in Normandy, Hitler believed, was to turn northeast across the Seine, link up with the presumed main force near Calais and make a concerted drive on Germany by the shortest possible route. It was thus of paramount importance to the Germans to hold the eastern flank of the Allies' bridgehead and, at all costs, to prevent the British and Canadians from breaking out across the Orne to the Seine. And to hold the eastern flank, they would have to hold Caen. The Germans therefore opposed the British and Canadian advance with all the means at their disposal.

On the 10th of June, Montgomery launched a pincer attack against Caen. Since he had had no success in attacking Caen directly from the beachhead north of the city, he decided to try to encircle the place. He would send the 51st Division and 4th Armored Brigade on a southward sweep from their sectors east of the Orne; these forces would link up with the famous 7th Armored Division, the Desert Rats, which would make a sweeping arc from left to right, south of the city through the town of Villers Bocage.

But before the British drive on the left flank could get under way, it was thwarted by an attack by the 21st Panzer Division. And the 7th Armored almost met disaster in their counterclockwise sweep around Caen. They had roared through Villers Bocage in their new light and swift Cromwell tanks and, finding a long stretch of empty road before them, were storming toward their objective southeast of Caen. Suddenly they met a unit of SS heavy tanks—four Tigers concealed in positions on either side of the road. The odds were heavily in favor of the Desert Rats, but the German company commander, Lieutenant Michel Wittman, was a formidable foe, a tank killer with 119 victories to his credit on the Russian front.

From hiding, Wittman opened fire at the leading British tank with his 88mm gun. The vehicle burst into flames and shuddered to a halt, blocking the entire British column. Then, as the Cromwells deployed to attack, Wittman rolled his 50-ton Tiger out from cover and moved down the stalled line of British vehicles, firing as he went. The thin-skinned British personnel carriers and the unprotected half-tracks exploded in geysers of flame and metal. Armor-piercing rounds from the few British tanks that tried to shoot back bounced like peas off the Tiger's thick steel plate.

A second company of Tigers, with eight tanks, now joined the fray, and in less than 10 minutes the leading brigade of the 7th Armored Division was nothing but scrap metal: 25 tanks, 14 half-tracks and personnel carriers. The Tigers plowed on into Villers Bocage, where the British soldiers, supported by a handful of tanks, were holed up with bazookas in houses. The Tigers shot up the houses and harried the British tanks, but the big panzers had outrun their infantry support. In the close quarters of the village, Tommies with bazookas began knocking out the Tigers, including the one operated by Wittman, who had to abandon it. Finally, the Germans were forced to retreat. But 12 of their tanks had smashed the spearhead of an armored division and stalled the whole attack. Again, the campaign for Caen bogged down in a grim slogging match between tanks.

Montgomery later claimed that events had gone exactly according to his master plan. His plan, he maintained, was to draw the main strength of the Germans against the British and Canadians in the east so that the American First Army could more easily gain territory and break out in the west. "In the Caen sector," Montgomery wrote, "the acquisition of ground was not so pressing; the need *there* was by hard fighting to make the enemy commit his reserves."

If this was so, it appears to have been news to Eisenhower, who became increasingly impatient at the lack of progress on the British front, as did some senior British air chiefs, who were anxious to capture and use important German airfields east of Caen.

Over the next month the Germans around Caen fought with determination, skill and strength. The hardened veterans from Montgomery's old Eighth Army were used to the sweeping freedom of the North African desert and took a while to adapt to the strangely cramped and inhibiting conditions imposed on tank fighting by the Bocage country with its maze of hedgerows. But they held on. So did the 6th Airborne, which stood firm on the east bank of the Orne against persistant German counterattacks. South of Bayeux the 50th British expanded their bridgehead inland, aiming for a line beyond Villers Bocage. But for the moment the fighting at Caen was a standoff.

For men new to battle, the front was a bizarre place and rarely matched their preconceptions of a battlefield. It was a place full of incongruities. Few soldiers—few generals, even—really understood what was going on around them. Woodrow Wyatt, who was with the British Liberation Army, was impressed not by the violence at the front line but by the absence of it.

"When the battle was stationary for a while I often drove down to visit the forward units," Wyatt wrote later. "The approach was always the same. The quick change from the hubbub and noise of the jumbled convoys in the back areas to roads deserted save for an occasional civilian walking very slowly. A few cattle in the fields grazing among the dead and swollen bodies of their fellows, but no farm-workers. A complete silence—not even the sound of birds, a sense of being in an unreal world with no life, so that even the people in the villages timidly looking out of their shell-damaged houses don't seem alive. There is no reality be-cause no one is doing his normal job. Even the war does not exist—until you see a notice 'You are in the sight of the enemy now' and a little further on 'Drive slowly'—dust causes shells,' and then a few steel helmeted soldiers cau-tiously poking their heads out of slit trenches to see who is going by. . . . The opening exchange of courtesies wasn't the weather but 'How many times have you been shot up today?' followed by a visit to the latest shell or mortar holes, much as one might go and see how the sweet peas were coming on in a country garden."

Perhaps the greatest burden of the battle fell on the German tank crews, many of whom were relegated to a strange new role in the thrust-and-parry fighting that was characteristic of the battle to defend Caen and contain the western flank of the Allies. Low on fuel and ammunition, pinned down and practically immobilized by the Allied fighter-bombers and naval shellfire, the panzers dug in, hull down, among the dense hedgerows of the Bocage area. Their crews led lives more suited to U-boat men waiting for a kill than to the erstwhile practitioners of blitzkrieg and mobile armored warfare. The use of crack offensive units in a static defense was a novel event in World War II.

The Panzer Lehr tanks defending the German perimeter around Caen became simply armored antitank guns. Each tank was the nucleus of an infantry unit, for without it no position could be either taken or held. A small squadron of perhaps four Mark IV tanks, with crews of five infantrymen hanging all over the outside, would move off for "outpost duty." With their tanks concealed in well-reconnoitered sunken lanes, orchards and hayricks, the tank crews would busy themselves for hours camouflaging. The tanks were festooned with branches cut from a hedge until not an inch of turret could be seen. Then the crew would obliterate their tracks by painstakingly straightening each flattened blade of grass or stalk of corn. Then they would board their tanks and take up their duties as a forward antitank screen against the British armored spearheads. Only under the cover of darkness could they emerge again for a breath of fresh air and a stretch. All day they would be on lookout, peering intently at the landscape ahead of them through their binoculars.

It was like living in a tomb—a tomb that served as gun position, arsenal, barrack, toilet, galley and radio post. The first two days were bearable. After that it was unsufferable. There was no hot food. The men, cooped up in the steamy, tiny space of the tank interior, soon got on one another's nerves. With no water to wash in they soon became intoler-ably smelly. In the daylight hours they would have to relieve themselves in empty shell cases. Under such circumstances an enemy attack was almost welcome.

So it was for the crew of a Mark IV stationed outside of Tilly, a village eight miles to the west of Caen. At 2 o'clock in the afternoon on the third day of outpost duty, the tank driver suddenly shouted:

"Alarm! Tommies!"

The crew immediately came awake.

"Ten Tommies with a manhandled antitank gun. They're crossing the field now. They're taking up position."

"High explosives," the skipper ordered calmly.

"Four hundred meters."

"Fire!"

The 75mm shell burst in front of the antitank gun. Of the 10 British soldiers, only three were still on their feet; they ran toward an apple tree with low, spreading branches.

"Turret eleven o'clock."

"High explosives."

"Four hundred and twenty meters."

"Fire!"

The shellburst shredded the top of the tree.

"Fire!"

The trunk of the tree was smashed.

"Fire!"

The tree was destroyed. The Tommies were torn to pieces by shrapnel. The Mark IV stayed where it was, waiting.

It was a brutal moment, but less brutal than some. The combat troops grew accustomed to encountering the daily horror, but they rarely became used to the horror itself.

Colonel Ralph Ingersoll found himself in the square of a small inland village. "The sight that fascinated me most," he later wrote, "was a corpse of a German soldier in a roadway near the corner. It had been run over by so many tracked vehicles that it was ironed flat like a figure in a comic strip—really—absolutely flat, the arms of its grey uniform at right angles to its pressed and flattened coat. Its black boots and the legs that were in them were just as flat and thin as if they had been cut from a sheet of dirty cardboard."

The dead were everywhere, but the dead were easier to stand than the dying. "The thing I hated," a Canadian soldier recalled, "was when they'd call up a carrier with a flame thrower to burn out one of their pillboxes. I can still turn sort of green when I think of it. I remember once there was this pillbox, and we could hear the guys inside yelling. We didn't know what they were yelling and I told the sergeant maybe they wanted to surrender but the door was jammed. I said it might have taken a hit and buckled and they couldn't get out. But the sergeant yelled to the guy with the flame thrower to turn on the heat, and you should have heard those Germans in that pillbox screaming. God, it was awful."

It was in this atmosphere of casual brutality that the British and Germans traded advances and retreats in their bloody fight for Caen. The Americans, meanwhile, were making intermittent gains in the west. After their relatively eventless landing on Utah, the men of the VII Corps had run into increasing German resistance in their push toward Cherbourg and had been finally halted at Montebourg on the main Cherbourg road.

The soldiers of the V Corps, on the other hand, after having suffered so heavily at Omaha, had picked themselves up and dusted themselves off and with remarkable resilience had penetrated deep beyond the German defensive line along the River Aure. By June 10, the V Corps had linked up with the British on their left flank at Port-en-Bessin. By the 11th the V Corps had advanced south of Omaha to capture Caumont—10 miles inland—and had drawn level with the British who were battling for possession of Tilly on the road to Villers Bocage. Farther west, they had moved inland to capture Isigny and were threatening to link up with the VII Corps on their right.

Rommel's pressing priority now was to stop them from crossing the Vire estuary and giving the Allies a continuous bridgehead. The key to this engagement was the town of Carentan, which lay on the main road to Cherbourg.

During the 10th of June the 502nd Regiment, 101st Airborne Division, advanced on Carentan down a long, exposed causeway north of the town. This causeway, some six to nine feet above the level of the marshes on either side, was utterly devoid of cover, providing a perfect field of fire for German snipers and machine gunners hidden in the thickets and hedgerows of the high ground at the edge of the marshes. Strung out in single file down the length of the causeway, crouching and crowding, the regiment advanced toward Carentan with great difficulty, suffering heavy losses from the withering fire that was pouring down upon them.

After enduring endless hours on this lethal causeway, I Company of the 3rd Battalion was bombed and strafed by two German planes at dusk of that June day; within a few seconds it lost 30 men dead or wounded. A curious thing then occurred. I Company was finishing several days of hard fighting. Its soldiers had been drenched, shelled, sniped at, strafed and bombed. Many of them had slept only briefly. And now they succumbed to combat fatigue, a malady born of heavy and prolonged action that had also begun to infect other Allied units all over the Normandy front by this stage of the campaign.

The men of I Company had thrown themselves to the ground to escape the air attack, and now they lay there in a kind of bewitched torpor. They had almost no interest in what had happened and no curiosity about who had been killed or wounded. The officer in charge found that no matter how hard he tried he could not keep them awake. Some were asleep within two or three minutes of the strafing, and he found it impossible to tell which of his men were asleep and which of them were wounded. Some had rolled down the embankment of the causeway and lay half in the marsh. Believing that these were the wounded, he went down to them but found they had simply fallen into the water in their sleep and had not even wakened as they hit the icy water. Others lay on the ground completely soaked through, sleeping the sleep of utter spiritual exhaustion. For the next four hours they took no part in the battalion's attack.

The next day, the weary and depleted 502nd went into reserve, and another 101st Airborne regiment, the 506th, resumed the advance down the causeway to Carentan. At the same time, the 101st's 327th Glider Infantry attacked the town from the east. On June 12 the two American pincers gradually closed on Carentan. U.S. troops entered the town and found little opposition. The Germans, almost out of ammunition, had retreated, leaving behind a small and ineffectual rear guard. The fall of Carentan enabled the V and VII Corps to join up; the Allies now had an unbroken lodgment about 10 miles deep by about 60 miles wide. It was yet another step down the grinding road that would lead to the heart of France and on to Germany itself.

As the German line buckled under American pressure,

Hitler issued one of his standfast orders that had cost the Germans so much in the war on the Eastern Front: "There can be no question of fighting a rearguard action, nor of retiring to a new line of resistance. Every man shall fight and fall where he stands." But there were not even enough men for that. German reserves had been delayed and mauled en route to the front by Allied air strikes. There were only two bicycle battalions available to reinforce the defenses and stem the breakout of the V Corps from Omaha. The crack 352nd Division, which had opposed the Americans on the beach, was cut to shreds and, according to the 84th Corps, had "small combat value." With the panzer divisions locked in a wasting battle with the British Second Army, Hitler's entire army group was strained and off balance.

On June 12, Rommel informed Keitel, chief of OKW, that he proposed to switch his point of attack to the Cotentin Peninsula, in order to avert the danger of Cherbourg, before launching a major attack between the Orne and the Vire. But he could not even achieve this. He was forced to continue using his panzer divisions to hold Caen and had to content himself with cordoning off the Allied bridgehead to prevent a major breakout. But as the British kept up the pressure on Caen, and the Americans on Saint-Lô, the German line came to a breaking point.

Rommel had always counted on defeating the Allies on the coast. The Germans thus had no defense in depth. Reserves arrived late and were committed to action piecemeal so that offensive units were soon reduced to static defense. Neither the Luftwaffe nor the German Navy was in any position to interrupt the Allies' reinforcement by sea and movement by land. On June 17, Rommel and Rundstedt met with Hitler to discuss the Germans' plight.

The meeting took place at Margival near Soissons in northeast France in the bombproof bunker constructed in 1940 as Hitler's headquarters for the invasion of England. The meeting lasted from 9 a.m. until 4 p.m., with a break for lunch (at which Hitler bolted down a heaping plate of rice and vegetables—after it had been tasted for him to make sure it was not poisoned). According to Rommel's chief of staff, General Speidel, Hitler "looked pale and sleepless, playing nervously with his spectacles and an array of colored pencils which he held between his fingers. He sat, hunched upon a stool, while the Field-Marshals stood."

Rommel and Rundstedt had asked to hold the meeting for two reasons. They wanted to let Hitler know that they considered the situation on the Normandy front hopeless, and they wanted Hitler to make a visit to the front, to see the situation for himself and to encourage his troops by a personal appearance.

The meeting did not go well. Rundstedt told Hitler that no effective German counteroffensive could be launched so long as the Allies enjoyed total supremacy in the air. Rommel, who had been up all night inspecting the front, was tired and touchy and became increasingly blunt with the Führer as the day wore on. He told Hitler that he wanted to withdraw the Caen front to the Orne River so he could disengage his panzers and let them reorganize. As Rommel warmed to his argument, he became more and more outspoken. He told the Führer that he believed the Italian front would fall, the Russian front would fall and the Western Front would fall, and that there would be nothing to stop the Allies from sweeping into Germany. He proposed the unthinkable to Hitler—end the War.

Hitler told him not to worry about the future course of the War but to look to his front. Withdrawal was inconceivable; capitulation was unmentionable. The course of the War was about to change, Hitler informed them. New wonder weapons would see to that. V-1 flying bombs, already in service, were about to be launched against London in such large quantities that they would ensure the collapse of Britain. The Luftwaffe was about to introduce their first jet fighters into the War, and they would soon sweep Allied aircraft from the skies.

As the disconsolate Rundstedt and Rommel made their way back to their doomed troops and their lost causes, one of Hitler's wonder weapons, a V-1 destined for England, did a U-turn over the Channel coast and flew back across France. Immediately above Hitler's headquarters at Margival, its engine cut out and a few seconds later the errant war head exploded near the *Führerbunker*. Hitler, safely secreted under many feet of protective concrete, was unhurt. But he wasted no time. He canceled his visit to the Normandy front. He leaped into his car and was driven to his airplane. He never returned to France, and before long it would not matter. There the walls of his fortress Europe were slowly but inexorably crumbling.

NEW WORK ON THE BEACHES

At the end of D-Day, amid the ruins of battle on Omaha Beach, Normandy fishermen stare thoughtfully at American dead, assembled for transport to England.

BUILD-UP TIME IN NORMANDY

On June 7, the day after D-Day, the invasion entered its second critical phase on the Normandy beaches. Even as the Allied dead were being gathered for shipment to England and the French civilians were struggling to return to normalcy, great flotillas of ships began pouring ashore more men and matériel from England. The task of the new units was to reinforce the D-Day assault troops, who were fighting to link up the individual beachheads and to expand their front inland. By D-plus-24, hundreds of thousands of soldiers and vehicles and 570,000 tons of supplies had to be landed on beaches that had never before seen cargoes larger than the catch of local fishing boats.

That June afternoon, a motley convoy of antiquated ships arrived offshore. The ships were to be sunk as part of two giant artificial harbors designed to increase the flow of supplies by creating an area of sheltered water with piers on which to land vehicles and bulk cargo difficult to land on the open beaches. To supply the 25 divisions that would arrive in the next 20 days, these ports, code-named Mulberries, would have to handle 6,000 tons of supplies daily by D-plus-5, 9,000 tons by D-plus-12, 12,000 tons by D-plus-18.

By the evening of D-plus-10, the massive movement of men and tonnage from England had shifted into high gear, and though the two artificial harbors were still incomplete, some 183,000 tons of supplies and 81,000 vehicles had already been landed in Normandy. Despite the fact that troops were arriving an average of two days behind schedule, some 557,000 soldiers had landed and were hurrying into combat. Hordes of landing craft, freighters and outboard Rhino ferries had transformed Omaha Beach and Gold Beach into major ports.

Supreme Commander Eisenhower set foot on French soil on D-plus-6. Ike was delighted with the progress of the invasion. Though the British were still battling to capture Caen, American troops were at that very moment driving into the streets of Carentan, eight miles inland, opening a vital main road and linking British and American forces in the interior. The Second Front was secure.

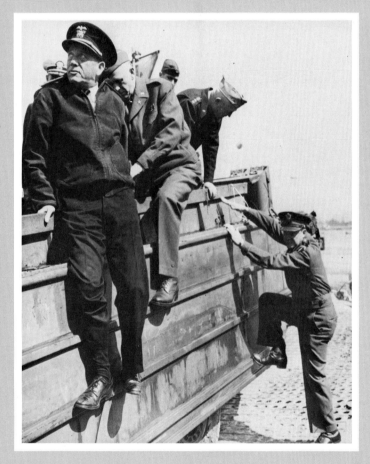

General Eisenhower (lower right) and three American commanders disembark from an amphibious vehicle to survey the Normandy build-up.

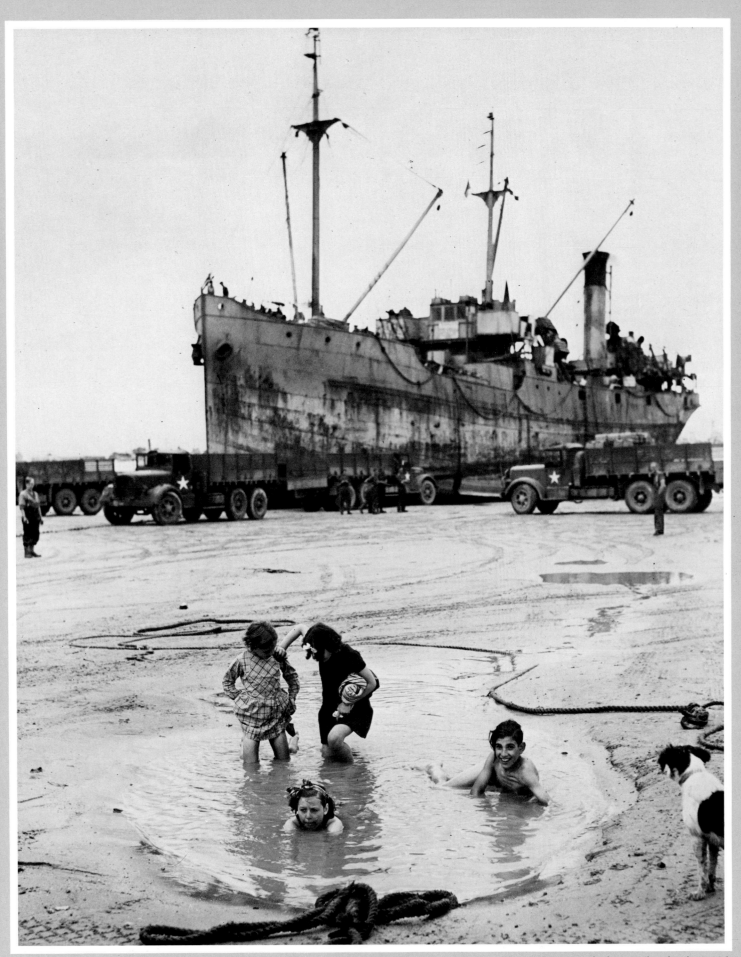

Oblivious of the ships and trucks laden with supplies around them, French children play in a tidal pool on Gold Beach, which was taken by the British.

Protected by barrage balloons, Omaha Beach swarms with ships and trucks funneling supplies inland to support the American troops, some of whom were pushing toward the vital port of Cherbourg. By D-plus-24, almost 180,000 tons of supplies and 50,000 vehicles had landed at Omaha.

Troops of the U.S. 2nd Division land on Omaha Beach on D-plus-1 and begin their trek inland to fight for the crucial high ground of Cerisy Forest, 12 miles to the south. On the way, the infantrymen captured the town of Trévières on D-plus-4. Then they took the forest with little difficulty.

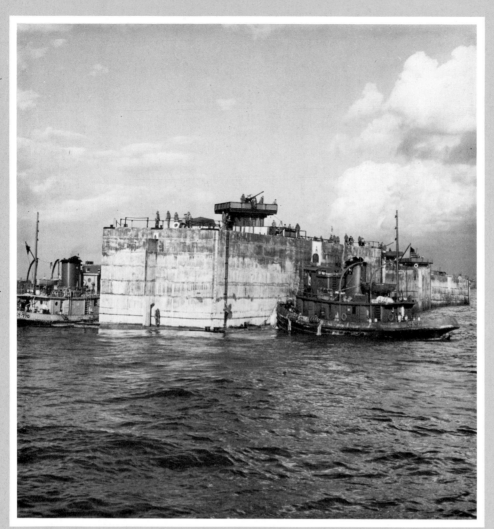

A concrete caisson, one of 213 used in the artificial harbors, is pushed into place off Omaha Beach.

A "LITTLE RIPPLE" IN THE FLOOD OF SUPPLIES

In the days after the landings, work forged ahead on the assembly of the two artificial harbors, Mulberry A for the Americans at Saint-Laurent and Mulberry B for the British at Arromanches. "The whole project was majestic," Churchill said, and indeed it was. In a period of approximately eight months some 20,000 British workmen had fashioned two million tons of steel and concrete into 600-odd sections that were towed piecemeal across the Channel by more than 100 tugs and assembled into two enormous floating ports.

At 4:30 in the afternoon on D-plus-10, an LST landing craft dropped its ramp onto the first completed pier runway of Mulberry A. Two days later, 24,412 tons of supplies and ammunition rolled ashore from the two Mulberries.

But then the capricious Channel weather intervened. On the morning of D-plus-13, gale-force winds and heavy surf began to pound the Normandy coast, driving landing craft against the piers and tearing sections of the piers from their moorings and crashing them against each other. By daybreak on D-plus-16, Mulberry A was a useless mass of twisted wreckage. Mulberry B, protected by a reef, suffered considerable but not disastrous damage.

Yet so powerful was the momentum of the build-up that the great storm caused, in Eisenhower's words, "little more than a ripple" in the flow of Allied supplies. When unloading resumed on D-plus-17, the British Mulberry, repaired and reinforced with salvageable parts from Mulberry A, went back into business, and the Americans landed 16,400 tons on the open beaches. By August 1, the armies that had established the Second Front were strong enough to break out of their Normandy beachhead and begin the liberation of the rest of France.

Sixty-foot-high caissons, sunk in place in 30 feet of water by opening intake valves at their bases, form a breakwater of the British Mulberry at Arromanches. On platforms atop the caissons, antiaircraft guns face the English Channel. The gun crews had living quarters inside the caissons.

The British Mulberry could harbor 500 vessels at once. Ships entered from top right and lower left; the sheltered area lay within the breakwater of sunken ships and caissons at right. Supplies were unloaded at the floating piers at center and trucked to shore on the roadways at upper left.

On Utah Beach, a jumbled pile of discarded underwater obstacles, removed by Allied combat engineers during the landings, attests to the success of the invasion.

BIBLIOGRAPHY

Allied Forces, Supreme Headquarters, *Report by the Supreme Commander to the Combined Chiefs of Staff on the Operations in Europe of the Allied Expeditionary Force (6 June 1944 to 8 May 1945)*. Government Printing Office, no date.

American Forces in Action Series:
  Omaha Beachhead (6 June–13 June 1944). Historical Division, War Department, 1945.
  Utah Beach to Cherbourg (6 June–27 June 1944). U.S. Department of the Army, Historical Division, no date.

Barker, Theo, ed., *The Long March of Everyman, 1750-1960*. Penguin Books, 1978.

Belfield, Eversley, and H. Essame, *The Battle for Normandy*. B. T. Batsford Ltd., 1965.

Blumenson, Martin, *Eisenhower*. Ballantine Books, 1972.

Blumentritt, Guenther, *Von Rundstedt, the Soldier and the Man*. Odhams Press Limited, 1952.

Bostick, William A., *England under G.I.'s Reign*. Conjure House, 1946.

Bradley, Omar N., *A Soldier's Story*. Henry Holt and Company, 1951.

British Broadcasting Corporation, *War Report*. Oxford University Press, 1946.

Brown, Anthony Cave, *Bodyguard of Lies*. Bantam Books, Inc., 1976.

Buckley, Christopher, *The Second World War, 1939-1945: Norway, The Commandos, Dieppe*. His Majesty's Stationery Office, 1951.

Butcher, Captain Harry C., USNR, *My Three Years with Eisenhower*. Simon and Schuster, 1946.

Capa, Robert, *Images of War*. Grossman Publishers, 1964.

Carell, Paul, *Invasion—They're Coming!* E. P. Dutton & Company, Inc., 1963.

Churchill, Winston S.:
  The Second World War. Houghton Mifflin Company.
  Closing the Ring, 1951.
  The Hinge of Fate, 1950.
  Their Finest Hour, 1949.

Craven, Wesley Frank, and James Lea Cate, eds., *The Army Air Forces in World War II*, Vol. III, *Europe: Argument to V-E Day (January 1944 to May 1945)*. The University of Chicago Press, 1951.

Crookenden, Napier, *Dropzone Normandy*. Ian Allan Ltd., 1976.

Cruickshank, Charles, *The German Occupation of the Channel Islands*. Oxford University Press, 1975.

Desquesnes, Rémy, *Le Mur de l'Atlantique en Normandie*. Editions Heimdal, 1976.

Eisenhower, Dwight D., *Crusade in Europe*. Doubleday & Company, Inc., 1948.

Eisenhower Foundation, *D-Day, The Normandy Invasion in Retrospect*. The University Press of Kansas, 1971.

Ellis, Major L. F., *Victory in the West*, Vol. I, *The Battle of Normandy*. Her Majesty's Stationery Office, 1962.

Esposito, Brig. General Vincent J., USA (Ret.), chief ed., *The West Point Atlas of American Wars*, Vol. II, *1900-1953*. The Department of Military Art and Engineering, The United States Military Academy, Frederick A. Praeger, 1959.

Ewing, Joseph H., *29 Let's Go! (A History of the 29th Infantry Division in World War II)*. Infantry Journal Press, 1948.

Funcken, Fred and Liliane, *The Second World War, Part 4: Arms and Uniforms*. Ward Lock Limited, 1976.

Gamelin, Paul, *Le Mur de l'Atlantique, Les Blockhaus de l'Illusoire*. Archives de Guerre Collection Dirigée Par Gérard Guicheteau, Editions Daniel & Cie, 1974.

Goerlitz, Walter, *History of the German General Staff: 1657-1945*. Frederick A. Praeger, 1953.

Greenfield, Kent Roberts, ed., *Command Decisions*. Department of the Army, Office of the Chief of Military History, 1960.

Halle, Armin, *Tanks: An Illustrated History of Fighting Vehicles*. New York Graphic Society, 1971.

Howarth, David, *D-Day—The Sixth of June, 1944*. McGraw-Hill Book Company, Inc., 1959.

Icks, Lieut. Colonel Robert J., *Tanks and Armored Vehicles, 1900-1945*. WE Inc., no date.

Ingersoll, Ralph, *Top Secret*. Harcourt, Brace and Company, 1946.

Leasor, James, *Green Beach*. Corgi Books, 1975.

Leventhal, Albert R., *War*. A & W Visual Library, A Ridge Press Book, 1973.

Liddell Hart, B. H., ed., *The Rommel Papers*. Harcourt, Brace and Company, 1953.

Longmate, Norman:
  The G.I.'s: The Americans in Britain, 1942-1945. Hutchinson of London, 1975.
  How We Lived Then. Arrow Books, 1977.

Lund, Paul, and Harry Ludlam, *The War of the Landing Craft*. W. Foulsham & Co. Ltd., 1976.

McKee, Alexander, *Last Round against Rommel: Battle of the Normandy Bridgehead*. The New American Library, 1964.

Macksey, Kenneth:
  Armoured Crusader—A Biography of Major-General Sir Percy Hobart. Hutchinson of London, 1967.
  Tank Warfare, A History of Tanks in Battle. Stein and Day, 1971.

Macksey, Kenneth, and John H. Batchelor, *Tank: A History of the Armoured Fighting Vehicle*. Charles Scribner's Sons, 1970.

Maguire, Eric, *Dieppe: August 19th 1942*. Corgi Books, 1963.

Majdalany, Fred, *The Fall of Fortress Europe*. Hodder and Stoughton Limited, 1968.

Mallory, Keith, and Arvid Ottar, *The Architecture of War*. Pantheon Books, 1973.

Marshall, S. L. A., *Night Drop: The American Airborne Invasion of Normandy*. Little, Brown and Company, 1962.

Masterman, J. C., *The Double-Cross System in the War of 1939 to 1945*. Yale University Press, 1972.

Maule, Henry, *The Great Battles of World War II*. Galahad Books, 1972.

Mills-Roberts, Brigadier Derek, *Clash by Night: A Commando Chronicle*. William Kimber, 1956.

Montgomery of Alamein, Field Marshal the Viscount:
  The Memoirs of Field Marshal the Viscount Montgomery of Alamein, K.G. The New American Library, 1959.
  Normandy to the Baltic. Houghton Mifflin Company, 1948.

Moorehead, Alan, *Eclipse*. Harper & Row, 1968.

Mordal, Jacques, *Dieppe: the Dawn of Decision*. Souvenir Press, 1962.

Morgan, Lieut. General Sir Frederick, *Overture to Overlord*. Doubleday & Company, Inc., 1950.

Morison, Samuel Eliot, *History of United States Naval Operations in World War II*, Vol. XI, *The Invasion of France and Germany, 1944-1945*. Little, Brown and Company, 1975.

Moulton, J. L., *Haste to the Battle: A Marine Commando at War*. Cassell & Company Ltd., 1963.

Partridge, Colin, *Hitler's Atlantic Wall*. D. I. Publications, 1976.

Piekalkiewicz, Janusz, *Secret Agents, Spies and Saboteurs*. William Morrow & Company, Inc., 1973.

Pyle, Ernie, *Brave Men*. Henry Holt and Company, 1944.

Ramsey, Winston G., ed., *After the Battle: Number 5 (Dieppe, Eben-Emael)*. Battle of Britain Prints International Ltd., 1974.

Rapport, Leonard, and Arthur Northwood Jr., *Rendezvous With Destiny—A History of the 101st Airborne Division*. 101st Airborne Division Association, 1948.

Ridgway, General Matthew B., USA (Ret.), *Soldier: The Memoirs of Matthew B. Ridgway*. Harper & Brothers, 1956.

Robertson, Terence, *Dieppe, The Shame and the Glory*. Hutchinson of London, 1962.

Roosevelt, Eleanor B., *Day Before Yesterday: The Reminiscences of Mrs. Theodore Roosevelt, Jr.* Doubleday & Company, Inc., 1959.

Roskill, Captain S. W., *The War at Sea 1939-1945*, Vol. II, *The Period of Balance*. Her Majesty's Stationery Office, 1956.

Ryan, Cornelius, *The Longest Day*. Popular Library, 1959.

Ryder, Commander R. E. D., *The Attack on St. Nazaire, 28th March, 1942*. John Murray, 1947.

Saunders, Hilary St. George:
  The Green Beret: The Story of the Commandos 1940-1945. Michael Joseph Ltd., 1949.
  The Red Beret: The Story of the Parachute Regiment at War 1940-1945. Michael Joseph Ltd., 1950.

Shirer, William L., *The Rise and Fall of the Third Reich*. Simon and Schuster, 1960.

Speidel, Hans:
  Invasion 1944. Henry Regnery Company, 1950.
  We Defended Normandy. Herbert Jenkins Ltd., 1951.

Stacey, Colonel C. P., *The Canadians in the Second World War*, Vol. I, *Six Years of War: The Army in Canada, Britain and the Pacific*. Edmond Cloutier, 1955.

Stagg, J. M., *Forecast for Overlord, June 6, 1944*. W. W. Norton & Company, Inc., 1971.

Sulzberger, C. L., and the Editors of American Heritage, *The American Heritage Picture History of World War II*. American Heritage Publishing Co., Inc., 1966.

Summersby, Captain Kay, WAC, Army of the U.S., *Eisenhower Was My Boss*. Prentice-Hall, Inc., 1948.

Thompson, R. W.:
  Dieppe at Dawn: The Story of the Dieppe Raid. Hutchinson & Co. Ltd., 1956.
  The Price of Victory. Constable and Company Ltd., 1960.
  Spearhead of Invasion D-Day. Ballantine Books Inc., 1968.

Tourtellot, Arthur B., ed., *LIFE's Picture History of World War II*. Time Incorporated, 1950.

Turner, John Frayn, *Invasion '44 (The First Full Story of D-Day in Normandy)*. G. P. Putnam's Sons, 1959.

Tute, Warren, *D-Day*. Macmillan Publishing Co., Inc., 1974.

United States Army in World War II, The European Theater of Operations. Office of the Chief of Military History, United States Army:
  Harrison, Gordon A., *Cross-Channel Attack*, 1951.
  Pogue, Forrest C., *The Supreme Command*, 1954.
  Ruppenthal, Roland G., *Logistical Support of the Armies*, Vol. I, *May 1941—September 1944*, 1953.

Warlimont, Walter, *Inside Hitler's Headquarters 1939-45*. Frederick A. Praeger, 1964.

White, William, ed., *By-line: Ernest Hemingway*. Charles Scribner's Sons, 1967.

Wilmot, Chester, *The Struggle for Europe*. Collins, 1952.

Wilt, Alan F., *The Atlantic Wall: Hitler's Defenses in the West, 1941-1944*. The Iowa State University Press, 1975.

Young, Desmond, *Rommel, The Desert Fox*. The Berkley Publishing Corporation, 1965.

Young, Brigadier Peter, *Commando*. Ballantine Books, Inc., 1969.

PICTURE CREDITS

Credits from left to right are separated by semicolons, from top to bottom by dashes.

COVER and page 1—The Public Archives of Canada, Ottawa.

HITLER'S ATLANTIC WALL—6, 7: Bundesarchiv, Koblenz. 8: Ullstein Bilderdienst, Berlin—Courtesy Manfred Rommel, Stuttgart. 9: Ullstein Bilderdienst, Berlin. 10, 11: Bundesarchiv, Koblenz—Zentralbild, Berlin—Bildarchiv Preussischer Kulturbesitz, Berlin; Bundesarchiv, Koblenz; Bundesarchiv, Koblenz. 12, 13: Bundesarchiv, Koblenz, except left, Ullstein Bilderdienst, Berlin (2). 14, 15, 16: Bundesarchiv, Koblenz. 17: Bundesarchiv, Koblenz—Courtesy Hellmuth Lang, Captain (Ret.), Schwäbisch-Gmünd. 18, 19: Courtesy Hellmuth Lang, Captain (Ret.), Schwäbisch-Gmünd.

REHEARSALS FOR INVASION—22: *Daily Mail*, London. 24, 25: Imperial War Museum, London. 26: Map by Elie Sabban. 28: British Official. 30: Imperial War Museum, London.

AFTERMATH OF A TRAGIC RAID—34, 35, 36: Bundesarchiv, Koblenz. 37: Ullstein Bilderdienst, Berlin. 38: Bundesarchiv, Koblenz—Ullstein Bilderdienst, Berlin. 39: E.C.P. Armées, Paris. 40 through 43: Bundesarchiv, Koblenz.

OVERTURES TO OVERLORD—46: Map by Elie Sabban. 49: U.S. Army. 50: Imperial War Museum, London. 53: Bundesarchiv, Koblenz. 55: By kind permission of *The Daily Telegraph*, London. 57: U.S. Air Force—Public Records Office/Nautic Visual Services, London (2). 60: U.S. Air Force. 62: Imperial War Museum, London.

THE BIG BUILD-UP—64, 65: U.S. Army. 66: Radio Times Hulton Picture Library, London. 67: Bob Landry for LIFE. 68: U.S. Navy, National Archives. 69: Radio Times Hulton Picture Library, London. 70, 71: U.S. Army (2); Imperial War Museum, London. 72 through 75: U.S. Army. 76, 77: Bob Landry for LIFE.

SUPREME COMMANDER—78, 79: Popperfoto, London. 80: U.S. Army—Dwight D. Eisenhower Library. 81: Imperial War Museum, London. 82, 83: UPI—Derek Bayes, London; UPI. 84, 85: Bob Landry for LIFE—U.S. Office of War Information; Imperial War Museum, London—National Archives. 86, 87: Imperial War Museum, London; UPI (2). 88, 89: Dwight D. Eisenhower Library; Wide World.

THE AIRBORNE ASSAULT—92: Imperial War Museum, London. 94: U.S. Army. 96, 97: Map by Elie Sabban. 99: Imperial War Museum, London. 100: Bundesarchiv, Koblenz. 101: The Netherlands State Institute for War Documentation, Amsterdam. 103: Musée de Sainte-Mère-Eglise.

YANKS IN BRITAIN—106, 107: Imperial War Museum, London. 108: U.S. Army. 109: Radio Times Hulton Picture Library, London. 110: Keystone Press, London. 111: Imperial War Museum, London—Keystone Press, London. 112, 113: UPI—Topix, London—U.S. Army; U.S. Army. 114: *Punch*, London, except bottom right, Express Newspapers Ltd., London. 115: *Punch*, London (2)—Mrs. B. H. Stillings, Dorset; Strube for *The Daily Express*, courtesy John Frost Historical Newspaper Service, New Barnet, Hertfordshire. 116, 117: Radio Times Hulton Picture Library, London. 118, 119: Ralph Morse for LIFE; Imperial War Museum, London.

THE INVASION ARMADA—120, 121: U.S. Army. 122: Imperial War Museum, London. 123: Royal Canadian Navy. 124, 125: David E. Scherman for LIFE; Imperial War Museum, London—Imperial War Museum, London; David E. Scherman for LIFE—Frank Scherschel for LIFE; Imperial War Museum, London; David E. Scherman for LIFE. 126, 127: Imperial War Museum, London; National Archives.

AMERICAN LANDINGS—130: U.S. Air Force. 132, 133: Schutz Photo Panorama from Historical Print Division of Ankers Capital, Washington, D.C., courtesy Jack Mitchell. 135: Robert Capa for LIFE. 136: National Archives. 139: UPI.

ORDEAL AT OMAHA—142 through 151: Robert Capa from Magnum for LIFE.

BRITISH BEACHHEADS—154: Janusz Piekalkiewicz, Rösrath-Hoffnungsthal. 156: Public Records Office/Nautic Visual Services, London. 158: Ralph Crane for LIFE. 159: Helmut Laux.

BRITAIN'S SHOCK TROOPS—162, 163: Popperfoto, London. 164 through 171: Imperial War Museum, London.

THOSE WONDROUS TANKS—172, 173: Art by John Batchelor. 174: Imperial War Museum, London. 175: Art by John Batchelor—Imperial War Museum, London. 176, 177: Imperial War Museum, London; Art by John Batchelor—Art by John Batchelor; The Royal Armoured Tank Corps Museum, Dorset. 178: Art by John Batchelor—The Royal Armoured Tank Corps Museum, Dorset. 179: Art by John Batchelor—Imperial War Museum, London. 180, 181: Art by John Batchelor—Imperial War Museum, London; John Batchelor; Imperial War Museum, London—Art by John Batchelor.

THE FIGHTING INLAND—184, 185: U.S. Air Force. 186, 188: Imperial War Museum, London. 191: Popperfoto, London.

NEW WORK ON THE BEACHES—194, 195: Robert Capa from Magnum for LIFE. 196: UPI. 197: Imperial War Museum, London. 198, 199: U.S. Coast Guard, National Archives; UPI. 200, 201: U.S. Navy, National Archives; Popperfoto, London—The Netherlands State Institute for War Documentation, Amsterdam. 202, 203: U.S. Army.

ACKNOWLEDGMENTS

The index was prepared by Mel Ingber. For help given in the preparation of this book the editors wish to thank Dana Bell, U.S. Air Force Still Photo Depository, Arlington, Virginia; Antoinette de Bérender, Curator, Musée du Débarquement, Arromanches, France; Eva Bong, Ullstein Bilderdienst, Berlin; Carole Boutté, Senior Researcher, U.S. Army Audio-Visual Activity, The Pentagon, Washington, D.C., Cornell (Director) and Edith Capa, International Center of Photography, New York; Charles Chevrot, Montivilliers, France; Cécile Coutin, Curator, Musée des Deux Guerres Mondiales, Paris; Claude-Paul Couture, Barentin, France; V. M. Destefano, Chief, Reference Library, U.S. Army Audio-Visual Activity, The Pentagon, Washington, D.C.; Directorate of History, National Defense Headquarters, Ottawa, Ontario, Canada; Hans Dollinger, Wörthsee, Germany; Geneviève Duboscq-Troszczynski, Paris; Paul Gamelin, Nantes, France; Government Institute for War Documentation, Amsterdam; Jeanne Grall, Archives du Calvados, Caen, France; Charles R. Haberlein Jr., Photographic Section, Curator Branch, Naval History Division, Department of the Navy, Washington, D.C.; David Haight, Archivist, Dwight D. Eisenhower Library, Abilene, Kansas; Dr. Matthias Haupt, Bundesarchiv, Koblenz, Germany; Werner Haupt, Bibliothek für Zeitgeschichte, Stuttgart, Germany; T. C. Hine, Imperial War Museum, London; Heinrich Hoffmann, Hamburg; Colonel P. H. Hordern, D.S.O., O.B.E., The Royal Armoured Corps Tank Museum, Wareham, Dorset, England; Richard Huyda, Division Chief, National Photography Collection, The Public Archives of Canada, Ottawa, Ontario; Philip Jutras, Curator, Museum of Sainte-Mère-Eglise, France; Heidi Klein, Bildarchiv Preussischer Kulturbesitz, Berlin; Dr. Roland Klemig, Bildarchiv Preussischer Kulturbesitz, Berlin; Hellmuth Lang, Captain (Ret.), Schwäbisch-Gmünd, Germany; Roger Le Blanc, Mayor of Arromanches, France; William H. Leary, National Archives and Records Service, Audio-Visual Division, Washington, D.C.; James Leyerzapf, Supervisory Archivist, Dwight D. Eisenhower Library, Abilene, Kansas; J. S. Lucas, Imperial War Museum, London; Colonel Marcel Dugué MacCarthy, Curator, Musée de l'Armée, Paris; Peter Masters, Bethesda, Maryland; Brün Meyer, Bundesarchiv, Freiburg, Germany; Henri Michel, Président du Comité d'Histoire de la Deuxième Guerre Mondiale, Paris; Brigadier D. Mills-Roberts, C.B.E., D.S.O., M.C., North Wales; Jack Mitchell, Bedford, Virginia; Jonathan Moore, London; Meinrad Nilges, Bundesarchiv, Koblenz, Germany; J. W. Pavey, Imperial War Museum, London; Janusz Piekalkiewicz, Rösrath-Hoffnungsthal, Germany; Marianne Ranson, Comité d'Histoire de la Deuxième Guerre Mondiale, Paris; Manfred Rommel, Lord Mayor of Stuttgart, Germany; Professor Admiral Friedrich Ruge, Tübingen, Germany; Axel Schulz, Ullstein Bilderdienst, Berlin; Albert Speer, Heidelberg; Jim Trimble, National Archives and Records Service, Audio-Visual Division, Washington, D.C.; Michel de Vallavieille, Curator, Utah Beach Museum, Sainte-Marie-du-Mont, France; A. Williams, Imperial War Museum, London; Joy Williams, Reference Consultant, National Photography Collection, The Public Archives of Canada, Ottawa, Ontario; M. J. Willis, Imperial War Museum, London; Marjorie Willis, Radio Times Hulton Picture Library, London; Marie Yates, U.S. Army Audio-Visual Activity, The Pentagon, Washington, D.C.

INDEX

Numerals in italics indicate an illustration of the subject mentioned.

Printed in U.S.A.